Cultural Sociology

Cultural Sociology

An Introduction

Les Back
Andy Bennett
Laura Desfor Edles
Margaret Gibson
David Inglis
Ronald Jacobs
Ian Woodward

WILEY-BLACKWELL

A John Wiley & Sons, Ltd., Publication

This edition first published 2012
© 2012 Les Back, Andy Bennett, Laura Desfor Edles, Margaret Gibson, David Inglis, Ronald Jacobs, Ian Woodward

Blackwell Publishing was acquired by John Wiley & Sons in February 2007. Blackwell's publishing program has been merged with Wiley's global Scientific, Technical, and Medical business to form Wiley-Blackwell.

Registered Office
John Wiley & Sons Ltd, The Atrium, Southern Gate, Chichester, West Sussex, PO19 8SQ, UK

Editorial Offices
350 Main Street, Malden, MA 02148-5020, USA
9600 Garsington Road, Oxford, OX4 2DQ, UK
The Atrium, Southern Gate, Chichester, West Sussex, PO19 8SQ, UK

For details of our global editorial offices, for customer services, and for information about how to apply for permission to reuse the copyright material in this book please see our website at www.wiley.com/wiley-blackwell.

The right of Les Back, Andy Bennett, Laura Desfor Edles, Margaret Gibson, David Inglis, Ronald Jacobs, and Ian Woodward to be identified as the authors of this work has been asserted in accordance with the UK Copyright, Designs and Patents Act 1988.

Library of Congress Cataloging-in-Publication Data

Cultural sociology : an introduction / Les Back . . . [et al.].
    p. cm.
  Includes bibliographical references and index.
  ISBN 978-1-4051-8985-9 (hardback) – ISBN 978-1-4051-8984-2 (paper)
1. Culture.   2. Sociology.   I. Back, Les, 1962–
  HM621.C85346 2012
  306–dc23   2011036315

A catalogue record for this book is available from the British Library.

Set in 10/12.5pt Minion by Aptara Inc., New Delhi, India
Printed in Singapore by Ho Printing Singapore Pte Ltd

1   2012

Contents

Notes on Authors		vii
Preface		ix
Glossary of Terms		xiii

Part I: Theory and Method

1	Starting to Write a History of the Present Day: Culture and Sociology *David Chaney*	3
2	Defining Cultural Sociology	19
3	Methodological Issues in Cultural Sociology	31

Part II: New Cultural Identities

4	Class, Culture and Social Difference	47
5	Gender and Sexuality	63
6	Racism, 'Race' and Difference	77
7	Bodies and Identities	91

Part III: Fragmented Ideology

8	Politics and Culture	107
9	Globalization	121
10	Culture and Religion	133

Part IV: Leisure and Lifestyle

11 Popular Music: Place, Identity, Community   151

12 Fashion Logics and the Cultural Economy: The Social Power of Tastes,
Aesthetics and Style   163

13 Food, Eating and Culture   177

14 Media, Culture and Public Life   189

References   201

Index   219

Notes on Authors

Les Back is Professor of Sociology at Goldsmiths College, University of London, United Kingdom. His books include *The Art of Listening* (Berg, 2007), *Out of Whiteness* (with Vron Ware, University of Chicago Press, 2002) and *The Changing Face of Football: Racism and Multiculture in the English Game* (with Tim Crabbe and John Solomos, Berg, 2001). He is also a journalist, and has made documentary films.

Andy Bennett is Professor of Cultural Sociology and Director of the Griffith Centre for Cultural Research at Griffith University, Queensland, Australia. He has authored and edited numerous books, including *Popular Music and Youth Culture* (Palgrave Macmillan, 2000), *Cultures of Popular Music* (Open University Press, 2001) and *Music Scenes* (with Richard A. Peterson, Vanderbilt University Press, 2004).

David Chaney is Professor Emeritus of Sociology at the University of Durham, United Kingdom. He has published extensively on aspects of cultural change in the modern era. His books include *The Cultural Turn* (Routledge, 1994), *Lifestyles* (Routledge, 1996) and *Cultural Change and Everyday Life* (Palgrave, 2002).

Laura Desfor Edles is Professor of Sociology at California State University, Northridge. She is the author of *Symbol and Ritual in the New Spain: The Transition to Democracy After Franco* (Cambridge University Press, 1998), *Cultural Sociology in Practice* (Blackwell, 2002), *Sociological Theory in the Contemporary Era* (Pine Forge Press, 2nd edn, 2010) and *Classical and Contemporary Sociological Theory* (Pine Forge Press, 2nd edn, 2011).

Margaret Gibson is a Senior Lecturer in Cultural Sociology in the School of Humanities, Griffith University, Queensland, Australia. She is author of numerous publications on death, mourning and material culture, including *Objects of the Dead: Mourning and Memory in Everyday Life* (Melbourne University Publishing, 2008).

David Inglis is Professor of Sociology at the University of Aberdeen, United Kingdom. He is founding editor of the journal *Cultural Sociology*, published by Sage and the British Sociological Association. He is the author and editor of many books and papers, including *The Globalization of Food* (with Debra Gimlin, Berg, 2010), *Culture and Everyday Life* (Routledge, 2005) and *The Sociology of Art* (with John Hughson, Palgrave, 2005).

Ronald Jacobs is Associate Professor of Sociology at the University at Albany, State University of New York. His most recent books include *The Space of Opinion* (Oxford University Press, 2011) and *The Oxford Handbook of Cultural Sociology* (Oxford University Press, 2011).

Ian Woodward is a Senior Lecturer in Sociology in the School of Humanities, Griffith University, Queensland, Australia. He is the author of *Understanding Material Culture* (Sage, 2007) and co-author of *The Sociology of Cosmopolitanism* (with Gavin Kendall and Zlatko Skrbis, Palgrave, 2009).

Preface

This book has been written by a diverse group of researchers who have in common a fervent belief that it is essential to give priority to cultural processes as a primary element of any social explanation. Moreover, the authors are committed to the development of a cultural sociology, which means that they give great weight to aspects and dimensions of social life that have received little or marginal consideration from previous generations of sociologists. To believe in the value of a cultural sociology is to perceive such matters as emotion, affect, discourse, narrative, reflexivity, and the visual and material basis of social life as crucial to social experience and indeed as basic elements of any considered, viable theory of social life. In addition, to believe in the value of cultural sociology is to understand that culture should not be reduced to other aspects of social explanation, or explained in terms of factors such as the economy or ideology, for example. Rather, culture is an independent force and deserves to be treated as central to the many and varied areas sociologists have traditionally studied.

While cultural sociology has become a very influential area of research, there are diverse ways of applying a cultural sociological approach. As we emphasize above, what the authors have in common is a belief in the value of studying culture, cultural forces and cultural processes as a way of understanding society. A broad distinction can be made between the general sociological study of culture and what might be called a 'cultural sociology'. The former can be taken to refer to the use of already widely used sociological methods and concepts to study cultural phenomena, while the latter refers to the belief that sociological approaches require a more systematic conceptual and methodological overhaul to account for the way contemporary society works. Although the question of the relative merits of each approach is a matter of some contention within the global field of cultural sociology, we believe that it is valid to call both of these styles of analysis 'cultural sociology', and to recognize advocates of each as providing a distinctive model for doing cultural sociology. These distinctions are elaborated further in the introductory chapters of this book. However, it is enough to say at the present time that the chapters in this book represent scholarship from across the spectrum of cultural sociological analysis. Naturally, because of the book's diverse authorship, some chapters might seem closer to a sociological take on cultural matters, while others are firmly in the camp of a style of cultural sociology, which advocates a separation from older, conventional styles of analysis. We see this diversity as a strength of the book and a reflection of the fact that the global cultural sociology movement is indeed a product of researchers drawing upon plural theoretical and empirical traditions, each of which has been shaped in unique ways by the central sociological canon and also refracted by distinct forces within national and regional spheres of scholarship.

The book is divided into four general parts. The contents of and rationale for each are outlined below.

Part I of the book gives an introduction to the field and methods of cultural sociology. *Chapter 1* is a special feature of the book. In this scene-setting chapter, founding cultural sociologist David Chaney provides a critical reflection and commentary on the factors that gave rise to the emergence of cultural sociology as a distinctive element of sociological theory and research. His account constitutes a particular narrative detailing the growth of cultural sociology as a distinctive sub-field. In doing so, Chaney's chapter is also a valuable statement on the contemporary vitality of the field. Because it is written by a contemporary founder of the field, it gives a historical perspective on the way cultural sociology developed. We suggest that readers would benefit by coming back to Chaney's chapter a number of times as they progress through this text and as their understandings of the field develop. *Chapter 2* discusses the emergence of cultural sociology as a particular field of sociological inquiry. It outlines the way particular traditions of cultural sociology have developed, especially in British, European and American settings. The chapter also addresses the differences between cultural studies, cultural sociology and the sociology of culture. *Chapter 3* considers the methodological tools sociologists typically use in their analyses, as well as the particular types of conceptual frames which guide how they undertake their research and how they see social phenomena. Rather than being a guide to methods, which is the standard approach used in textbooks that inform the reader about the difference between the types of possible research interviews, or matters of sampling, for example, this chapter considers the special methodological toolkit from which cultural sociologists can draw.

Part II of the book is entitled 'new cultural identities'. In fact, what the chapters in this section of the book do is to take some of the very oldest and central ideas about identity from the traditional sociological canon and render them anew, in ways afforded through the cultural sociological lens. Thus, existing sociological understandings of basic identity categories – class, gender and race – have been challenged by cultural sociological perspectives which argue that contemporary socio-cultural identities are also informed by images, objects and attendant resources which exist within people's everyday lives. Such resources are appropriated from the media and cultural industries and function to problematize conventional sociological interpretations of identity as structurally determined. Although these fundamental categories of social life remain relevant, to a substantial degree their capacity to fix identities has also been significantly undone by processes of globalization, the spread of media and popular culture, and the individualization trends that have defined the last few decades. Moreover, skilful cultural analyses have shown that factors such as class, race and gender are to a large degree constructed or performed 'from the ground up', utilizing a range of everyday discourses and practices. Appropriately, then, this section concludes with a chapter on theories of the human body as a cultural object. The body constitutes a new site for political intervention and governance, as well as offering potential for challenging and breaking hegemonic discourses.

Part III of the book looks to important realms of ideology and belief within the contemporary world in which there have been huge recent changes. These chapters highlight the way traditional forms of religious and political authority have been challenged by characteristic processes of late modernity, including the dissolution of traditional forms of authority, the rise of life politics and the politics of lifestyle, and the global spread of media, celebrity and opinion cultures which fundamentally alter the way we understand and experience political and civic life. Also included in this section is a chapter on globalization. If one wishes to understand the conditions in which different groups of people live today, it seems increasingly impossible to ignore the aspects of those conditions that are seen to be characterized, or influenced, by 'global' forces, movements and phenomena. Globalization intensifies the spread of hegemonic capitalist forms, but also sows the seeds for bubbling forms of cultural difference to take hold which complicate and possibly challenge Western modernity.

Part IV of the book analyses a variety of media, leisure and lifestyle forms including music, fashion, food and the media. Such cultural forms have become more prominent aspects of everyday life due to the onset of late modernity and the increasing prominence of consumerism and leisure. Thus, there is a need to apply cultural sociological perspectives in order to fully understand their role and significance as primary cultural forms in the context of contemporary everyday life. The cultural sociological perspective sets out not necessarily to endorse or celebrate fashion, popular music or television, or the pleasures of eating out, nor to analyse them just because they are important new industries. Rather, the cultural perspective shows how such cultural forms represent and embody diverse social ideals and provide resources for giving meaning and forging social solidarity or difference among people, how such cultural formations help to contour and narrate aspects of personal lives and social events, and how they provide us with entertainment, pleasure and a relationship with very basic human desires and energies.

Each chapter features a range of words that are highlighted in **bold text**. These words are defined in the glossary of terms included at the front of the book. At the end of each chapter you will find a list of carefully selected additional readings and a series of relevant discussion questions.

Glossary of Terms

Aesthetic. The socially communicative capacities of the decorative, visual and material dimensions of culture.

Aesthetic public sphere. Public discussions about entertainment media and matters of aesthetic concern.

Aestheticization. A general process by which the qualities of decoration, style and design have increasingly become important to individuals, the economy and society in general.

Category. A class of things or group of people. Categories are basic ways by which the world is ordered and organized. New categories emerge as a way of acknowledging changes or shifts in identities and group affiliations, family organization, and so on.

Class analysis. A mode of social analysis that focuses on categories of economic attainment and stratification to illuminate social inequality.

Codes. The pattern of underlying beliefs and modes of judgement, developed over a long period of time, that structure how individuals perceive events, objects and other people. Codes are relatively obdurate cultural structures, and provide the narrative material necessary for navigating everyday culture.

Collective consciousness. A concept developed by Émile Durkheim, referring to the commonly shared beliefs, values and ways of thinking that create and sustain social cohesion. The word 'consciousness' is etymologically linked to conscience, and the collective consciousness is both internalized in the development of a social conscience and externally enforced via institutionalized (laws) and non-institutionalized social rules (norms). In modern pluralistic societies, the collective consciousness is harder to create, sustain or claim at the level of mass individual forms of conscience, as diversities in religion, beliefs, values and identities fragment collective forms of solidarity and identity.

Cosmopolitanism. A mental condition whereby individuals understand themselves to be part of a world made up of people of multiple different cultures, all of whom are seen to be profoundly connected to each other; this situation is accepted and welcomed rather than feared and disliked.

Creolization. *See* Hybridization.

Cultural capital. A term developed by Bourdieu in examining the nature of contemporary social identity, taste and lifestyle as produced through aesthetic and ideological sensibilities associated with class and its impact on educational achievement and occupational status. Refers to valuable economic resources possessed by individuals, including their education or other cultural learnings, which constitute non-financial assets that may assist people in becoming socially mobile.

Cultural heterogenization. A process whereby cultural life becomes more complex and elaborate over time.

Cultural homogenization. A process whereby previously different and separate cultures become replaced by one single culture that is the same in every part of the world.

Cultural imperialism. A situation where one region of the world – usually the West – is seen to dominate and control the media, and cultural life more generally, of other parts of the world.

Cultural policy. Public policies and discussions about how to organize and regulate the cultural industries.

Cultural politics. Conflicts that occur over values and meanings rather than actual public policies.

Cultural racism. A form of racism in which the biological notion of race is replaced by a pseudo-biological definition of culture that is defined as incompatible with the host culture.

Cultural turn. The turn among a variety of academic disciplines to culture as a means through which to understand and interpret everyday life in contemporary social settings.

Culture. The systematic sets of code, narratives, discourses and practices which structure the interpretation of social life and social action

Deterritorialization. A process where cultural phenomena cease to be located in one particular geographical location and potentially are spread out across the whole planet.

Dialectical. Describes a situation involving the complex interplay of diverse social forces, all of which come to have unanticipated effects on each other.

Difference. A means to describe human variety that does not fix or reduce human beings to essential qualities or categories.

Discourse. The socially productive ideas, beliefs and codes of thinking which circulate in a culture and influence how people perceive aspects of the social world.

Disembedding. A process whereby people's social relations are no longer limited to particular geographical locations, but are lifted out of those contexts and stretched across long distances.

Disenchanted world. A world drained of magic.

Embodied. Refers generally to a feature of social life that is related to the display, performance or exhibition of the body.

Essentialist. When an argument or theory is *essentialist*, it rests on the proposition or assumption of a unique female or male nature that is always already there as part of biology.

Ethics. Notions of right and wrong.

Ethnographic. A tradition of sociological methodology that emphasizes the use of multiple qualitative modes of inquiry, which focus on the participation and immersion of the researcher within the environment or community they are researching.

Field. The everyday socio-cultural environment of research subjects, often situated as the 'other' – a somehow self-contained or at least 'definable' world in relation to that occupied by the social researcher.

Fordism. Assembly line production systems; *see also* Taylorism.

Frame alignment. The ability to make an argument that resonates with the public agenda of the time.

Gender. The learned differences between men and women.

Gender identification. The internalized image of oneself according to socially available images of gendered subjectivity. Gender identification is largely an unconscious inner process but this is inevitably shaped and mapped by cultural and historical context, and particularly family cultures and social interaction.

Globality. A condition whereby the world is regarded by most people on the planet as 'one place', and everyone's existence is seen to be profoundly connected with everyone else's.

Globalization. A contested term with various competing definitions. In essence, it refers to processes that make different parts of the world connected to and dependent upon each other in complex ways.

Glocalization. The commingling of more local and more global cultures, creating complex social and cultural forms that are neither purely local nor purely global.

Habitus. Habitual ways of seeing, acting and understanding that are socially and economically conditioned by class location.

Hegemony. The attempt by dominant groups to make their worldview seem like 'common sense' to the rest of the population.

Heterogenization. A process whereby previously similar things become more different from each other.

Historical materialism. A method associated with Marx and the Marxist approach to the analysis of history and changes in human consciousness. Historical change is understood in terms of class struggle and transformations in the dominant mode of production.

Homogenization. A process whereby previously different and separate things become uniformly similar to each other.

Homology. A concept that explains the acquisition of cultural taste as a reflection of structural circumstances – for example, class, gender and ethnicity.

Hybridization (or Creolization). A process through which new cultural forms are created by the mixing of previously separate cultural traditions.

Informal public. Small-group discussions that take place among regular individuals in everyday settings.

Interactionist. Refers to the sociological tradition of symbolic interactionism, pioneered by Erving Goffman and others, which emphasizes the way social and cultural values are continuously reproduced and performed in small-scale interactions between people.

Intersexed. Refers to combinations of chromosomal characteristics and combinations of internal and external genitalia that differ from female and male sexed bodies and chromosome configurations (XY – male, XX – female).

Jim Crow laws. The legal framework for racial segregation in the United States, enacted between 1876 and 1965, which divided all public facilities along racial lines.

Legitimate authority. The belief that those in power are acting in the public interest, or that they have the proper authorization to make decisions, or both.

Life politics. As opposed to the politics of class, which is premised on emancipation and class conflict, this contemporary politics is focused on self-actualization and self-realization – for example, through ethical eating practices or wearing green fashion.

Life-course trajectories. The established and patterned pathways and milestones of people's lives, as influenced by factors such as social class, educational opportunities and gender, as well as by chance factors such as illness.

Lifestyle. A term initially used by Weber to describe the articulation of wealth and social status by social groups. The term was later adopted and developed by Chaney in examining the appropriation and inscription of cultural commodities into lifestyle projects by individuals in late modern, consumer-oriented societies.

Massification. A process whereby previously small-scale phenomena become greatly enlarged.

Material culture. This term emphasizes how apparently inanimate things within the environment act on people, and are acted upon by people, for the purposes of carrying out social functions, regulating social relations and giving symbolic meaning to human activity.

Methodology. The process of considering one's general approach to studying research topics and collecting evidence by highlighting the underlying normative assumption about research epistemology – for example, what *types* of knowledge do social surveys generate? How can we know if our interpretation of evidence is a valid one?

Methods. The particular techniques used by sociologists to collect data and evidence – for example, social surveys or visual analysis.

Modernity. The features of social and economic organization that consolidated in Western Europe and America around the 1850s and extended until late into the twentieth century. The bedrocks of modernity are to be found in the processes and ideologies encapsulated in scientific rationality, specialization and individualism, and commodification.

Moral panic. A heightened public fear of a group or public issue, usually created by those in power in order to maintain their control.

Narratives. Narratives consist of the accounts or stories people tell themselves, and others, in order to both *make sense of – and make through practical means –* their lives. Narratives can also have a collective orientation, referring to the way groups such as national collectives or identity groups have stories that help to define the nature of group beliefs.

Official public. Public discussions that take place between government officials, politicians, experts, journalists and other representatives of the public interest. Official publics are almost always organized within the largest media organizations: in major newspapers and television channels, and on web sites.

Ontological security. The feeling of psychological security a person must possess in order to experience his or her social world as stable and ordered.

Organic intellectuals. Individuals who are responsible for articulating the publicly held worldview of a particular group, and criticizing the competing worldviews being put forth by other groups.

Performance. The attempt made by an individual to authentically embody a particular set of meanings through a series of actions and symbolic activity.

Positivism. Positivist approaches make the assumption that aspects of the social and cultural world, such as a person's behaviours or attitudes, are amenable to description and measurement via approaches that adopt logical scientific procedures based on principles of empirical measurement.

Post-materialist. Refers to a shift in culture whereby people's behavioural and value orientations tend to be focused on matters of lifestyle and self-cultivation, rather than being directed towards matters of personal economic position and gain.

Postmodernity. A variety of rapid social and economic changes which have occurred predominantly in Western societies, but are also increasingly global in reach, since around 1970. Postmodernity is principally defined by the questioning of modern values and assumptions of progress, and questioning the values of scientific and economic rationality. Postmodernity also places an emphasis on matters of aesthetics and style in cultural life and on the importance of leisure and consumption in forming people's identities.

Post-positivism. Such approaches challenge the idea that scientific approaches can access a universally known external reality or truth, and suggest that the knower (the researcher) and ways of knowing (the methods employed) can never really be separated.

Profane. The everyday, mundane world.

Public sphere. Those places where individuals gather together to discuss matters of common concern. These spaces can consist of face-to-face or mediated discussion.

Qualitative. Refers to a variety of non-numeric data-collection techniques used by researchers, and includes visual, textual, discursive and narrative forms of research where data are preserved in their collected state, rather than being abstracted and assigned a numeric value.

Quantitative. Refers to data-collection procedures where numeric values are assigned to measure aspects of beliefs, values, orientations and sentiments, and where the data are aggregated and analysed in terms of statistical variance between sets of relevant variables.

Race. The classification of human beings into pseudo-biological types produced within European racial science, racial ideologies and common sense.

Racism. The ordering of humanity into racial hierarchies that confer on white racial majorities full political entitlements and civic and social rights while denying those same rights to racial minorities.

Rationality. The idea that people will give good reasons to justify their positions on an issue, and that the best argument will carry the day.

Rationalization of society. The increasing reliance on methodical procedures and calculable rules rather than tradition and emotion.

Reflexivity. The process though which individuals engage in social life, with a capacity to continually judge and evaluate the outcome of their actions, choices and motives.

Ritual. A series of events that are set apart from ordinary life, designed to convey a particular set of meanings. Rituals usually involve a heightened sense of emotional energy that binds people together.

Sacred symbol. Objects or ideas that are above and beyond the everyday world. Examples include the Christian cross, or the wine/wafer in the Christian Communion rite.

Sex. The biological differences between men and women.

Social class. A group of people within society who have a similar economic position and similar sets of political, cultural and social views and goals.

Social imagination. The set of cultural scripts that individuals use in order to make sense of themselves and the world around them.

Socialization. The sociological concept refers to the complex processes by which children become social beings. Socialization covers everything from toilet training and learning how to walk, speak and read to learning social manners, norms and values. Children learn by osmosis without consciously being aware that they are learning to become social beings.

Sociology of culture. A sociological model that emerged in the United States during the 1970s though pioneering work by, among others, Richard A. Peterson and Paul DiMaggio in the study of forms of cultural production as these related to, for example, music, art and literature.

Soteriology. A 'right' relationship with a higher power.

Status. The honour or prestige attached to one's position or role within society.

Strong program. A conceptual framework associated with Alexander, Smith and other US sociologists to connote a meaning-centred cultural sociology that attempts to map out the internal logics of cultural systems.

Structural determinism. The contention that social life is governed purely by socio-economic determinants such as class, educational attainment and occupation.

Surplus value. The difference between the money wages earned by workers and the economic value they create in their work. This difference becomes the basis of profit-making and exploitation within Marxist theory.

Symbol. A word, image or object that stands in for a larger set of meanings.

Symbolic boundaries. Refers to the role of cultural categories, beliefs and elements of visual and material life to signify differences between social and cultural groups.

Symbolic order. The meanings, representations and ideas that constitute ways of acting, thinking and understanding our selves and others. It is a concept running through Durkheimian sociology as well as psychoanalytic theory. In psychoanalysis, the symbolic order is a turning point in the child's acquisition of language and meaning-making skill as it is able to symbolize or represent its own self and significant others through words, images and objects.

Taylorism. Involved the development of time and motion studies, which closely documented the amount of time it took for workers to complete tasks in order to develop ways of increasing production and efficiency.

Theology. An explanation for evil.

Thick description. All human actions exist within a broader culture structure, consisting of multilayered symbols, texts and meanings. Thick description supposedly allows for a reading of a culture and its practices according to that culture's own concepts and circuits of meaning.

Transgender. Refers to people who identify with and live a gender style that does not normatively match their sexed bodies. This includes men who live as women but are anatomically male and women who live as men and are anatomically female. It can also include intersexed people and the way they combine gender identity with their sexed-body profiles. Transgendering clearly subverts normative category matches between sexed bodies and gender styles. Many societies recognize transgender identities as part of their culture.

Trans-local. Not confined to a particular locale or region but spread across the nation or nations.

Transnational corporation (TNC). A large company, such as Nike or Coca-Cola, which operates in many countries, both in terms of making goods and selling them. Its business model involves operating across national borders to make profits.

Part I
Theory and Method

1

Starting to Write a History of the Present Day: Culture and Sociology

David Chaney

The 'problem' of culture

In the second half of the twentieth century, a major innovation in the syllabus of academic sociology was the study of **culture**. The new theme was not exclusive to sociology, so it was also explored and caused major revisions in a number of fields within the human studies, such as philosophy, art history and English literature, among others. The topic also spawned its own distinctive field of cultural studies (Chaney 1994).[1] The idea that all this was an innovation might seem paradoxical, as culture had been central to the human sciences and particularly anthropology for at least a century. Thus we need to consider how and why the sociological syllabus was reshaped by a turn to culture. I suggest that in turning to culture sociologists revised and developed the fundamental sociological project of the characterization of modernity. It can now be seen that these revisions amounted to the beginning of writing a history of the present day.

An initial suggestion could be that a particular distinctiveness of the new perspectives lay in their concern with the culture of contemporary post-industrial societies. This is in itself insufficient, however. More broadly, we need to consider how culture was changing in later modernity, the social relationships between those who made and/or commentated upon culture and those who consumed it, and whether traditional distinctions between 'high' and 'low' culture were being changed.

In this chapter, I explore how and why culture was 'discovered' in Britain as a topic after a century of sociological work. I will use this particular episode in cultural history to begin a more general discussion of universal sociological questions that must be posed in the study of culture. These are:

- *What* is the culture being seen as problematic?
- And by *whom* and *how* is it being discovered?

Cultural Sociology: An Introduction, First Edition. Les Back et al. © 2012 Les Back, Andy Bennett, Laura Desfor Edles, Margaret Gibson, David Inglis, Ronald Jacobs and Ian Woodward. Published 2012 by Blackwell Publishing Ltd.

Answers to these questions will help us to understand the reasons why and the ways in which cultural sociology has become so central to the sociological syllabus at the beginning of the twenty-first century. In effect, this means looking at how sociological work has adapted to the cultural changes of late modernity. These are clearly major issues, and ones that this collection is intended to address. In this chapter, I say something about how culture came to be seen as distinctively problematic in the 1950s and 1960s in Britain – not just as academic study but in the broader politics of cultural and social change, as well as in terms of relationships between the heterogeneous **discourses** of cultural studies and the broader discourses of academic sociology.

As an introductory point, it is important to recognize that in certain respects the culture of the 'masses' had been seen as a problem by certain members of the intelligentsia and opinion-leaders since a new urban popular culture came into existence. To go back only to the first half of the twentieth century, culture was often considered as an element in wider concerns with ideological knowledge and the ways in which rationality could be defended and sustained in an era of mass demagoguery, particularly Nazism.

A central element in these fears over mass ideologies was the idea that new forms of mass entertainment and information (principally films and radio at the time) could easily subvert traditional forms of moral and political order. In the United States, for example, such a concern was focused by research known as the Payne Fund Studies on the effects of mass cinema attendance, particularly on the young. In Britain, an influential version of this concern was a book written on the dangers of popular literature by a Cambridge intellectual, Q.D. Leavis (1932; see also Eliot 1948).

These examples illustrate some of the ways in which sets of fears around 'culture' were being expressed at this time. In the immediate aftermath of the cataclysmic World War I, it was widely felt that a new society was emerging or would have to be made. In the process, there were concerns that much of what was romanticized as a shared culture between the ruling class and the lower orders was being undermined. It could be said, then, that culture was being seen as a problem because it was being threatened by mass audiences and mass tastes. These fears over the implications of cultural change persisted in the latter half of the twentieth century, although much of the work of cultural studies was to celebrate popular experience and cultural forms. To assume that fear was glibly replaced by celebration would be to miss much about the way the 'problem' of culture has more organically adapted in both academic discourses and the discourses of the wider society.

In part, this is because even those most dismayed by modernity have had to recognize that the culture of traditional pre-industrial society had been disappearing for a long time. As an often nationalist response, there had been a movement in several countries to collect and record the folk songs and traditions of a disappearing world (Storey 2003). This sense of a distinctive national culture under threat was further exacerbated by the early forms of a global mass culture such as the Hollywood film industry in the first half of the century. A concern to 'civilize' the new urban masses of industrial class society had been a recurrent theme in public discourse at least since the first popular national festival – the Great Exhibition of 1851. However, it was given new forms and a distinctive emphasis by the strength and vitality of a popular culture largely focused around forms of mass entertainment – radio, cinema and popular literature, and so on – that developed from 1900 onwards. In the British context, the perceived need to improve the culture of the masses was seen as the central role of the institution of public service broadcasting.

This was an institutional arrangement in which the possibility of commercial gain was sacrificed for ideological ends (Briggs 1970; Scannell 1991).

The complex of political forces that sustained the founding and hegemony of the British Broadcasting Corporation (BBC) throughout this period is too complex to be summarized adequately here. It was, however, a central aspect of the meaning of public service that an 'improving' culture had to be made available to – and was indeed insisted upon for – the national audience. The stratification of radio into audience segments and the early introduction of commercial television based on regional producers modified but did not seriously challenge the authority of cultural elites to shape a hierarchy of taste (McDonnell 1991). And to the institutional power of the BBC should be added the influence of the Arts Council, founded immediately after the war to spread culture outside elite bastions. In this setting, the role of intellectuals – not just those working directly for the BBC but also in universities and working for broadsheet newspapers and magazines – was of central importance: first, as shapers of how the national culture understood itself; and second, as articulators of how that culture was, more or less effectively, to be made accessible to mass audiences. It follows that, as an initial step, our understanding of the 'discovery' of a problem of culture must begin with the power and character of the intelligentsia. That is, a grasp of changes in the meaning and forms of culture in the contemporary era must be grounded in changes in the status, authority, recruitment and institutional hegemony of this intellectual class.

A number of relevant factors can briefly be mentioned. Some indication of the characteristic outlook of elites is provided by the training of those who constituted the influential intelligentsia of British culture. Looking back from today's vantage point, we might be surprised by the significance of departments of English literature. Even now a training in reading English literature has been the foundation for the careers of many cultural commentators, critics, producers and directors. This has been particularly relevant to a discussion of the policies around both the provision of culture and the sorts of culture that were appropriate because of the influence of the teaching of F.R. Leavis and his school (Leavis 1977). Leavis was understood to be concerned by a betrayal of cultural standards in public life, and emphasized the centrality of quality and the ways in which good literature is able to reflect imaginative experience truthfully. Although a Leavisite emphasis upon the significance and power of the greatest literature came to be rather excoriated in the more populist and wide-ranging emphases of cultural studies, it is significant that two books published in the late 1950s, and subsequently seen to have had an important role in redirecting concerns around the provision of culture (Hoggart 1957; Williams 1958), were both written firmly within Leavisite perspectives. It is also significant that both authors wrote from a self-consciously working-class background, and saw themselves as marginal to the institutionalized centres of cultural power in Britain.

In this opening section of the chapter, a two-part theme is introduced that resonates throughout the whole: (i) the idea that the 'discovery' of culture stemmed from fears about the implications of changes to a mass culture; and (ii) the importance of the relationship of cultural elites to mass audiences. Leavisite influences remained significant on cultural policies and the terms of culture debate, particularly in relation to a continuing commitment to the defence of 'quality' (Thompson 1964). There was in the 1960s, however, a realization that the values of 'high culture' were felt to be indefensible and inappropriate in an increasingly commercialized and consumer-driven culture. There is an interesting contrast, for example, in how fine artists in the late 1950s and 1960s increasingly turned away from the rather drab conventions of English fine art and began to explore for the first time the iconography of advertising and popular culture more generally in the movement known as Pop Art.

It could not escape the attention of even the most serious literary scholar that an explosive burst in creative energy occurred in fields such as advertising, fashion and mass media. From the late 1950s onwards, there was what George Melly (1970) later characterized as a 'revolt into style' – particularly among the young – which above all involved the pioneering of new sounds and movements associated with a mass, youth-oriented popular music (Frith 1992). It changed the cultural landscape. This shift in cultural hierarchies and agendas was also matched by an extraordinary pouring of creative energy into the making of popular television for both the BBC and commercial companies. For the first time in the era of modern life, it became fashionable for 'the brightest and the best' of cultural elites to work in the mass media. This meant that in the second half of the twentieth century, mass television was the most innovative and rewarding field of cultural production for both creative intellectuals and popular audiences (Corner 1991).

Confronting cultural divisions

For many, it was within this context of rapid cultural change that it became necessary to re-examine intellectual presuppositions about the role and nature of culture in the lives of ordinary people. Before discussing some of the ways in which that re-examination was undertaken in Britain, it is necessary to look briefly at the dominant hierarchy of cultural value during the first half of the twentieth century. Despite many intellectuals' commitment to an idea of a common culture in pre-industrial society, it is in fact clear that one effect of the massive changes of industrialization and urbanization was the development of distinct and separate class cultures. Considerable effort was put into segregating the spaces inhabited by different classes, such as the parts of a seaside resort visited (and the transport used to reach it), or the parts of a theatre if they were sharing a common entertainment. In the first half of the twentieth century, new forms of mass entertainment such as the cinema transcended these class divisions to some extent, although there were attempts – particularly in the early years of cinema – to segregate the social levels of the audience. In general, however, it is important to note that patterns of cultural activity were clearly differentiated by class and locality.

Sport had been promoted by Victorian and later reformers as a way of transcending aspects of these segregated and generally mutually antagonistic cultures, but where members of different classes might play on the same team they were given different titles – for example, gentlemen and players in cricket, who used separate entrances to the playing field. In general, though, sports did not overlap class boundaries so that the sport you played was a clear indication of your class affiliation (identifications which to some extent survive to the present day), although it is important to recognize regional differences in this. Association football remained a thoroughly working-class game in terms of both who played it and who watched it, and it was really only in the 1960s, facilitated by television and the popularity of the World Cup in 1966, that it started to become glamorized and to attract middle-class audiences (Mason 1989). Within this context, it becomes more comprehensible that where culture did figure in the sociological discourse it was generally as a way of describing community life, so that culture was being used to refer to a whole way of life rather than a set of cultural activities or tastes (Dennis, Henriques and Slaughter 1969; see also Williams 1958).

It is relevant in this context to note that one of the indices of cultural change in the 1960s was an attempt to represent the reality of working-class life in several cultural forms (for example, film, literature and television). Previously, members of the working class had been portrayed through comic or menacing stereotypes, so that they were effectively bowdlerized through patronizing portrayals as in the stock characters played by George Formby or Gracie Fields. Although these figures were often very popular and were important stars, they sentimentalized the realities of working-class life and were in stark contrast to the films, books, television and plays of the 1960s that garnered a generic label of social realist or kitchen sink dramas (see Hill 1986; Elsom 1976; Stead 1989).

The discovery of culture that is our theme thus has at least two distinct but related strands. The first is a gradual appreciation by cultural elites that popular culture was not coarsely vulgar and lacking in merit; the second is that the semi-autonomous and largely hidden domains of popular experience had to be experienced on their own terms. It is significant that this feeling of discovery was being undertaken at a time when the fundamental structures of working-class communities – the industries of coal, steel, shipbuilding, rail and dock work – were beginning their rapid contraction or even destruction. If we also consider massive programmes of rehousing and new town development, as well as suburban migration, then the frameworks of cultural communities were changing at the same time as new forms of youth culture and consumerism, and forms of mass entertainment, were emerging (Hebdige 1979).

For the intelligentsia, it must have seemed that everything that was solid was melting into air. Although recruitment to cultural elites was still predominantly from the ranks of the middle and upper classes, this was changing in response to a step-change expansion in the numbers of people attending universities and associated changes in degree structures and themes. At least partly as a consequence of these developments, the nature of politics was also changing – driven by new forms of radicalism. New single-issue political movements emerged to mobilize new political constituencies, most strikingly in relation to opposition to nuclear weapons and subsequently the US neo-colonial war in Vietnam. These campaigns also pioneered distinctive forms of protest, such as marches, mass demonstrations and non-violent civil disobedience (Gitlin 1993; Roszak 1971).

A new political culture was therefore developing in opposition to institutionalized authority, and this to some extent complemented new predominantly working-class youth cultures. There was then a more middle-class counter-culture in which there was an aspiration to emulate the avant-garde European art movements from earlier in the century, combined with a romantic Bohemianism from the United States fuelled by new forms of drug use (more accurately, drugs became common among middle-class youth rather than being confined to metropolitan ghettoes). Although inspired in part by innovations in modern art, this counter-culture engaged very strongly with contemporary popular culture, not least in the blues groups that came to symbolize an alternative lifestyle later in the 1960s (Sandbrook 2006).

The political culture was in these ways going through a process of rapid and fundamental change. This process was very significant for the discovery of culture. This is because, rather than culture being understood purely as a set of aesthetic concerns with interpretations and meanings, sociological issues were understood to be central to the broader 'cultural project'. These sociological issues can be summarized as:

1. how the nature of social order is to be understood;
2. how the ramifications of the relations of 'power, property and privilege' (to use Williams's phrase) were to be sought in every aspect of British society, particularly cultural forms (and not just the institutionalized politics of parties and the economy).

In this context, the reworking of socialist theory and historiography by a number of authors, and often focused in the British context by the newly founded journal *New Left Review*, was an important element. British political culture typically has prided itself on a pragmatic empiricism in approach, but at this time there was a significant turn towards Europe for theoretical inspiration.

More wide-ranging were new modes of struggles for emancipation that were initially particularly focused on situations in the United States. I am thinking here of movements for Black Power and Gay Pride, but such struggles quickly came to be seen as having a major relevance to understanding forms of oppression in contemporary Britain. Particularly important for social politics and cultural studies was the emergent Women's Movement (Thornham 2000; McRobbie 2009; Rowbotham 2001). In part growing out of new forms of political radicalism, this was a movement for liberation and analysis of oppression that was to become central to new forms of cultural theorizing.

The next section will discuss the significance of the various forms of the new politics for the theorizing of culture for sociological thought. Concluding this section, it is appropriate to note that the contemporary interdependence of culture and politics was dramatized particularly powerfully in '*les évènements*' of Paris in May 1968 (Willener 1970). In this 'moment', which seemed to offer the possibility of a cultural revolution, many elements of a changing political culture were clearly manifest. New ideas spawned in this intellectual and political ferment underlay many significant developments in the theorizing of cultural forms.

Culture and sociology

The purpose of this chapter so far has been to indicate the social and political context of changing cultural values. This section considers institutional innovations in the study of culture, and looks at how these new ideas were taken up in sociological practice. Thus the Centre for Contemporary Cultural Studies (CCCS) was founded at the University of Birmingham at the beginning of the academic year in 1964. It is unsurprising and appropriate that the Centre was an adjunct of the Department of English (initially inspired by the leadership of Richard Hoggart). While there were some close personal connections to the Department of Sociology, the dominant character of early work at the Centre was firmly within a framework of critical theorizing, and was based on methodologies of literary criticism adapted to ideology critique. (The intellectual history of the Centre and of cultural studies more generally has been discussed in a number of publications, such as Hartley 2003; Strinati 1995; Tudor 1999.)

It could well be argued that not only did the initial turn to culture take place outside the syllabus of sociology, but to a considerable extent in opposition to sociological discourse – although it is important to note that a number of quasi-ethnographic projects by graduate students and research associates attached to the Centre have proved important resources for social theory (see, inter alia, Willis 1978; McRobbie 1991; Hall and Jefferson 1976). The main point to emphasize is that the cultural forms and formations of contemporary society that were being 'discovered' by those drawn to the new focus were principally seen as topics for critiques of ideology (particularly under the leadership of Stuart Hall). It was felt by many drawn to cultural studies that sociology had largely failed to emancipate itself from the ideological hegemony of a repressive social order. This meant that the relations between sociology as it was being developed and the emergent themes of cultural studies covered a range from excited enthusiasm to mutual suspicion. Aspects of either end of this range will be considered in turn.

We begin by looking at the more positive responses to the cultural initiative. The rather clumsy formulation 'sociology as it was being developed' has been used because British sociology more generally was going through a process of rapid change at this time. First, many more young people were participating in tertiary education, so colleges were expanding with new departments being founded. Second, the young people being recruited to the discipline were far from immune to changes in the contemporary political culture. Many were actively involved in new forms of radicalism, and these interests and commitments were expressed in new ways of teaching, as well as in new emphases and additions to the established syllabus. These trends combined to create a fundamental radicalism in conceptions of social order. For example, the study of crime and criminal behaviour shifted from an emphasis upon control to a more celebratory concern with deviance and other forms of transgressive social action. This shift in stance had strong links to a more cultural approach, not least with representations of 'dis-order' (Cohen 1985). There were other similar innovations in perspective in fields such as education, the family, political sociology and social theorizing. Above all, the subsequent development of gender as a key analytic resource for the study of social order, as well as the development of women's studies as foci for research and theorizing in their own right, had major implications for the sociological syllabus (Shiach 1999; O'Sullivan 1982).

There were, then, many opportunities for an emphasis on culture to be consistent with other themes in contemporary sociology. Unsurprisingly, from the late 1960s appointments were being made to lecture on culture in departments of sociology. There was great variation in how the brief for such positions was interpreted – from, for example, a commitment to theorizing in cultural studies, to film studies and popular culture more generally, to more traditional concerns with the sociology of art and literature (the extent to which form and content – particularly in high art – can be interpreted from sociological perspectives). A number of innovations in related work also occurred, which have continued to reshape the academic syllabus under a variety of disciplinary rubrics. These included studies in folk and popular music, leisure and entertainment, mass communications, and consumer culture and fashion.[2] Such a variety of topics generated an equivalent variety of styles of work, from exclusively theoretical to various modes of empirical study; however, perhaps the greatest interest was in the area of social theory (the title of the influential journal *Theory, Culture & Society*, founded in 1982, locates these overlapping interests very clearly).

Faced with the self-evident inadequacies of the repressive regimes of self-styled communist states, in conjunction with the stuttering compromises of social democratic movements in Western Europe, it is not surprising that those caught up in a radicalized environment felt the need for new ideas regarding how to proceed. Neither should it be surprising that in the rapidly expanding sociology departments of the 1970s, the syllabus of social theory moved well beyond the previously dominant perspectives of American social theory. This broadening of horizons was greatly facilitated by translation and publication in English of a range of authors who quickly came to be seen as central to the concerns of those working in both cultural studies and sociology. Rather than review this enormous bibliography, it is sufficient to say that in the 1970s work by authors as diverse as (and not in any order of significance) Foucault, Barthes, Elias, Simmel, Benjamin, Adorno, Bourdieu, Habermas and Brecht, as well as others, was either published in English for the first time or the corpus of their work expanded.

One effect of this new body of work, particularly in the context of a revived interest in and reworking of the Marxist tradition, was that sociologists in general reoriented their work from the perspectives of American to European social thought. Sociologists increasingly saw themselves as engaging in a normative critique of late capitalist society as an empirical analysis, and under this rubric there was a strong sense of a common bond between staff and students, which sometimes acted to exclude 'unbelievers'. A sense of a common ground between those addressing issues in cultural theory and social theory more generally – also grounded in a common commitment to European social thought – was intensified by the rise of a diverse body of work loosely interested in notions of postmodern society and postmodernism (Harvey 1989; Seidman 1994; Owen 1997).

While in certain respects an emphasis upon contemporary culture in sociological work was consistent with other changes and developments in the discipline, there were at the same time many working in sociology who saw cultural studies as a cuckoo in the nest. This constitutes the second, more negative, response to the cultural turn. Within the ranks of the broader sweep of sociology departments that were likely to contain social policy specialists – perhaps criminologists or even anthropologists as well as more traditional sociological specialists – there was a considerable amount of distrust and even resentment of what might have been seen as the glamour attaching to the now-fashionable cultural studies.

This can be attributed to a combination of attitudes. First, British sociology was greatly influenced by strong traditions of commitment to social amelioration (or, more pejoratively, social engineering). Second, there was a strong suspicion of a lack of methodological rigour among cultural theorists. These attitudes were expressed as scepticism over the relevance of the topic of culture – a scepticism reinforced by the greater salience of philosophy as a meeting ground for social theorists and those working in cultural studies. English philosophy had been so sterile for at least a century that new philosophical currents (particularly from Europe) were very welcome, but often seemed alien in both manner and terminology to the sensibilities of conventional sociology. The suspicion was also undoubtedly heightened by the subsequent association of cultural themes with postmodernist ideas, together with a presumption that this implied uninhibited relativism.

To many, the new concern with culture as a sociological topic thus seemed to challenge the character of the sociological perspective. Because the main concerns of the 'culturalists' were with meaning, ideology and a background of critical reading, it seemed that the focal problem should be seen as the character of representation in cultural forms and social discourse more generally. Although I have stated that a commitment to deconstructing social order and associated relations of power and privilege are central to the cultural project, for many in sociology it was hard to see these aims being addressed in readings of cultural forms – however critical. An emphasis on representation, with its consequential implication that 'everything that passes for knowledge' in society can be subject to a critical reading, should not have been surprising to those familiar with work in the sociology of knowledge. However, a large proportion of the constituency of sociology proved to have an obstinate commitment to the graspable – indeed self-evident – reality of the social world, thus finding deconstructing reflexive representations at best distracting and at worst perverse.

An attempt to bridge the gulf between positive and negative attitudes to cultural perspectives can be found in the collection of papers from the first national conference of the British Sociological Association (1978), focused on culture (Barrett *et al.* 1979). The organizers of the conference saw themselves as opening new territory: 'Given the virtual non-existence of any sociology of culture we were confronted by a field that was largely unmapped' (Barrett *et al.* 1979: 9).[3] In practice, though, the novelty of the situation was neglected by these authors in favour of a more traditional sociological determinism.

Thus their approach was to treat the representations of cultural practice as essentially epiphenomenal – that is, as something determined by forces 'outside' cultural practice. Such an approach is locked into an epistemology of material 'reality' and representational 'illusion'. It neglects the constitutive power of narratives to make experience meaningful – that is, to become ways of staging social practice that frame and shape actors' understandings of meaning and possibility. Second, an epiphenomenal perspective effectively leaves those who use representations – audiences, consumers, and so on – as passive cultural dupes. In the years that have followed this conference, there has been a massive amount of work on how audiences actively interact with representations in making them meaningful (Morley 1992). One can go further and make a more subversive sociological critique of an account of culture in which the determination of representation is emphasized above all else. In this critique, key features of the character of representation in modernity which would otherwise have been neglected are rescued. Three themes in this critique are outlined briefly below.

First, a persistent strand in the culture of modernity is that critical representation has typically sought to escape being explicit or too clearly determined by what it represents (Eagleton 2008). Our words, pictures, films, sounds and buildings are, to differing degrees, abstract allusions to the reality of the world we inhabit. In this lies much of the power of representation, but it also entails an essential open-endedness in interpretation. The second theme is almost self-evident in a culture of spectacle. As the world has become more modern, the illusions and spectacles of entertainment and persuasion have moved out of specialist sites such as theatres and cinemas to become universally present and thus pervasive in every aspect of life. In important ways, culture has become the basis for rather than the reflection of social life (Chaney 1994: ch. 5). Third, an epiphenomenal approach assumes that there is 'a real', which somehow exists prior to the way in which it is represented; yet in so many ways what we take to be real is that way because of how it is mediated or represented. Our grasp of the real is therefore doubled or made reflexive through the ways in which we can represent, narrate, account for and dramatize an iconography of social life (Chaney 1996, 2002).

These critiques are based on an account of representation in culture in which representation both helps to shape the world of meaning and is at the same time formed or determined by the social relations of that world. In writing a history of the present day – that is, an interpretation of social process and cultural change as it is unfolding – we need to be aware of both the constraints on and possibilities for action and understanding.

It should be becoming clear that, in turning to the study of culture, sociology was at last engaging with the character of modernity. This was not an arbitrary fashion of a particular era but rather an expression of a complex battle over who was going to be able to write the history of the present day, and in what ways. Modernity is a historical phenomenon, and thus one that will change over time. Modernism as a movement of distinctive aspirations in the representation of modernity may well be exhausted (Clark 1999), but the problems posed by, as well as the achievements of, modernism have not been discarded. There is an enormous literature on how culture has changed and is changing, but the ways in which we recognize, describe and interpret these changes shows that they are not meaningless. It may well be that one of the most fruitful ways of beginning to open up the character of recent change is through recognizing that, as contemporary culture has changed the status, authority and social character of the intelligentsia – the group particularly charged with the production and interpretation of culture – that group has changed too (Bauman 1987).

Cultural change

The turn to culture as a sociological topic led to a fundamental reconsideration of the sociological project and appropriate methodologies. Sociological engagement with the nature of cultural representation – that is, all the ways we have of talking about, picturing and understanding ourselves, the repertoire of social knowledge in effect – requires a concern with how to write a history of the present day – or, to put it more simply, how to write about cultural change. In this section, some contemporary developments in the theme that has run throughout the chapter – the interrelationships of popular taste and the culture of social and intellectual elites – will be discussed.

The mode of change to be considered concerns the relationship of popular taste with the orthodoxies of elite culture. The argument will not be that cultural hierarchies have disappeared, or the even less likely proposition that social hierarchies have disappeared, but that their persistence has been masked by a display of cultural ordinariness. This takes two main forms: first, that the boundaries differentiating class hierarchies of taste are ostensibly denied; and second, that the tastes of ordinary people are not only not ignored, but ostensibly celebrated. These modes of populism will be characterized by the – ironic – heading of radical democratization.

To begin, we should be reminded of the points already made concerning the class-based segregation of cultural taste in earlier phases of the modern era. Although the character of popular culture changed to an extraordinary degree in the first half of the twentieth century, class cultures remained largely separate, with the middle and upper classes maintaining an effective monopoly of high culture and the discriminations of good taste. From the perspective of elite standards, popular culture was trite, formulaic, lacking in sensitivity and reliant on spectacular effects rather than a nuanced exploration of character. The primary responsibility of elite institutions such as universities was therefore understood to be to defend cultural standards, and where possible help to elucidate them and make them accessible to the less advantaged. It has also been noted that the authority of these standards and the elites' confidence in them began to wane in the years following World War II.

Popular culture in the 1960s began to break out of its ghetto, and hierarchies of taste became considerably more confused. One way of illustrating this point is to say that when 'toffs' patronized the music halls at the beginning of the twentieth century, they were self-consciously slumming it, enjoying the vulgarity of popular taste. When young men at art schools (or private schools) started forming rock bands (such as Pink Floyd), they were aping popular taste – but now because it was fashionable, even avant-garde. Another area in which boundaries between class cultures became blurred was television audiences. Television became a mass medium for the first time in the 1960s, as coverage became nationwide and sets were a lot cheaper to buy. There were still presumptions of a stratification of taste, as in the distinction between BBC2 and the other channels, but mainstream television became fashionable and innovative too. Or one could mention the development of popular holiday-making outside Britain at this time, with innovations in transport such as cheap air travel making mass tourism possible (Rojek and Urry 1997). More generally, fashion itself became fashionable, with a vast expansion of consumer culture and youth culture as heterogeneous melting-pots for new lifestyles.[4]

Of course, it is essential to emphasize that discriminations in taste remained potent indices of class affiliations. Holidaying on the Costa Brava was not the equivalent of a holiday cottage in the French countryside, and shopping at even Marks & Spencer was not the same as patronizing Harvey Nichols. In a society structured by inequalities in class and **status**, such distinctions were essential in order to sustain the social fabric (the power and persistence of class-based discriminations has been demonstrated most powerfully in Bourdieu's (1984) study of taste; see also Bennett *et al.* 2009). It is also important to recognize that certain high arts, such as opera, literary novels and abstract art, retained their privileged status and were certainly not opened up to popular audiences.

Yet it remains true that the terrain of the cultural landscape began to change markedly towards a more widespread acceptance that the forms and styles of popular culture were no longer to be patronized only by social elites. In all sorts of ways, the opinions of the masses were continually sought and ostensibly given equal weight with so-called experts. As part of this shift in perspective, academic commentary on culture was no longer confined to high art in fields such as art history, literary criticism and music schools. Film studies, popular music, media studies and mass leisure became – albeit gradually – recognized as respectable fields for academic study.

There has been a development then of a strong populist current in which aspects of the privileges of established elites were increasingly called into question. This current was not confined to cultural hierarchies, but became part of a general social climate. For example, the Thatcherite revolution was not just an attack on public services or professional autonomy, but also involved unseating the land-owning gentry from their dominance in Conservative politics. Margaret Thatcher's political heirs – most markedly Tony Blair – have attempted to mask their privileged backgrounds by putting on 'mock-ney' or 'estuarial' accents, and lying about a childhood commitment to regional football. More generally, the form of address in public life has shifted as the demotic has become standard and marks of education or privilege are avoided. Even the Queen has shifted the social register of her public voice downwards. The tone of public discourse displayed by the BBC, as the guardian of a national culture, has broadened very considerably and become more popular. Even what used to be called broadsheet or quality newspapers have in general shrunk to tabloid size and adopted more populist forms of presentation and subject matter.

In a recent book (Chaney 2002), I summarized this current with the label of radical democratization. I mean by this term that, although Britain formally became a popular democracy early in the twentieth century, the structures and privileges of social hierarchy continued to dominate the institutions of public life, such as law, medicine, education and politics, as well as culture. In the latter years of the twentieth century, the populist current purported to complete the unfinished revolution of democratic change, and thus its radical import. In this current, every opinion is presumed to be of equal value, and the authority of expertise is widely discredited.

Despite this, it is of course accepted – although some find this surprising – that a democratization of tone has served only to mask the persistence of social and cultural inequalities. Not only has Britain *not* become a more egalitarian society, with differences in standard of living between social groups widening it has actually become *less* equal. My use of the term 'radical democratization' is therefore meant to be ironic, and thus to direct attention to how and why a populist ethos functions as an ideology in which the illusions of choice mystify the inequalities of contemporary society.[5]

While critical research into the character and function of populism should not be confined to the cultural sphere, this is an area in which populism has become more pervasive. The changing character of culture is particularly relevant to both the status and character of the intelligentsia and creative producers, and to the nature of cultural objects. What have the implications of changes in the production and marketing of culture been for creative personnel? The production of culture for mass audiences has always necessitated distinctive modes of industrialization (Power and Scott 2004; Hesmondhalgh 2002). Typically, culture industries have sought to rationalize processes of distribution as far as possible, while allowing production units high degrees of autonomy and informality in order to facilitate innovation.

One way in which forms of change might be addressed is by considering changing roles and functions associated with new technologies. It has, for example, frequently been remarked that the 'news' function of newspapers has been changed by the development of rolling news channels on radio and television, as well as news access on web sites. Newspapers have been forced to shift away from an emphasis on breaking news – apart from occasional pieces of investigative journalism, although those are becoming increasingly exceptional with greater reliance on agency sources (Davies 2008) – to a much more extensive use of columnists providing commentary on public affairs and/or a concentration on entertainment news, principally the activities of celebrities and sports stars. Curiously, their diminished role in generating news seems to have been associated with a greater influence over shaping news, so that politicians are now more influenced by newspaper-set agendas than previously. However, even this conception of journalism as a print medium is hard to sustain in light of falling advertising revenues, and is changing with increasing use of web sites set up by newspapers and the rise of the blogosphere. It is therefore possible that the future newspaper is more likely to function as a gateway or set of portals to more specialized news resources or commentaries.

Clearly, these sorts of changes have major implications not only for columnists, journalists and other public figures mediating the news, but also for the character of public discourse. The traditional model of the public sphere has been a small focus of metropolitan sources radiating out through gatekeepers and other influentials to mass audiences. Whether or not such ideas of mass-ness were ever justified, changes in the organization of the production and marketing of culture partly induced by technological developments have meant that audiences are no longer masses in the same sense. Increasingly, it seems that older conceptions of 'the performance' that is the cultural text – whether it be film, book, sports event or art exhibition – which is the object of their collective attention are being superseded.

Traditionally, performances were resourced by charging audiences an admission fee to the event. In an era of mass production, that model could be retained while it was possible to sell audience members individual copies of a cultural good. Newspapers and television developed an alternative model in which the good was itself subsidized or free, but resourced through the willingness of advertisers to pay for the right to hitch their marketing to the object. In both cases, though, the distinctiveness of the cultural good being sold was enshrined in a notion of copyright so that ownership of the good was restricted – usually to the distribution agency. Now both of these models are being undermined – in one way, because the good (for example, a book or record or film) can be accessed online and copying by downloading cannot be controlled, and in another way, because the good might not exist as a discrete event but simultaneously be happening over a multiplicity of sites. In effect, this has meant that copyright has become intensely contested and, in the judgement of some commentators, is being superseded to the point of becoming irrelevant.

The significance of the legal notion of copyright is that it makes a cultural production into a marketable commodity. It has therefore underlain the character of cultural work since at least the Renaissance in fifteenth-century Europe. It is in this sense that the concept of the artist is inseparable from the notion of a commodity, with value that can be bought and sold. If the notion of copyright – and thus the uniquely valued object – is changing, then the character of authorship is also changing. A notion of individual authorship traditionally has been more significant in the sphere of high culture where value – both commercial and aesthetic – typically has been very dependent upon an attribution of particular authorship. Thus marginal and trivial jottings can be found to have a significant value if they can be reframed by being shown to be the work of a high-status individual. A deconstruction of authorship is thus likely to prove particularly tricky for aesthetic and commercial discourses.

One solution to the problem of selling cultural goods when they are produced in digital formats that can be copied quickly, infinitely and in ways that cannot be controlled has been to abandon the 'good' as the object being sold. In this approach, the object – for example, a recording of a group performing a collection of songs – is given away free or for a nominal sum in the expectation that substantial revenues can be generated by associated para-textual goods such as live performances by the group or endorsed clothing. These new forms of marketing will require a considerable amount of ingenuity on the part of those selling culture, and clearly many organizations have been reluctant to abandon entirely the traditional conception of 'the work of art' as that which is being sold. More generally, it seems that contextual or supplementary 'cultural goods' may be becoming more significant in their social effects.

An interesting example is provided by the ways in which high cultural objects have been found to be important factors in schemes of social and cultural regeneration. A number of unlikely places – such as the Baltic Centre, the Sage concert hall and the Angel of the North, all on the South Tyneside bank in the United Kingdom – have found that investment in prestigious cultural developments works very effectively to generate new housing developments and generally to completely change the character and perceived identity of an area. In part, these developments work through attracting tourists, both nationally and internationally, as in the case of the Guggenheim Museum in Bilbao or the Tate Modern gallery in south London, and in part they function through changing the meaning of a place. In these situations, the culture that is being produced is less about individual works – indeed, the content of museums and galleries often seems fairly irrelevant – than a claim for a distinctive identity as in the European City of Culture appellation. Culture becomes integral to the marketing of a place that is usually, but not exclusively, a city and as such has come to function as an end in itself.

Conclusion

I should clarify that my central concern has been with some aspects of how the syllabus of sociology has changed and developed in response to cultural change, and how continuing processes of change will present further challenges in understanding both the character of contemporary culture and the forms of the social world. I hope to have shown that the essential cultural change to which all those concerned were responding was everything that was involved in the emergence of a mass culture. The implication of the discovery of culture for academic sociology was that it put the theme of the character of modernity firmly back at the heart of the sociological enterprise. It is a perfectly reasonable argument to say that the meaning and implications of modernity have been the key problematic of sociology for and since the 'founding fathers'; too often, though, the practice of sociology has drifted or been directed into the management of social order. Themes of cultural sociology require us instead to consider the ways in which social order has been, and is being, made meaningful for the new publics of modern experience – to write a history of the present day. Only in the light of these reflections can we begin to contest and change the terms of that order.

Notes

1   In the book referenced here, I characterized the emergence of culture as a distinctive focus as a 'cultural turn', punning on the use of the term 'linguistic turn' to refer to the distinctive focus on language studies earlier in the century.

2   Later developments in fields such as the sociology of the body and everyday life were excavations of neglected themes in the sociological perspective that can largely be attributed to the influence of the discovery of culture.

3   Williams (1980) is interesting both for what it says about the time and for illuminating how far Williams had moved in the nearly 20 years since he began to shape 'the discovery of culture'. See also Eagleton (1989).

4   A contemporary view that class structures were becoming less entrenched was expressed by Harold Macmillan after being elected prime minister in 1959 when he wrote to the Queen about the current state of the nation: 'The most encouraging feature of the Election . . . is the strong impression that I have formed that Your Majesty's subjects do not wish to allow themselves to be divided into warring classes or tribes filled with hereditary animosity against each other. There was a very significant breakdown of this structure of society' (quoted in Hennessy 2006: 1). However, some may feel that this 'optimistic' view was more likely to be held by a member of traditional social elites such as Harold Macmillan.

5   Recently Ross McKibbin (2008) has also sought to describe this trend: 'In its social manners Britain has rapidly become a very democratic society. Old forms of respect and the deference due to traditional hierarchies have not altogether disappeared, but they have been profoundly weakened. In the daily exchanges of life Britain is now very like North America or Australia'. However, he does go on to note that: 'Britain is now a very much more unequal and less socially mobile society than it was thirty years ago' (McKibbin 2008: 22).

Acknowledgement

I am really grateful for the helpful advice Stephanie Lawler and Andy Bennett gave me in the preparation of this chapter.

2

Defining Cultural Sociology

Learning objectives

- To examine the origins of cultural sociology and the impact of the cultural turn on its development.
- To understand cultural sociology as a field of research distinct from cultural studies.
- To consider the distinctions between British and US approaches to cultural sociology.
- To comprehend the ongoing development of cultural sociology in an international context.

Introduction

Over the last two decades, cultural sociology has developed quickly from a relatively minor sub-field of the broader sociology discipline to an established and internationally acknowledged approach. Driving this rapid development is an increasing concern among theorists and researchers about culture as a focus for understanding the processes and systems of relations through which societies are arranged. This cultural approach challenges earlier sociological models, which have tended to regard culture as merely a by-product of structural experiences of class, gender, race, and so on, by re-representing culture itself as a driving force for the creation and representation of social life. As a critical part of this mission, cultural sociology also recasts culture not just as the representation of elitist definitions and understandings of culture – art, literature, classical

Cultural Sociology: An Introduction, First Edition. Les Back et al. © 2012 Les Back, Andy Bennett, Laura Desfor Edles, Margaret Gibson, David Inglis, Ronald Jacobs and Ian Woodward. Published 2012 by Blackwell Publishing Ltd.

music, and so on – but rather as encompassing a broad range of everyday social practices and conventions, from the spectacular to the mundane. The rapid impact of cultural sociology can be measured by significant developments towards establishing a series of foci for cultural sociological research. This can be seen, for example, in the establishment of the Yale University Center for Cultural Sociology (founded in 2004) and the publication of the UK journal *Cultural Sociology* (launched in 2007).

This chapter provides a series of key definitions of cultural sociology together with a description and critical evaluation of the central conceptual tenets underpinning the cultural sociological approach. Taking as its starting point cultural sociology's concern with culture as a dynamic process characterized by an interrelationship between structure and agency, the chapter then goes on to examine the significance of cultural sociology as a means by which it is possible both to critically address established sociological models and to map out new understandings concerning the role of culture in the production and re-production of social relations. Key to this discussion will be the rendering of cultural sociology as an approach exhibiting features that make it characteristically distinct from cultural studies. Thus it will be argued that, although cultural studies is similarly concerned with the portrayal of culture as the product of 'ordinary' discourses and practices of everyday life, the orientation of cultural studies around issues of power and conflict based in pre-assumed **categories** of class, race, gender, and so forth places this approach much closer to traditional forms of sociological theory and practice. For cultural sociology, issues of power, conflict and struggle, as these contribute to the cultural fabric of society, are recast as the product of a multifarious range of ideological and aesthetically informed discourses and sensibilities in which class, gender, race and other articulations of identity are reflexively constructed and articulated.

The cultural turn

The emergence of cultural sociology as a distinctive theoretical and empirical approach is strongly linked to the **cultural turn** (see Chaney 1994). In general sociological parlance, the cultural turn refers to a revised emphasis on culture, not as the product of class relations and a concomitant positioning of ideological and economic power with the ruling elite, but rather as a dynamic process centring around the redefinition of individuals and groups as reflexive agents of cultural production. Within this new arena of analysis, culture is considered inseparable from the capabilities of individuals to act upon and influence cultural practices, norms and values as embedded within social categories such as class, gender, ethnicity and social institutions like the family, school and workplace. It is also acknowledged that such *everyday* production of culture centres around an interplay of local and global influences, with the latter continually feeding off each other as a means through which individuals construct identities and **lifestyle** practices (Giddens 1991; Chaney 1996).

A critical development in this repositioning of culture has been its wresting away from more or less exclusive associations with high art (literature, paintings, music, and so forth). Important in this respect were the formative observations of British literary theorist Raymond Williams, whose 1958 essay 'Culture is ordinary' was an early acknowledgement of the fact that culture in its broadest sense, including aspects of traditional and vernacular practice, needs to be acknowledged as integral to any understanding and analysis of culture (see Williams 1958). In his later work Williams qualifies this position:

> The analysis of culture . . . is the clarification of the meanings and values implicit and explicit in a particular way of life, a particular culture. Such analysis will include . . . historical criticism . . . in which intellectual and imaginative works are analysed in relation to particular traditions and societies, but will also include elements in the way of life that to followers of the other definitions are not 'culture' at all: the organization of production, the structure of the family, the structure of institutions which express or govern social relationships, the characteristic forms through which members of the society communicate . . . It seems to me that there is value in each of these kinds of definition. For it certainly seems necessary to look for meanings and values, the record of creative human activity, not only in art and intellectual work, but also in institutions and forms of behaviour.
>
> (Williams 1961: 57–8)

The ideas of Williams, together with those of fellow British scholar Richard Hoggart (1957), were an instrumental influence on a field of study that came to be known as cultural studies. Founded in 1964 and directed by Hoggart, the Birmingham Centre for Contemporary Cultural Studies was an early indication of the widespread influence that cultural studies was to quickly establish on critical thinking in the humanities and social sciences. Taking Williams's interpretation of culture as 'a whole way of life' as a central tenet for cultural analysis, cultural studies set about the task of investigating how the class struggles that had characterized British society for over a century and a half continued to be played out through a series of everyday, seemingly mundane, cultural practices. This embraced the key tenets of Gramsci's (1971) cultural Marxist approach, critically the concept of hegemony. Gramsci coined the term hegemony as a means of expressing the dominant system of ideas and beliefs through which the ruling class is able to exert power over society. According to Gramsci, the hegemonic order is susceptible to challenges from below. Although such challenges are in themselves incapable of usurping the ruling class from their dominant position, they nevertheless can produce a 'crisis of authority' (Bennett *et al.* 1981: 199). Utilizing this position as a means of reinvestigating cultural life, and in particular the impact of popular culture, cultural studies challenged the cultural pessimism of European critical theorists such as Adorno and Horkheimer. The latter had argued that the mundane and ephemeral products of the emergent twentieth-century media and cultural industries conspired to extend the controlling influence of the ruling elite over the working class; mass broadcasting and mass consumerism, it was suggested, merely signalled a new form of hegemonic control over the ordinary masses (Bennett 2005). By contrast, cultural studies theorists contended that, while the products of the media and cultural industries could be fashioned with intended meanings in mind, the ultimate everyday significance that such images, texts and products assumed could not be controlled. In this way, it was argued, new and subversive meanings could be attached to media and cultural resources that supplied new challenges to the hegemonic order.

Sociology and the 'rediscovery' of culture

The origins of sociology in the late nineteenth century had seen the emergence of a number of writers, among them Georg Simmel and Max Weber, whose work on aspects of status and distinction in the growing urban metropoles paid critical attention to the place of social actors in shaping and performing the cultural life of the city through various modes of conspicuous consumption. Simmel, for example, in what is largely considered to be the first sociological essay on fashion, attributed the significance of fashion in urban contexts to the need among city-dwelling individuals to assert a level of individualism among the large and anonymous crowds that populate public spaces (see Simmel, in Frisby and Featherstone 1997). Despite such early interest in everyday cultural practice, throughout much of the twentieth century sociological interest turned away from issues of meaning and focused instead upon structural institutions and practices, as manifested through the social relations of capitalism. To this end, studies of social institutions such as the family, school, work and religion, together with social categories such as class, gender, race and ethnicity, were positioned and explained in terms of their relationship to patterns of social stratification, inequality and exclusion, based upon socio-economic status.

In many ways, it was precisely the mission of cultural studies to reinvestigate such patterns in the social relations of capitalism through questions of culture. Yet within this approach, the questions asked about culture continued to work from a position where cultural identity and practice were perceived to be fixed and trapped by the structural circumstances in which individuals found themselves. Towards the end of the twentieth century, however, de-industrialization and the shift from production to consumer- and leisure-based societies in the West prompted new questions about the nature and significance of culture and its relationship to society. This 'cultural turn' in academic thinking radically altered the prevailing conceptualization of culture. Thus, rather than perceiving culture, as well as associated concepts such as identity and lifestyle, as in any way rigidly fixed by the imposition of social structure, this new approach sought to prise such assumptions about culture apart – to view questions of culture, identity and lifestyle as far more complex, locally nuanced and, above all, inextricably bound up with the reflexive agency of social actors. It was in the wake of the cultural turn that sociology made a return to culture as a basis from which to examine social life. Indeed, a number of sociologists were themselves important in the realization of the cultural turn, and thus created a significant basis from which to mount a new exploration of culture from a sociological perspective.

Cultural sociology in a British and European context

A figure central to the re-emergence of culture as a focus for sociological research is French theorist Pierre Bourdieu. In his celebrated study *Distinction*, Bourdieu (1984) develops ideas introduced in the work of Weber and Simmel in relation to the connections among class, lifestyle and social status. According to Bourdieu, while at one level lifestyles appear to be autonomously constructed and reflexively articulated forms of cultural practice, they nevertheless remain inextricably bound up with the socio-economic circumstances of the individual. Extending this argument, Bourdieu coins the term **habitus** to articulate how an individual's entire field of cultural competence is linked to the accumulation of five forms of capital: cultural, social, educational, economic and political. For Bourdieu, there are close connections between each of these forms of capital – particularly cultural and economic capital – and these directly reflect the class status of the individual. According to Bourdieu (1984), in the context of late capitalist consumer-based society, the fact of class itself becomes a mediation, something that is learned and understood through particular forms of consumption practice in relation to an array of goods and services:

> class constitutes a relatively autonomous space whose structure is defined by the distribution of economic and **cultural capital** among its members, each class fraction being characterized by a certain configuration of this distribution to which there corresponds a certain life-style.
>
> (Bourdieu 1984: 260)

It follows that, in Bourdieu's interpretation, as individuals become more socio-economically mobile, the experience and shaping influence of class remain integral to social identity as this is articulated at both the individual and collective levels. Subsequent work has challenged Bourdieu's interpretation of lifestyle as the subconscious practice and articulation of rigidly established class-based sensibilities. For example, according to Chaney (1996), Bourdieu's insistence on the structuring role of class amounts to a crude negation of the reflexive and oppositional qualities that late modern consumerist practices have introduced into the cultural sphere of the everyday. Thus, argues Chaney:

> To assume that objectifications [of cultural capital] are only displays of a lesser or greater mastery of cultural codes is to presume that there is a pre-existing and unchanging hierarchy of codes – or perhaps more accurately, it is to presume that culture is an inescapable environment which envelops social action in the way that social structures envelop individual experience.
>
> (Chaney 1996: 66–7)

These ideas form part of a body of work that has emerged in Britain over the last 30 years, and that now forms an important dimension of cultural sociology, alongside an American tradition led by the Yale Center for Cultural Sociology (see below). As noted elsewhere in this book, a watershed moment for the development of cultural sociology in a British context was the 1978 British Sociological Association and the subsequent conference proceedings publication (see Barrett *et al.* 1979). In his important book *The Cultural Turn*, published some years later, Chaney (1994) explores the background of this return to questions of culture among British sociologists, noting as a central point an increasing dissatisfaction with theories of hegemony as these were being applied in cultural research. Summing up this position, Chaney observes:

> Such theories cannot allow the free play of irony and reflexivity in cultural discourse . . . Putting it at its simplest, such theories assume that social entities such as class exist, one might say in the real world, and then they are talked about, represented and experienced as cultural matters. It follows that the dynamic relations of the former can be used to explain the character of the latter.
>
> (Chaney 1994: 48–9)

Central to Chaney's argument here – and also explored in his later work (see Chaney 1996, 2002), and in the work of Giddens (1991) and Bauman (1992) – is the notion of the individual as an active and reflexive agent, capable of making choices in relation to issues of identity and lifestyle rather than accepting these as being imposed from above. In particular, Chaney considers the cultural resources produced and disseminated by the cultural and media industries to be important in the marking out of new aesthetic and ideological territories through which individuals actively participate in the cultural production of everyday life. For Chaney, the cultural and media industries act as new frames of reference for individuals in the construction of identity and associated lifestyle projects (see Chaney 2002). A broadly similar observation is made by Abercrombie and colleagues regarding 'the centrality of consumer desires to the conduct of life' (1994: 45).

For some advocates of a cultural sociological approach, this shift in the nature of social identity was to be explained in terms of a waning of modernity and the emergence of a new 'postmodern' state (see Bauman 1992). Indeed, some observers went so far as to suggest that postmodernity signalled an end of ideology and historical narrative (for example, see Lash 1990). Within this new social situation, it was argued, individuals became key controlling agents – authors of their own identities, masters of their own fate. A notable example of such an approach is seen in the work of Bauman (1992), who argued that the postmodern shift, and the concomitant breakdown of modernity's control of cultural relations and identities, had given rise to a new cultural terrain in which social bonds and the forms of identity to which they gave rise become inherently unstable and fleeting. Applying this interpretation of identity-formation in a more extreme fashion, the German social theorist Ulrich Beck (1992) regards postmodernism as inextricably bound up with the rise of the post-industrial society. For Beck, the slackening of social controls and regulation associated with the era of industrial capitalism has given rise to increasing levels of risk and uncertainty, and has resulted in a rapid process of individualization. This, argues Bauman, is centrally defined by a new era of self-interest among individuals and a breakdown of social and cultural bonds, as these are more conventionally understood as drivers of social cohesion.

For other early advocates of a cultural sociological approach, the cultural turn is characterized not by a shift from modernity to postmodernity, but rather by the emergence of a new state of modernity referred to as 'reflexive modernity'. Coined by British sociologist Anthony Giddens (1991), reflexive modernity – like postmodernity – argues that the increasing influence of media and consumerism has given rise to new ways for individuals to construct their identities and understand their relationships with others. For Giddens, this resulting process of individualization does not result in a weakening of social bonds; rather, it gives rise to new possibilities for the formation of social relationships and groupings. Giddens argues that these are grounded not in structural experiences of class, gender and ethnicity, but rather reflect contemporary individuals' reflexive appropriation and everyday articulation of cultural resources:

> What to do? How to act? Who to be? These are all focal questions for everyone living in the circumstances of late modernity, and ones which, on some level or another, all of us answer, either discursively or through day to day social behaviour . . . Everyday choices about what to eat, what to wear, who to socialise with, are all decisions which position ourselves as one kind of person or another.
>
> (Giddens 1991: 70, 81)

Although in some ways analogous to the notion of identity as a postmodern construct – unstable and apt to change – there is in Giddens's description scope for a different interpretation of identity. For Giddens, rather than engaging in a fickle 'pick and mix' mode of engagement with the manifold images, texts and objects produced and disseminated by the contemporary media and consumer industries, individuals structure their reflexive appropriation and use of these in ways designed to produce and uphold particular systems of cultural meaning.

A fruitful means of conceptualizing such a process of reflexive appropriation is the theory of 'lifestyle' developed by Chaney (1996). Utilizing Weber's work on status groups, Chaney applies lifestyle as a way of explaining the symbolic transformation of media and consumer products and resources into culturally meaningful aspects of contemporary everyday life. Key to this process of cultural transformation, argues Chaney, is an understanding of the value and significance that individuals inscribe within such images, texts and objects. Chaney elaborates on this through a theoretical model that he refers to as lifestyle 'sites' and 'strategies'. According to Chaney (1996: 92), lifestyle *sites* refer to the 'physical metaphors for the spaces that actors can appropriate and control', while *strategies* denote the 'characteristic modes of social engagement, or narratives of identity, in which the actors concerned can embed the metaphors at hand'.

It is evident that, in denoting the importance of sites and strategies for the operationalization of lifestyle in an everyday, lived context, Chaney is moving beyond the notion of reflexive appropriation as an inherently individual project. Rather, lifestyle is established as both an individual and collective project. Through their symbolic transformation of images, objects and texts, individuals actively contribute to the production of new, collectively understood cultural meanings and associated forms of cultural practice. Important in this respect is the distinction that Chaney makes between a way of life and a lifestyle. For Chaney, a way of life 'is typically associated with a more or less stable community. It is displayed in features such as shared norms, rituals, patterns of social order and probably a distinctive dialect'. Lifestyles, on the other hand, connote 'creative projects, they are . . . displays of consumer competence' (Chaney 1996: 92, 97). In this sense, lifestyles can be viewed as means through which individuals negotiate traditional ways of life, using cultural resources to construct new identities at both an individual and a collective level. As such, lifestyles are, as Chaney observes, inherently creative – indeed, as a number of cultural sociologists have sought to illustrate, lifestyle projects draw on a broad variety of influences and sources, often producing richly nuanced renderings in which popular and vernacular culture are reflexively intertwined to evoke new everyday understandings and enactments of previously taken-for-granted social descriptors such as ethnicity (Back 1996), local identity (Bennett 2000) and youth (Miles 2000).

Cultural sociology in the United States

If cultural sociology emerged in Britain as a dialogue with cultural studies, its development in the United States was somewhat different. This story has been told elsewhere, primarily by Jeffrey Alexander and Philip Smith (Alexander and Smith 2003, 2010; Alexander, Jacobs and Smith 2011). But it is important to recount the US history here, because we want to suggest that cultural sociology today is shaped in important ways through a trans-Atlantic dialogue that incorporates insights from and the trajectories of both regions.

In the early decades of US sociology, culture was one of the central sites of investigation. At the University of Chicago, Robert Park and his colleagues spent a great deal of time investigating urban culture, in particular the impact that this had on the assimilation of new immigrants (for example, Park 1922, 1938). Integration and urban culture were also the focus of sociologists at Columbia University, where Paul Lazarsfeld and his colleagues undertook a number of studies examining the dynamics of mass persuasion on urban populations, the most well-known of these being a study of the Orson Welles *War of the Worlds* radio broadcast (Cantril, Gaudet and Herzog 1940; Lazarsfeld, Berelson and Gaudet 1944). Around the same time, at Harvard University, Talcott Parsons was developing a comprehensive theory about how culture functions to produce social order and social integration.

These early developments in American cultural sociology differed in several respects from the British case. As David Chaney argued in Chapter 1, the British debates about culture during the first half of the twentieth century were organized around an abiding concern with the relationship between mass culture, 'civilized taste' and social class. While cultural critics in the United States also debated the effects of mass culture, American social scientists at the time were much more interested in urban culture, social order and immigration. Indeed, American sociologists were quite suspicious of claims about 'mass society', whether those concerns were being voiced by conservatives concerned about the erosion of taste or by radicals concerned about the diffusion of capitalist ideology.

A second key difference was the way in which British cultural studies emerged during the 1960s as an alternative to sociology. This opening was made possible partly by the fact that British sociologists were not asking questions about culture and cultural processes. Combining cultural Marxism with French theory, British cultural studies infused the 'cultural turn' with a sense of radical challenge – not only to the prevailing social order, but also to the disciplinary organization of British sociology. This left an opening in the 1970s for British sociologists to challenge the mainstream of their discipline by taking the cultural turn, and doing so in a broad academic climate where important developments had been made in fusing cultural Marxism with French cultural theory. In the United States, by contrast, sociologists during the 1950s spent a good deal of energy criticizing the cultural Marxism of the Frankfurt School scholars, arguing instead that media had rather limited effects, which were much less powerful than the social networks and relationships that intervened between the media message and the individual (Katz and Lazarsfeld 1955; Katz 1960). The result was an academic climate much less open to cultural Marxism or ideological critique. Not surprisingly, from this point of view, American sociologists during the 1960s and 1970s were much more likely than their British counterparts to turn against culture, through a series of important anti-cultural polemics. Scholars such as Charles Tilly, Barrington Moore and Michael Mann argued that while attitudes, values and beliefs may help in the reproduction of inequality, culture was much less important in the organization (and potential transformation) of these inequalities than 'real' things such as organizational structures and resources (Tilly 1984).

Because of the turn away from culture in the 1970s, it was not until the mid- to late 1980s that sociologists in the United States began to think seriously about culture. Indeed, the American Sociological Association did not form a section on culture until 1988. When

US sociologists did begin to examine culture more seriously, they tended to do so by focusing on organizational structures, resources and other material factors that shaped the institutional production of culture. Key early contributors in this movement included Richard A. Peterson (sociology of music), Vera Zolberg (sociology of art), Diana Crane (sociology of art), Muriel Cantor (sociology of media) and Paul DiMaggio (sociology of art). What all of these scholars had in common was their concern for studying the organizational resources, routines and structures that determined the production and the success of specific cultural products. What tended to get left out of, or marginalized in, these analyses was a consideration of how social actors made their world meaningful, or how these social meanings operated to help organize action.

Against the **sociology of culture** that was emerging in the United States, others argued for a different kind of cultural sociology that privileged meaning-centred social analysis. Central to this alternative approach were two scholars, Ann Swidler and Jeffrey Alexander. For both, the starting point for any cultural sociology was a commitment to 'thick description', an idea that Clifford Geertz describes in the following way:

> Believing, with Max Weber, that man is an animal suspended in webs of significance he himself has spun, I take culture to be those webs, and the analysis of it to be therefore not an experimental science in search of law but an interpretive one in search of meaning.
>
> (Geertz 1973: 5)

Swidler (1986) adopted an action-centred and pragmatic approach to the interpretive project of thick description, emphasizing that culture provides a common repertoire of habits, skills and styles from which people can develop their own specific 'strategies of action'. In other words, culture provides a pragmatic 'toolkit', consisting of 'symbols, stories, rituals, and worldviews, which people may use in varying configurations to solve different kinds of problems' (Swidler 1986: 273). Emphasizing that 'real cultures' contain multiple and usually conflicting symbols and rituals, she sought to highlight the different ways in which actors draw upon these cultural materials in order to craft their own context-specific guides to action.

For Alexander, the key starting point for an effective cultural sociology was to take seriously what he called the 'autonomy of culture'. This meant that the social webs of meaningfulness could be described as if they had their own logic, which could be mapped according to certain basic rules, or cultural structures. Alexander argued that it was a mistake to enter cultural analysis having already decided that social meanings were determined by class relationships, by organizational structure and routines, by elite conflicts, or by any other external force. The problem with this approach is that it encourages the analyst to consider the social world to be 'pre-interpreted'. The causal arguments that result from such an approach may be strong, but the descriptions of social phenomena that accompany them tend to be too 'thin'. Alexander and Smith proposed a two-stage approach, which he felt would produce a stronger cultural sociology:

> What is needed here is a Geertzian 'thick description' of the codes, narratives, and symbols that create the textured webs of social meaning. The contrast here is to the 'thin description' that typically characterizes studies inspired by the weak program, in which meaning is

either simply read off from social structure or reduced to abstract descriptions of reified values, norms, ideology, or fetishism . . . [Only] after the internal pattern of meaning has been reconstructed . . . does it become possible to discover in what ways culture intersects with other social forces, such as power and instrumental reason in the concrete social world.

(Alexander and Smith 2003: 13–14, emphasis added)

The main point that Alexander and Smith are trying to make here, with their plea for a 'strong' cultural sociology, is that sociologists need to treat meaning on its own terms, before considering the relationship between culture and society. Their criticism is directed primarily against the sociology of culture perspective, which explains cultural outcomes almost completely through non-cultural explanations. But they are also critical of British cultural studies, for many of the reasons that Chaney (1994) has put forward elsewhere, specifically that it is too ready to align social meanings with social class and too quick to equate cultural resistance with class resistance. With this similar line of criticism, the conditions for a trans-Atlantic dialogue in cultural sociology were clearly established – a point to which we will return shortly.

Reflecting on the distinctive history of cultural sociology in the United States, Spillman (2002) identifies three general approaches to studying culture that we can find in US cultural sociology today. The first approach is to study 'culture in practice'. Reflecting Swidler's pragmatic theory of culture and action, this approach studies how people use culture to get things done and to solve problems. The most typical methods used in this approach are ethnography and extended interviews. The second approach identified by Spillman is cultural production studies. Reflecting the influence of the 'sociology of culture', this approach studies cultural workers in cultural industries, with an eye to how they are able to act creatively within organizational constraints. This approach uses a wide-ranging set of methodological approaches, including ethnographies, interviews, historical research and quantitative analysis. Finally, there is the study of cultural frameworks. Influenced by Alexander and his call for a **strong program** of meaning-centred cultural sociology, this approach attempts to map out the internal logics of cultural systems. The favoured approaches here tend to use various techniques of interpretive textual analysis, though there have been some innovative recent attempts to use quantitative techniques as well.

To summarize, the US development of cultural sociology followed its own trajectory, which is characterized by the following distinctive features and key differences from the British case:

1. In the United States, cultural sociologists have tended to be less concerned with the relationship between culture and social class, and more concerned with race, ethnicity and urban culture.
2. In the United States, cultural agency has been conceptualized in a more pragmatic way, as the specific ways that actors use culture in order to accomplish specific tasks and to solve specific problems. As a result, the link between cultural agency and cultural resistance is weaker than it has tended to be in the United Kingdom.
3. In the United States, ideology critique has not been very influential as a way of doing cultural sociology.

4. Reflecting the strong position of the 'sociology of culture', and the sociology of organizations more generally, cultural sociologists in the United States have probably spent more time studying cultural production than cultural consumption.
5. In the United States, one of the key debates in cultural sociology concerns the 'autonomy of culture', or the extent to which cultural frameworks have an internal logic of their own.

This is not to suggest that cultural sociology in the United States developed in complete isolation from things that were happening in the United Kingdom or in Europe. To be sure, American sociologists were reading the monographs that were coming from British cultural studies, and they were reading many of the same French cultural theories. In addition, there was a continuous trans-Atlantic flow of scholars, which brought the distinctive perspectives of the two continents into frequent dialogue. However, it does help to explain some of the different emphases that we see in the two countries. It also helps to explain the different contexts of reception in which cultural sociology had to establish itself. For example, in the United Kingdom, the project of pursuing a meaning-centred cultural sociology is more readily accepted, but there is a need to create a clear distinction between cultural sociology and cultural studies. In the United States, by contrast, the main challenge is to create a clear distinction between cultural sociology and the sociology of culture. There is also a deep distrust of cultural studies by the mainstream social science establishment in the United States, informed in large part by the development of a more postmodern version of cultural studies in that country, which is committed more to a radical social constructionism and a strong view about the indeterminacy of meaning. This distrust was magnified and publicized by the 1996 Sokal affair, in which a physics professor managed to publish a fake article about the 'transformative hermeneutics of quantum gravity' in the leading cultural studies journal in the United States, *Social Text*.

These different contexts of reception create challenges for creating a trans-Atlantic cultural sociology, which can combine the different insights from the two intellectual contexts while avoiding the kinds of translation problems described above. Nevertheless, it is precisely this kind of trans-Atlantic dialogue that has developed in the twenty-first century, leading to a cultural sociology that is more vibrant than ever.

Conclusion

This chapter has examined the emergence of cultural sociology as a distinct sub-discipline of the academic field of sociology. The chapter began by examining the context in which questions of culture became important for research on society and social life. Critical here, as shown, was the emergence of the cultural turn – a process through which academics began to consider culture as something more than a reflection or by-product of socio-economic circumstances. An important development in this respect was the emergence of cultural studies as a field of research that set about considering how everyday life was characterized by a hegemonic struggle in which the appropriation and use of cultural resources by individuals was pivotal. The chapter then went on to map the emergence of cultural sociology as a response to some of the argued limitations of cultural studies, notably its reduction of everyday struggles around culture to issues of social class. In its survey of the British and European cultural sociological field, the chapter considered the work of key theorists such as Bourdieu, Chaney, Giddens and Beck, each of whom attempted to rethink the relationship between social structure and individual agency by using frameworks of cultural capital, reflexivity, risk and lifestyle. The final section of the chapter focused on the development of cultural sociology in the United States. As was illustrated, although sharing some concerns with its British and European counterparts – namely criticisms of the cultural studies tradition – cultural sociology in the United States has also been engaged to build its own 'strong program', as distinct from that characterizing the sociology of culture as a means through which to recast the study of culture as something not limited to issues of industrial production and dissemination, but rather an integral, active element in all aspects of social life and social interaction.

Review questions

2.1 What do you understand by the term 'cultural turn'?

2.2 What are argued to be the key differences between cultural studies and cultural sociology?

2.3 What differences and similarities can be identified between British and American approaches to cultural sociology?

Further reading

Alexander, J.C. (2003) *The Meanings of Social Life: A Cultural Sociology*, Oxford University Press, New York.

Chaney, D. (1994) *The Cultural Turn: Scene Setting Essays on Contemporary Cultural History*, Routledge, London.

3

Methodological Issues in Cultural Sociology

Learning objectives

- To understand the distinctions between various research styles and strategies in sociological research.
- To appreciate some of the common analytic frames cultural sociologists use in their research.
- To understand some of the particular methodological concerns of cultural sociology.
- To be aware of the interdisciplinary heritage of research in cultural sociology.
- To appreciate some of the important methodological approaches employed by cultural sociologists.

Introduction

As discussed in the previous chapter, the emergence and development of cultural sociology owes much to the cultural turn and the increasing emphasis on the interpretation of cultural production as a reflexive process. This chapter turns its attention to the topic of methodology in cultural sociology – that is, the means through which cultural sociologists collect data about the social world for analytical and writing purposes. It follows that the principles guiding the theoretical development of cultural sociology must also have implications for the ways in which empirical data are collected, analysed and interpreted by cultural sociologists. Research methods fall broadly into two categories: qualitative and quantitative methodologies, each of which embodies a distinctive approach to the study and interpretation of the social world. The purpose of this chapter is to consider

Cultural Sociology: An Introduction, First Edition. Les Back et al. © 2012 Les Back, Andy Bennett, Laura Desfor Edles, Margaret Gibson, David Inglis, Ronald Jacobs and Ian Woodward. Published 2012 by Blackwell Publishing Ltd.

how existing research methods drawn from both qualitative and quantitative approaches can be utilized in cultural sociological research. The chapter also considers how the emergence of cultural sociology places new demands on the research process to the extent that existing methodologies are challenged. The final section of the chapter focuses on ethical issues as these apply to cultural sociological research.

Reinterpreting the field?

A common starting place for instruction manuals dealing with the principles and practice of qualitative sociological research is the need for *objectivity* and *empathy* when engaging with research subjects and their everyday socio-cultural environment (commonly referred to as the **field**). The field is often situated as the 'other' – a somehow self-contained or at least 'definable' world in relation to that occupied by the social researcher. Classic examples of the field include the street gang, the shop floor and the lobby group. The process of 'hanging out' in the field for a period of time is often considered key to an informed understanding of the 'social' world at the centre of one's research.

In many respects, this kind of approach mirrors many of the assumptions informing traditional sociological theory. Social actors are considered somehow cemented into particular social worlds, where they are invisibly tethered to forms of cultural practice that may only reveal themselves once a sustained level of methodological rigour has been employed. The role of the sociologist is to uncover and objectify the subjective truth of the research subjects – a truth that, more often than not, is revealed in sociological writing as inherently connected to a structurally informed relationship to the everyday world.

While such a connection between traditional sociological theory and the methodological approaches employed to generate data is unsurprising, it does beg an important question regarding the ready transference of research methodologies between sociology and cultural sociology. While, in the final analysis, the process of collecting and analysing empirical fieldwork data may serve a critical role in the establishment of cultural sociology as a distinctive approach, the rationale underlying the fieldwork process, and perhaps the methodology employed, may differ to a significant extent. As already asserted in Chapter 2, from a cultural sociological perspective, a critical objective is to shift the relationship between structure and agency in such a way that scope is given to explore the often nuanced and intimate dynamic that exists between them in the production of everyday life. It follows that empirical investigation conducted by the cultural sociologist must seek to explore and interpret the socio-cultural landscape to the same end.

Global–local

In Chapter 2 it was suggested that Chaney's (1996) rendering of lifestyle provides a potentially fruitful theoretical model for our understanding of social actors' reflexive engagement with their everyday life-worlds. Chaney's interpretation of lifestyle also serves as a useful template for empirical research on contemporary social life. In particular, lifestyle raises critical issues about the importance of 'everyday life' as a space in which to conduct empirical research concerning the production and reproduction of culture. More pointedly, there is a need within the field of cultural sociology to represent the highly complex interplay between the global and the local. It is fair to say that, in the past, empirical investigations conducted by sociologists in specific locations served largely as a means of uncovering social systems, whose workings were then applied across a broader – transnational or global – set of social relations. Such was the case even with the 'classic' ethnographic studies of, for example, the Chicago School, where *close-up* accounts of social groups were argued to reveal deeply embedded social structures based around distinctions of class, gender and ethnicity, which were then deemed applicable in a macro sociological context.

This is not to suggest that cultural sociology should abandon the task of interpreting social life in a macro sense. Rather, given cultural sociology's central claim that culture is a process that is produced through a reflexive engagement on the part of individuals with their everyday circumstances, an empirical cultural sociological approach must be aware of the ongoing dynamic between the local and global, each acting upon the other in the production of the contemporary cultural landscape.

The case of hip hop culture serves as a pertinent example in this respect. Although comprising a diverse series of musical and stylistic influences spanning Jamaican reggae and German electronica, it is generally acknowledged that hip hop began to coalesce as a genre in the South Bronx district of New York during the early 1970s, with important cultural innovators being former street gang member Afrika Bambaataa and DJ Kool Herc (see Gilroy 1993; Rose 1994). Today, hip hop culture is a globally established youth cultural form with a high profile in the global commercial media. During the course of its transformation into a global cultural form, however, elements of the hip hop genre were appropriated and reworked in the context of a variety of different multi-ethnic cultures, including the United Kingdom and Germany (Bennett 2000), France (Huq 1999), Japan (Condry 1999), Australia (Maxwell 1994) and New Zealand (Mitchell 1996). The various inflections that such local appropriations have brought to hip hop have in turn fed back into understandings and interpretations of hip hop's cultural significance at a global level, among fans, critics and practitioners alike.

As this example illustrates, the task of the empirical cultural sociologist must involve an awareness of the intricate dynamic that exists between the local and the global, and an openness to the ways in which the everyday lives of social actors are implicated in the production of culture at both the local and global levels. The field then becomes not merely a means of investigating a set of social relations from which broader inferences can be drawn; rather, it is recast as a space in which a locally nuanced, spatially contingent set of social relations engender and reproduce a set of practices through which cultural transformation may occur simultaneously in both a local and global context.

Insider–outsider

A critical issue in empirical research involving fieldwork is the establishment and maintenance of field relations. This invariably involves careful negotiation of relationships with informants in such a way as to avoid both a loss of objectivity and impartiality (typically referred to as 'going native'), and the acquisition of data informed by the biased judgements of one or more individuals within a particular field setting. In respect to the latter issue, considerable emphasis is placed on the importance of securing reliable gatekeepers – individuals within the field with comprehensive insider knowledge and connections, who can be trusted to guide the researcher effectively in establishing field relations. Although clearly of importance in establishing sound procedural standards for generating data as objectively as possible, such methodological instruction also carries with it a series of assumptions concerning the nature of the relationship between the researcher and informant. Most strikingly, there is scant acknowledgement of the potential for the sociological researcher to enter a particular field of research with which they are already intimately familiar and within which they are, to all intents and purposes, an 'insider'. Recent years have seen an increasing shift in this direction among sociological researchers. Indeed, such is the frequency of insider researchers – particularly in sub-fields of sociology with an emphasis on culture, such as youth, music, consumption, dance and sport – that new questions now need to be asked about the practice of negotiating the field. The objective may thus be not to 'learn' about the field setting, but rather to relearn it from the point of view of an insider with a fully formed, pre-existing vernacular knowledge. Of equal salience here is the fundamental question of how the narrowing gap between the researcher and the researched informs methodological questions about issues of expertise in the understanding and interpretation of cultural practice and the methodological competence that goes along with this. Given the by no means insignificant number of published ethnographic studies that cite insider knowledge and/or status as a critical advantage in the data-collection and interpretation process, what correlations can be established between lived experience and the sociological imagination – and how does this interface with the methodological basis of cultural sociology?

The blurring boundaries between researcher and researched have been flagged through a number of recent innovations in the research process: action research, for example, encourages the participation of research respondents in the data-gathering process by granting them varying degrees of licence in the interpretation and representation of the data; auto-ethnography provides an avenue for a researcher or research group to produce descriptive narratives through deep reflection on their own involvement within a given field setting. Insider research may encompass elements of each of these approaches, although as a form of cultural sociological inquiry such considerations may be secondary to an understanding of how a pre-existing vernacular knowledge of a research setting to be re-examined 'sociologically' can be refashioned as a research tool through which to position the field as a cultural space and those within it as reflexive agents of cultural production.

The insider researcher's long-term investment in the everyday 'organic' life of a particular social setting and their first-hand experience of how cultural practices are acquired and operationalized therein are, in themselves, important points of departure. Although sociological research involves a significant level of retraining, the transformation of the subject from pure 'insider' to insider-researcher must allow scope for the effective synthesis of everyday know-how with academic rigour in a way that allows for these skills to be applied equally and equitably in the research process.

Surface–depth

An enduring theme in cultural sociology, which runs an intellectual line from the very earliest forms of linguistic theory and structural anthropology in the first decades of the twentieth century to much contemporary work, is the idea that patterns on the observable surface of social life – from diverse areas such as clothing to social etiquette, violence, discourses in the media and the ways individuals spend their leisure time – are patterned by underlying culture structures that govern their expression on the social surface. Therefore, although the 'surface' of social life can appear complicated, diverse and unpredictable, there are generative processes beneath it that guide the playing out of such minutiae. In order to come to grips with all that we observe and identify at the face of social life, we need to look to the constructive processes of culture. In the personal reflections contained in his book *Tristes Tropiques*, the anthropologist Claude Lévi-Strauss (1973) notes that in his intellectual life he has '*trois maîtresses*' (three mistresses) – geology, psychoanalysis and Marxism. What these three fields have in common is a basic notion that what is observable at the surface is determined by generative processes beneath it. Thus, in the case of geology, the features of the earth's surface make full sense if we can account for the generative processes beneath the surface of the earth's crust. In the case of psychoanalysis, human behaviours can be explained by reference to conscious and unconscious processes. In the case of Marxism, social relations are seen to be governed by basic features related to the organization of economic life. For Lévi-Strauss, these deep generative principles of culture are there to be discovered; however, everyday social actors who are immersed in them take them for granted, along with most aspects of and events in social life, and consequently they are not able to identify such structures. Lévi-Strauss believes that the patterns these structures create on the surface of cultural life can best be observed and analysed by objective, detached scientific investigation that employs a structuralist analytic approach.

Just as there are discernible culture structures, people have a drive to classify and categorize people, events and things, and these classifications – while being the basis of forms of everyday cultural work – evaluate, partition and assign these things according to regimes of cultural value. Durkheim and Mauss's (1963) argument is that classification is a process of marking-off, of demarcating things that are related, but have distinct points of difference to another. In the process of making ongoing distinctions and demarcations, social life becomes consolidated partly through the practical accretion of classifications. These systems of ideas of relation and difference serve to connect and unify knowledge about the world. They build up a hierarchical system where ideas form chains of meanings, and where values can be assigned and competing discursive constructs weighed up. In the mature, contemporary form of cultural sociology, this idea that there are 'culture structures' – just as there might be economic structures – is pervasive. It is expressed most strongly in the so-called 'strong program' advocated by Alexander and Smith (2003), associated with the Yale Center for Cultural Sociology.

On sociological methods: some traditional distinctions

First, we need to distinguish most basically, and importantly, between methods and methodologies. The term **methods** refers simply to the techniques, strategies and actual data-collection procedures researchers use for compiling their data. Thus the social survey is a method, as is a face-to-face interview, participant observation or photograph analysis. Cultural sociologists use a range of social research methods, effectively drawing from the same methodological toolkit as other researchers in the social and cultural sciences.

While cultural sociologists do tend to favour interpretive, discursive, textual and broadly qualitative methodologies, this does not rule out the use of quantitative and statistical methods. In the case of survey research, the challenge with the latter methodology is to devise questions that can measure dimensions of the culture structure effectively. Using Likert-scale style questions to measure such dimensions is surely equivalent to creating and reifying such structures (see Reed and Alexander 2009). The resulting statistical outputs and generalizations can be subjected to cultural sociological scrutiny, and be shown to bear the hallmarks of academic ritual, iconic representation and the capacity to carry their own performative power (see Mohr 1998; Biernacki 2009). Thus skilful statistical analysis remains something of a rarity in cultural sociology, working from textual and structuralist assumptions, though in work that is more concerned with the sociology of culture – for example, cultural consumption studies – the use of complex statistical reasoning is common. For example, Bourdieu's (1984) famous matrix diagrams of what he called 'the space of lifestyles' might be seen by some as innovative and powerful sociological explanation, but by others as equivalent to ink blots. As Mohr (1998: 367) notes, 'any visual representation of a meaning structure is still largely a Rorschach test upon which one must seek to project an interpretation'.

The term **methodologies** refers to the reflective study of methods, and particularly the study of the philosophical assumptions behind methods and the types of knowledge they generate; often, this is referred to as the field of 'epistemology'. Thus a methodological assumption of traditional positivist research approaches is the idea of a universally accepted objective reality that is amenable to scientific study, while interpretive methods are premised on the methodological assumption that reality is constructed via interpretations, codes, narratives and symbols, best understood through interviews, discourse or ethnographic methods and the application of models of genre, narrative and codes to decipher the meaning of cultural events and fields. It is therefore best not to assume that methods are objective, but rather that they give partial, and somewhat prejudiced, information about the objects they study.

Second, following on from the above discussion, it is useful to distinguish between the two broad schools of qualitative and quantitative methods. **Quantitative** methods involve the numericization of observed phenomena and the statistical analysis of these. Thus aspects of everyday practices, such as the frequency of certain behaviours or the degree of particular value and attitudinal orientations, can be measured quantitatively – for example, on a numeric scale. Alternately, **qualitative** methods look to the qualities and textures of experiences, attitudes, outlooks and practices through non-numeric methods. Most commonly, these methods collect textual data based on interviews or the analysis of written documents, images or materials. Sometimes researchers use these methodological approaches in combination, or convert one form of data to another. For example, the frequency of themes or keywords within a consumer interview could be quantified and reported in numeric form.

Third, we can distinguish generally between positivist, post-positivist and postmodern research paradigms. While this distinction broadly follows the qualitative–quantitative distinction, it adds an extra and important epistemological dimension. **Positivist** approaches make the assumption that aspects of the social and cultural world, such as a person's behaviours or attitudes, are amenable to description and measurement via approaches which adopt logical scientific procedures based on principles of empirical measurement. In summary, positivist approaches suggest that there is an objective world that can be studied and known through the scientific approach. Most positivist research is likely to be quantitative in design, though some qualitative research can also be positivist. In contrast, **post-positivist** approaches challenge the idea that scientific approaches can access a universally known external reality or truth and suggest that the knower (the researcher) and ways of knowing (the methods employed) can never really be separated. Thus knowledge produced by researchers is always contingent upon a range of factors, constructed and interpreted by them in the form of research narratives and susceptible to various types of unacknowledged irrationalities and cultural biases. While post-positivism does not necessarily throw out all the entrenched methods for studying social life, it does force researchers to become more reflexive and cautious about interpreting the meaning and validity of their results. The **postmodern** paradigm is similar in many respects to the post-positivist paradigm, but gives weight to a greater diversity of approaches and research models. For example, it might emphasize the narrative construction of reality, the plurality of different interpretations of objects and events, and the uncertainty and instability of regimes of semiotic signification. Postmodern research is also likely to incorporate innovative and experiential methods, which give priority to things like emotion, bodily senses and feelings, using qualitative and interpretive approaches. In addition, rather than looking for a unitary or comprehensive understanding of social behaviour, the postmodern perspective acknowledges the fragmented and performative aspects of social role, identity and cultural action.

Points of methodological inspiration for cultural sociology

While the dynamics of insider and outsider, surface and depth, and the local and global guide the ways cultural sociologists tend to think about the constitution of the social world, there are a number of particular methodological ideas – both historical and more contemporary – that guide the way cultural sociologists go about interpreting and reconstituting the social world in their own research. Some of the most important frames are examined below.

Verstehen

In cultural sociology, as in sociology more generally, Max Weber's methodological principle of *verstehen* – a German word that means 'to understand' – is a major point of inspiration. Weber argued in his book *Economy and Society: An Outline of Interpretive Sociology* (1978) that sociology should develop as a social science, in contrast to the models of the natural sciences. Dealing with human beings, sociology should concern itself with being a science of social action, and Weber asserted that this action must be understood from the perspective of the social actors themselves. Thus, Weber made the point that sociology's task was to identify the meanings and motivations that people attributed to their own behaviours. No external, objective valid criteria could exist for understanding these behaviours except the meanings actors subjectively attributed to them, which reveal a sociological logic of their own.

Working from a different perspective, but similarly making the case for a sociology founded on understanding the individual, Georg Simmel (1997a) urged sociologists to look to the person as the focal point of their studies, arguing that society was no more than a collection of individuals. What we take from Weber is an insistence on the meaningfulness of social action. That meaning forms the basis of social action is an irreducible aspect of the cultural sociological approach. Cultural sociology extends this dimension of meaningfulness to show not just that meanings are important for individuals – for example, in their own narratives or personal relations to others – but as principles of social collectives and events. Thus meaning penetrates individual actions and collective imperatives alike. Clearly, such a principle is set in contrast to the positivist and quantitative paradigm that sought to aggregate, abstract and generalize about social behaviours via quantitative methods, rather than individualize them.

Thick description

In anthropology, ethnographic methods exemplifying the qualitative approach were pioneered by eminent scholars such as Malinowski, Evans-Pritchard and Mead, and were absolutely essential to the discipline's formation. More recently, the anthropologist Clifford Geertz's (1973) methodological premise of 'thick description', famously explicated in his study of Balinese cockfighting and demonstrated in his important book *The Interpretation of Cultures*, has become essential for understanding the interpretive approach in the social sciences. Pointing back to Max Weber's definition of culture as consisting of the complex webs of significance that people both create and routinely reproduce in their everyday practices, the essential idea of **thick description** is that all human actions exist within a broader culture structure, consisting of multilayered symbols, texts and meanings, and that it is the task of the cultural analyst to uncover these. By using such a practice, the researcher could locate the meanings participants themselves assigned to events and practices in their own culture. Instead of proclaiming to be an 'objective' reading of cultural practices by an outsider, thick description supposedly allows for a reading of a culture and its practices according to that culture's own concepts and circuits of meaning. In terms of a rationale for understanding culture, there is a clear implication that researchers should look to the meanings people articulate and also that they must locate these social practices and meanings within wider circuits of cultural narrative and symbolism.

Codes and systems

A foundational element of cultural sociology is its claim that social life is governed by a series of codes, which in essence are drivers of how people interpret and understand both aspects of their personal everyday life and the role of governments, media, firms and other organizations. These **codes**, learnt through growing up in a culture, are the frames for social action. In essence, they provide a type of working language for understanding social life. The Swiss linguist Ferdinand de Saussure (1966) was elemental in forming a basis for this approach early in the twentieth century. An important feature of de Saussure's approach is his interest in synchronic, rather than diachronic, studies of language. Previous scholarship within the field of linguistics had focused primarily on the historical evolution of language systems over time – their diachronic features. De Saussure argues that, at any particular point in time, language must exist as a system – a series of related parts that are inseparable and form a system of linguistic communication. This system is not necessarily closed, inviolable or inflexible – for, as we know, language conventions change over time. Yet at any point in time language can be analysed as a communicative system. Accordingly, rather than attending to the proliferation of 'speech acts' – words, sounds, sound images and alphabetic texts – de Saussure argues that scholars must understand these linguistic structures as: (i) irreducibly psychological; (ii) intrinsically contoured by social-communal codes; and, above all, (iii) as a system. Thus language is a social institution, whose structures must be understood on their own terms – 'in itself', and as a system of relations (de Saussure 1966: 16). Conceptualized through de Saussure's systemic perspective, language becomes a 'self contained whole and a principle of classification' (de Saussure 1966: 9) – a system of signs (de Saussure 1966: 15). The 'systemness' of linguistic phenomena is further emphasized by de Saussure's distinction between 'langue' and 'parole'. In shorthand, one might think of langue as referring to language, while parole refers to speech. To elaborate, langue refers to the underlying rules and principles that govern the use of language, and is used by de Saussure to refer to its systemic quality – for example, the order in which we combine words to make sense. On the other hand, parole refers to the phonic and psychological manifestations of language – talk, utterances and sounds – that comprise the surface of language. If scholars could look to uncover the langue – meaning the system of related codes and ideas that structure our social language – then this could become a type of key for social explanation.

One of the most striking and revolutionary cultural theories of the twentieth century, emerging from the anthropological theories of Claude Lévi-Strauss (1966, 1973, 1979), constituted an important application of de Saussure's linguistic theory. The ideas of Lévi-Strauss are crucial to what has been called the 'strong program' in cultural sociology (Alexander and Smith 2003) because Lévi-Strauss is able to show how culture is built on classifications and linguistic systems that operate in a way which is autonomous, meaning that culture stands alone as a type of independent system for reproducing the social. This does mean that it is unchanging, however. The powerful ambition of Lévi-Strauss's analytic model is apparent in the subtitle to his book *Myth and Meaning* (1979), 'Cracking the Code of Culture'. We can see from this subtitle that Lévi-Strauss's *oeuvre* is of no small ambition – to apply the structuralist model developed by de Saussure to studies of culture in order to uncover the underlying laws: to 'crack its code'. In *The Savage Mind* (1966), Lévi-Strauss investigates the scientific practice of the 'primitives'. Resisting attempts to portray primitive thought as inferior (Smith 2001: 105), as people in the West often assumed, he showed how primitive forms of classification and cultural ordering were akin to what we in Western societies have called 'science'. In fact, the processes of primitive ordering were analogous to the processes of advanced 'science', having both practical and intellectual uses. Working with de Saussure's fundamental principle of communicative systems in mind, Lévi-Strauss argues that the universe is ordered according to systems of classification and taxonomies. Thus cultural events and objects can be understood within particular contexts where systemic cultural rules and codes operate to inform and contextualize their meaning. Cultural things therefore have appropriate places. As Lévi-Strauss (1962: 162) famously points out in a brief, yet widely quoted and instructive, section toward the end of his book *Totemism*, 'natural species are not chosen because they are "good to eat" but because they are "good to think"' ('*bonnes á penser*'). From this insight, we can conclude that a fundamental tenet of Lévi-Strauss's theoretical model is that culture does not exist just to serve straightforward, utilitarian purposes. In fact, the more important symbolic role of events, people and objects is to allow humans to construct and assign meanings within their cultural universe.

Genre, narrative, social drama

Without storylines to interpret it, the events of the media-saturated, mobility-obsessed, enclave-ridden and wildly unequal world we inhabit (and continuously make and re-make) would remain merely the 'blooming, buzzing confusion' (James 1918: 462) it is when we are infants. In their manifesto statement on the strong program in cultural sociology, Alexander and Smith (2003: 25) point to the consolidation of interest in narrative and genre theory within cultural sociology. Social actors make their judgements and determine their courses of action by reference to their personally held beliefs and values, but since their behaviours are public, they are always open to interpretation and possible dispute. In essence, social behaviours must attach to stories, accounts and narratives. **Narratives** refer generally to stories or accounts that are told individually and at the macro, societal level. At an individual level, narratives consist of the accounts or stories people tell themselves, and others, in order to both make sense of – and make through practical means – their lives. Narratives are thus reflective, accounting for events that have already taken place. But they are also active as a site for articulating an individual's values and beliefs – they provide the resources and frames for constructing a person's future. Individuals tell their lives through stories, though these stories are not simply there waiting to be told; they are actively constructed for particular audiences, plots and contexts. This process of narrativization tells us about the meanings people apply to their lives.

There is a second type of narrative that is relevant to the concerns of cultural sociology. Narratives are not only mentalistic or idealistic aspects of selfhood, but important components of culture. That is, narratives are not just told by individuals to others or to oneself. They circulate within culture, telling members of a group about the meaning of events in their own culture. Using the work of literary and genre theorists such as Frye and Propp, Philip Smith (2005) argues that the machinations of wars have less to do with realist struggles for resources and interests and more to do with interpretations and storylines held by their protagonists. For example, public discourses about the value of the 'Iraq War' invoke a series of dramatic elements, based on performances by key political, media and military players. The way the public understands the war, including aspects of a war's legitimacy, is based upon the prevailing genre in which it is held to rest – for example, a war could be seen as a tragedy, or a necessary act of self-defence, or an equally necessary defence of democratic or religious values. The dominant genre switches according to ongoing events and becomes the way we actively construct our own history.

Social performance

Recent developments in performance theory have emerged from a range of theoretical traditions, becoming influential in a range of fields of cultural and social theory to demonstrate the contingent, emergent and practised dimensions of social reproduction. Goffman (1959) uses the concept of performance to explain the enactment of social roles according to the logic of status management. More recent developments in performance theory (Alexander 2004a, 2004b; Butler 1997; Geertz 1973; Schechner 1993, 2002; Turner 1982) seek to understand the performative character of identity and social collective by drawing upon theoretical resources of symbolic action, ritual and social drama to show how social action is contingent upon history and collective sentiments, but must be brought into existence by continuous performative acts that actualize and reproduce the identities of social actors and groups (Butler 1997: 409). In his exposition of the elements of performance, Alexander defines cultural performance as:

> the social process by which actors, individually or in concert, display for others the meaning of the social situation. This meaning may or may not be one to which they themselves consciously adhere; it is the meaning that they, as social actors, consciously or unconsciously wish to have others believe. In order for their display to be effective, actors must offer a plausible performance, one that leads those to whom their actions and gestures are directed to accept their motives and explanations as a reasonable account.
>
> (Alexander 2004b: 529)

Based on his account of the 11 September 2001 terrorist events in the United States, Alexander (2004b) goes on to develop a model of the elements of cultural performance. These include a variety of things that compose a social performance, such as a body of collective representations to which social actors orient their actions (goals, morals, beliefs); actors and audiences; *mise-en-scène* (the elements of the scene within which people act); and social power (some performances are understood as natural and appropriate, others as inherently challenging and iconoclastic). A final element of Alexander's model is the means of symbolic production. By this, Alexander is referring to the range of 'mundane material things' (2004b: 532) that allow and empower people to act socially. This consists of objects that serve to represent things to others, frequently through iconic means. These material things are a crucial part of any social performance because they assist social actors to 'dramatize and make vivid and concrete the invisible motives and moral they are trying to represent' (Alexander 2004b: 532). In an important and fascinating recent study, Alexander (2010) applies the performance model to understand the way the US political and electoral system operated in the lead-up to the election of Barack Obama as president in 2008. Alexander shows that the ability of politicians to win over the electorate depends on the orchestration of drama, emotion and powerful imagery, and the use of cultural codes to try to master the way in which they and their competitors are seen by the voting public and media.

Visual and material research methods

In the last decade or two, there has been a significant move in sociology, cultural studies and also some historical and literary studies towards studying both the image and the object. In one sense, this is a turn against bottom-line references to discourse, narrative and speech as the bottom-line explanations of social dynamics. Thus we have the rise of visual research methods and also **material culture** or materialities research. Rather than studying human subjects, as most methods do, in a very direct way through interviews, observations or experiments, new approaches have advocated looking to the role of non-human or apparently inanimate things in creating, reproducing and directing crucial aspects of social life. Historically, the technique of semiotic analysis has dealt with analysing the linguistic characteristics and structure of the visual and material world, classically exemplified in Roland Barthes's seminal study *Mythologies* (1993); however, these new approaches look more closely at the visual and material constitution of social life (Tilley *et al.* 2006; Emmison and Smith 2000; Woodward 2007). This point seems increasingly relevant to a range of fields of research in cultural sociology, from studies of consumer culture and consumption practices, and media and music studies, to studies of political life which at their core are inherently and fundamentally visual. For example, think of advertising and its use of colour, or its visual portrayal of consumer dreams and ideals, and its reference to the direct physical engagement between people and material objects. Or consider the way visual images contained in newspapers or Internet sites can help us to understand the nature of global culture and our place in it. Through their powerful storytelling capacity, such visual objects allow us to empathize with some groups or individuals and reject others.

Review questions

3.1 What is the difference between 'the sociology of culture' and 'cultural sociology', according to proponents of the strong program in cultural sociology?

3.2 Discuss how cultural sociology draws on a large set of interdisciplinary influences in its methodologies.

3.3 Distinguish between methods and methodologies, and quantitative and qualitative research approaches. Does cultural sociology necessarily have an exclusive focus on qualitative methods?

Further reading

Alexander, J.C. (2003) *The Meanings of Social Life: A Cultural Sociology*, Oxford University Press, New York.

Bourdieu, P. (1990) *The Logic of Practice*, Stanford University Press, Stanford, CA.

Emmison, M. and Smith, P. (2000) *Researching the Visual: Images, Objects, Contexts and Interactions in Social and Cultural Inquiry*, Sage, London.

Geertz, C. (1973) *The Interpretation of Cultures*, Basic Books, New York.

Griswold, W. (2004) *Cultures and Societies in a Changing World*, Pine Forge Press, Thousand Oaks, CA.

Lévi-Strauss, C. (1979) *Myth and Meaning: Cracking the Code of Culture*, Schocken, New York.

Schechner, R. (2002) *Performance Studies: An Introduction*, Routledge, New York.

Smith, P. (2005) *Why War? The Cultural Logic of Iraq, the Gulf War, and Suez*, University of Chicago Press, Chicago.

Weber, M. (1978) *Economy and Society: An Outline of Interpretive Sociology*, University of California Press, Berkeley, CA.

Part II
New Cultural Identities

4

Class, Culture and Social Difference

Learning objectives

- To understand the importance of class to traditional sociological analysis and the fundamental frames of reference of sociologists.
- To understand the core historical accounts of class and class analysis within sociological theory.
- To understand the range of challenges recent sociological research has presented to the concept of class.
- To understand the range of cultural and post-class frameworks of analysing social difference and inequality.

Introduction

Class was – and indeed remains – a central concern of sociological investigation. Yet in recent decades there has been growing questioning of its relevance to social explanation. This chapter considers how post-industrialization, increasing social mobility and the turn to leisure and consumer-based societies have impacted on issues of class and class identity. While class distinctions and social inequalities have not disappeared, the everyday circumstances that now inform understandings of class have significantly altered the ways in which class identities are understood and enacted. Instead of narrow definitions of class, cultural capital becomes an important currency, and symbolic social exclusions are shown to work outside of old class structures on the basis of a diverse range of different cultural resources such as self-identity, place and material culture. Class will be revealed as something that is reflexively experienced and thus 'lived out' in a variety of different and highly particularized ways.

Cultural Sociology: An Introduction, First Edition. Les Back et al. © 2012 Les Back, Andy Bennett, Laura Desfor Edles, Margaret Gibson, David Inglis, Ronald Jacobs and Ian Woodward. Published 2012 by Blackwell Publishing Ltd.

The concept of class is central to the very constitution of the discipline of sociology, something that can be observed in two ways. Objectively, the concept has a long and established lineage, and has been fundamental to disciplinary theoretical and empirical explanation for a century and a half. This is especially the case within the Marxist and Weberian tradition of sociology. A general rule is that if one learns and practises sociological investigation, one must be aware of the centrality of class to the discipline. Although some (for example, Pakulski 1993; Pakulski and Waters 1996a; Clark and Lipset 1991) believe it is a concept that has had declining relevance and decreased explanatory value since the beginning of the post-industrial era, others (such as Wright 1997; Marshall 1997) have recently sought to reinvigorate the concept, showing how it works along new lines and structures that, although historically unique, continue to point to the salience of class as a crucial explanatory category.

If we take a step back and look at the concept more critically, both textually and from a broadly constructionist angle, we can see that the concept provides a key narrative for sociology's self-image, and is also pivotal to the development of sociology's ability to offer publicly valuable scientific diagnoses of social and economic problems. The debate on the usefulness and centrality of the concept pervades intellectual discussions. Traditional forms of sociological expertise need the concept's apparent claims of scientific power, precision and currency to establish and perform their disciplinary expertise and identity. Newer approaches wish to move beyond narrow conceptions of class, but cannot escape the intellectual cachet of the concept's critical pedigree. Class, it is often assumed, is elemental to any potent sociological critique of capitalist social organization. So can any viable analysis of Western society not rest on the concept of class? One of the principal aims of this chapter is to explore this question.

Defining class and class analysis: key terms and perspectives

In introducing the sociological idea of **social class**, we can say that it refers generally to a body of theory and evidence that is used to explain the structural reproduction of inequality within society. Its essence as a sociological concept is characterized by reference to an objective economic position, indicated by one's occupation, one's assets and the amount and source of one's income, which in turn shape one's life possibilities and chances, and continue to do so generationally within family structures in patterned ways through society.

Wright (2005) distinguishes between how the *word* 'class' is used and how the *concept* of class is understood. The former refers to general notions of structured inequality, while the latter refers more specifically to sociological operationalizations of the concept as a measurable entity. For Wright (2005), the 'anchoring questions' of **class analysis** – consisting largely of beliefs about the nature of society, regardless of the school of class analysis to which one subscribes – are distinguished by five major themes. These are outlined below.

Class as subjective location

Classes are subjective, everyday categories that refer to real existing differences within the social spectrum but can change depending on social location and historical timeframe.

For example, this dimension of class might hinge on people's sense of others' different lifestyles or their apparently different economic resources. These senses of economic difference are collectively shared by sub-groups within a society, and constitute a starting point for class analysis. However, they do not depend on objective definition or criteria but rather a lived awareness of social difference and distance that can be traced back to or evidenced by economic difference.

Class as social position

Class is often understood as a social location in relation to others, as measured by material achievements and standards of living – particularly family income, occupation and wealth. In this sense of the word, class is gradational, meaning that there will be a myriad of class locations and names for clusters along this continuum of grades – for example, upper class, working class and middle class. Objectively, a person's level of income becomes the elementary measure of social position. For example, one person might be ranked at the 90th percentile of income-earning Americans, meaning they sit at the edge of the bottom 10 per cent of income earners in that country, while another might be located in the 5th percentile, or top 5 per cent of income earners.

Class as life chance

As an explanatory concept linked to an extensive and complex set of social mechanisms that refer to the reproducibility of long-term social relations of inequality, class becomes an important predictor of a person's life chances. Such a usage is complex, for class factors must be analytically – often mathematically – disentangled from other influential variables such as geographical location, family status, race and gender.

Class as historical dimension of inequality

This dimension refers to the way in which systems of economic production allow for the extraction of profits from labour. In this sense, class is defined as a relationship to labour exploitation and the appropriation, ownership and distribution of economic profit.

Class as political category

In this sense, class is not just a measurable, objective concept integral to various strands of sociological explanation, but a powerfully normative concept that allows an analyst not just to explain social structural inequalities, but to explain how such systemic features can be challenged, overcome and transformed. In doing so, this tradition of the use of the class idea is firmly Marxist in orientation: it identifies and labels points of oppression and exploitation, and on the basis of these constructs a radical, emancipatory political project.

In understanding the concept of class, there are two inescapable and powerful so-ciological traditions that continue to provide direction for much contemporary class analysis. The first is a Marxist conceptualization of class, centring on the social and economic relations of labour and capital, and the central dynamic of the extraction of profit. Developed originally by Karl Marx, the concept of class is central to explaining the Marxian vision of capitalism. Writing in the mid-nineteenth century, Marx's analysis of capitalism is probably the most comprehensive and intellectually powerful theory of capitalism ever expounded. It has inspired rabid ideological followers and detractors alike and, because it forcefully and meticulously analyses some fundamental patterns within capitalist society, it continues to be an inspiration for many contemporary scholars.

Marx situated class differences as central to capitalism's dynamism, and elemental to what he saw as its inevitable downfall. In the Marxian tradition, capitalism essentially is structured by the existence of two classes: the owners of the means of production or capital, who were called the bourgeoisie; and the workers who had only their labour power to sell, called the proletariat. The bourgeois, capital-owning class may have owned factories, inherited wealth or possessed vast shareholdings that gave them economic and social power. By owning the means of production the capital-owning class also possessed the means to extract and appropriate profits from their capital. This was the basis of the private-enterprise capitalist economy, and continues to be an important ideological pattern in contemporary culture: those who risk investments of capital have the sole right to reap profits. In contrast to those who owned capital, the workers or proletariat had only their labour power to sell. This labour power commanded a comparatively low wage, but of course in reality it yielded much higher value for the capitalist owners of the means of production in terms of value-added production.

Marx called the difference between the monetary value that workers produced and what they were paid **surplus value**. Surplus value was the key to the perpetuation of a capitalist system of class. It allowed the owners of the means of production to amass large profits, which in turn could be used to strengthen their economic position and also their position as the dominant social class, supported by ideological apparatus like schooling and legal systems. The workers had their wages and conditions continuously squeezed by capitalists, to the extent that Marx believed the stability of capitalism would eventually be threatened. The result, Marx hoped, would be that the working class would come to understand their own exploitation within the capitalist system of economic production and eventually develop a revolutionary consciousness, which would lead to an overthrow of the system. Central to this Marxist vision of capitalism is a class system, which grows out of the way economic production is organized into basic groups of capital owners and workers. On the basis of one's position in relation to capital and ownership of the means of economic production, the development of a group class consciousness would be realized. On the one hand, the class system envisioned by Marx was ruthlessly exploitative and oppressive in extracting profits from the labouring class; on the other, this same tendency provided the impetus for the development of a class awareness and emancipatory mood among the exploited classes that Marx believed threatened the social stability of the capitalist system.

Max Weber's idea of class is multidimensional compared with Marx's. In outlining the processes whereby modern societies are stratified, Weber pointed to a basic distinction between class and status. He defined class in terms of an individual's market situation – that is, he understood class mainly by reference to the ownership or possession of various skills or abilities within labour markets, which commanded differential access to monetary rewards and income. In relation to market exchanges for one's labour, or the goods one made, differential rewards were allocated. Of course, under capitalist market conditions, individuals with greater skills, those who owned capital or various means of production, and the educated classes were likely to command greater incomes and profits. This differential access to material resources and its consequences for market positions were then basic determinants of life chances, which were in turn directly related to one's opportunities, outcomes and **life-course trajectories**. Classes were thus groups that had in common particular life-course trajectories, which were an outcome of their capacity to offer labour skills in the market. Weber also highlighted that societies were stratified not just by relationships to markets, but by various sorts of status dimensions, which he called the status order. Status does not directly affect material chances, but can do so indirectly by way of the influence of status and honour on one's capacity to participate within various social circles and fields. Status groups share particular types of lifestyles, meaning they have general normative agreements over such aspects of life as manners, dress, acceptable leisure activities, matters of taste and decorum. Though this is not directly a market phenomenon, it can have implications for reinforcing and supporting basic material inequalities. Status is not a basic determinant of life chances, but it goes hand in hand with particular stratifications based upon economic opportunities. Finally, Weber pointed to the concept of 'party' as a final determinant of life chances. Parties refer to the groups to which people belong, which in some way have an associational character and an agreed-upon set of goals and aspirations. Necessarily, parties try to effect or have power over social outcomes by way of their group character. The collective energies of parties are directed towards particular goals, and work in conjunction with both class and status characteristics in trying to reach these goals.

Challenges to class analysis: problems, debates and new forms of inequality and politics

Having outlined the most important principles and concepts of traditional class analysis, we will now go on to consider recent challenges to the concept. Since the 1990s, there has been a rush of debate about the usefulness of the concept of class for explaining social stratification and political conflict. This debate occurred within mainstream sociological fields of class and sociological theory, and was also sparked in new debates about identity and reflexivity that originated within what we can broadly think of as the cultural turn in sociology. This chorus of relatively recent critical commentary was preceded by a developing awareness of the utility of the concept, which had much earlier origins. For example, the Australian-based sociologists Pakulski and Waters cite Robert Nisbet's statement in 1958 to a meeting of the American Sociological Association that:

> the term social class is by now useful in historical sociology, in comparative or folk sociology, but that it is nearly valueless for the clarification of the data of wealth, power, and social status in the contemporary United States and much of Western society in general.
>
> (Pakulski and Waters 1996a: 667)

More than three decades later, Clark and Lipset began a well-known article in the journal *International Sociology* with the claim that:

> New forms of social stratification are emerging. Much of our thinking about stratification – from Marx, Weber, and others – must be recast to capture these new developments. Social class was the key theme of past stratification work. Yet class is an increasingly outmoded concept, although it is sometimes appropriate to earlier historical periods . . . Class analysis has grown increasingly inadequate in recent decades as traditional hierarchies have declined and new social differences have emerged. The cumulative impact of these changes is fundamentally altering the nature of social stratification – placing most theories in need of substantial modification.
>
> (Clark and Lipset 1991: 397)

In 1996, Pakulski and Waters (1996b) published a book with the triumphant – some might say reckless – title *The Death of Class*. In their introduction, they suggest that disciplinary ossification has occurred as a result of over-using the concept and hanging on to it for too long – most likely for sentimental and political reasons. They comment that sociologists have become so dependent on class as a fundamental platform of any social explanation that the concept no longer has any genuine analytic potency:

> This book confirms the good news that class has collapsed and is decomposing, leaving only the merest traces of its effects. If it ever was real and salient, and we are certainly prepared to admit that class was a sturdy historical reality, it is no longer. This means that sociologists cannot go relating and reducing every social phenomenon, from feminine subordination to taste in music, to class. We must begin the search for a new theoretical *terra firma*.
>
> (Pakulski and Waters 1996b: 7)

Despite their apparent rush to abolish the use of the concept, the proponents of such a view are careful to suggest a number of caveats. First, they are certainly not suggesting that inequalities are being narrowed or erased, or that class was – and remains – a fiction of theorists' minds. Rather, they point out that inequalities are greater now than ever, as well as more global than ever before, and that such current inequalities are being arranged along new lines of structuring force. That is, if we conceive it broadly as the socially structured reproduction of difference then class now operates through different mechanisms and systems and is being expressed in new ways. Furthermore, Pakulski and Waters (1996b) are careful to point out that the processes that structure these new forms of inequality best relate to specific regions of the world, in particular the advanced Western economies of the United States, Western Europe and Australia.

So what factors make class less analytically powerful in the view of these sociologists? First, traditional Marxist conceptions of class were based on the ownership of productive property and the capacity of such property to generate profits. Yet throughout the twentieth century there has been a weakening of the influence of property on social position as more and more people have begun to purchase and own their own homes, for example. This has meant that ownership of capital has slowly been distributed down the social ladder. Furthermore, since the 1980s capitalism has begun to dedifferentiate or 'disorganize' (see Lash and Urry 1987, 1994) in such a way that there is now less of a distinction between the capitalist class and the working class. Small businesses have grown in number, and the extent of share ownership in Western countries has expanded greatly. For example, in Australia and the United States over 50 per cent of the population have direct share ownership, while many more have indirect investments through their superannuation portfolios. The privatization of government utilities in many Western countries since the 1970s has ushered in a new phase of what some have labelled 'people's capitalism', where members of the middle and even working class can at least technically be part-owners of the means of production. The impact of this on the development of the revolutionary consciousness about which Marx talked should be clear – the working and middle classes have become gradually wealthier and more comfortable, and consequently less likely to challenge, or even identify, the exploitative basis of systems of production. This is not to say that economic downturns such as the one experienced globally since 2009 could not reactivate the perceived need for urgent global social change at some time in the future. However, it is more likely that a bundle of dimensions would come into play in this situation. Along with social class, factors relating to environmental and social sustainability would clearly be significant as people increasingly weigh up their economic gains against personal, environmental and cultural anxieties and degradations.

In addition to this, the nature of what constitutes a productive resource has drastically changed since Marx's time. Before the time when Marx was writing, ownership of land constituted the most valuable form of capital, useful for agricultural production. At the stage of still relatively early capitalism, when industrial expansion intensified, factories and machinery were clearly at the centre of economic productivity, and because they were expensive assets, only a relatively small segment of society was able to own them. However, as the twentieth century progressed and capitalism matured and moved into the post-industrial era, various forms of technical and professional knowledge come to be more highly valued, skilled workers began to command higher wages, and production became controlled not just by the bourgeoisie but by skilled technical and professional classes. For example, expertise relating to information technology, cultural business knowledge around branding and advertising, or various forms of creative, art-based business became more valuable because they could offer expert pathways to building culturally distinguished and meaningful commodity forms. Moreover, in the workplace work teams and cooperative forms of production become popular – workers had more flexibility and a little more say about how they worked, and in some instances they were able to demand more meaningful patterns of work. The workplace therefore became relatively de-hierarchicalized. Of course, this did not diminish social inequalities, erase historically entrenched patterns of exploitation or overcome the politics of social difference springing from visible and embodied social differences; however, it did offer workers the opportunity for more autonomy, status and meaning within their workplaces, which ultimately meant that a class consciousness – the feeling of belonging to a structurally disadvantaged social group – was less likely to develop.

A further factor challenging a strong version of class theory relates to changing patterns of political affiliation in Western, industrial democracies. In earlier times of industrial capitalism, political affiliations were fixed more closely to party loyalties, and voting options were often fewer and were attached more clearly to mainstream, big-party left- and right-wing political options. The working classes were typically affiliated with parties on the left, while the professional and bourgeois classes were affiliated with the right-wing parties. A set of group or collective interests, determined principally by one's relation to capital ownership and accumulated wealth, which translated directly and simply into traditional political affiliations, was assumed. Since World War II, however, voting according to this binary has become more complicated. For example, voters on the left may still come from traditional working-class backgrounds, but there is a growing section of voters from professional occupations who support left-wing social policy or green environmental policy (Clark and Lipset 1991). Voting patterns detach from class issues and focus more on what some have called **post-materialist** concerns (Inglehart 1990). The result is that voting becomes more directed at concerns very much distanced from class politics:

> Political issues shift with more affluence: as wealth increases, people take the basics for granted; they grow more concerned with lifestyle and amenities. Younger, more educated and more affluent persons in more affluent and less hierarchical societies should move furthest from traditional class politics.
>
> (Clark and Lipset 1991: 403)

In many Western nations we are now observing the rise of third parties, minority parties, single-issue parties and lifestyle parties, in preference to 'catch-all' political parties that many people perceived as too monolithic and traditional to respond effectively to urgent social issues. Given the fusion of political discourses with public perceptions and symbolism, single-issue and independent parties can have significant effects on political outcomes. Furthermore, individual voting habits are now less tied to master discourses of left and right political values, and have become more susceptible to volatility, depending on the political, social and environmental issues of the day.

Post-class social analysis: the rise of life politics

This detachment of voting and political affiliations from class location is complemented by increasing individualization of political concerns, a growing quest to cultivate and protect one's lifestyle, and an interest in self-cultivation and self-actualization generally. Politics becomes a social field that mirrors the logic of consumer culture more broadly, where choice triumphs over long-term commitment, experimentation over habit:

> whole areas of lifestyle and consumer choice are freed up and individuals are forced to decide, to take risks, to bear responsibilities, to be actively involved in the construction of their own identities for themselves, to be enterprising consumers.
>
> (Lash and Urry 1994: 61)

A large swathe of innovative, macro-social theory in the 1980s and 1990s focused on questions of identity, individualization, personal reflexivity, the decline of traditional forms of authority, sub-politics and subaltern politics, and the disorganization of economic and social forms. Associated with the cultural and postmodern turn in social theory, the monolithic concepts of traditional structural sociology – such as class – began to be challenged and, to some degree and perhaps more in theoretical terms than real terms, were dissolved. The assumption that social changes would arise from radical political interests that formed collectively based around class interests was challenged by the idea that a politics of the self, or 'life politics', could offer emancipatory possibilities. **Life politics** is based on the premise that people's personal decisions about the things that affect their own quality of life in social, cultural, personal and environmental ways can become infused with moral meaning and begin to replace class location as a signpost for ethical and political action and communal responsibility. For example, community actions to care for local waterways or sections of wild landscape might motivate citizens within a region. Or people may be driven by the idea that an urban life less reliant on the motor vehicle might become a dominant concern within a city as that city grows so large that it begins to experience significant traffic congestion and pollution issues. Finally, political battlegrounds might be drawn around cultural affiliations such as gender, sexuality or commodification within an inner-city area that is gentrifying rapidly. In all of these cases, interests and affiliations can form across social classes and also beyond them, decentring the role of class as the primary explanation of political mobilization and radicalism.

Cultural consumption and class reproduction: Bourdieu

The strongest attempt to link the traditional radical thrust of class theory to cultural concepts and a culture-based explanation of social inequality can be found in the work of French sociologist Pierre Bourdieu. One of Bourdieu's theoretical priorities is to avoid resting on either structure or agency – or, to put it another way, either objective or subjective features of social life – as the pivotal axes of sociological explanation. Hence his theory of social inequality is based on the relations between the personal, embodied and performed world of everyday cultural practices, with an account of how such subjective capacities bind to matters of reproduction of social inequality. For example, beyond the possession of forms of economic assets or capital, Bourdieu points to the increasingly important role played by cultural forms of capital. Bourdieu's class explanation is positivist in nature, evidenced most strongly in his work *Distinction* (1984), which makes extensive use of social surveys and complex statistical techniques but also rests on a complex theoretical framework. Central to this framework is the idea of **habitus**, the generative mechanism by which tastes, perceptions and everyday practices are cultivated and exercised. The habitus – something we all possess but of which we are mostly unaware – is the means by which people come to develop systems of likes and dislikes, the way they form and repeat social practices, and also the set of guiding principles and procedures that they use in their relations with objects and others. In short, it is a set of dispositions for use in practice that orientates individuals in their relations with people and objects in the social world. The habitus is formed in individuals through historically and socially situated conditions of its production, and can be thought of as 'class internalized'. Bourdieu (1990: 54) says it is the 'active present of past experiences'. He theorizes the habitus as both *structured and structuring*. That is, while the habitus is a product of a determinate class of conditions, Bourdieu stresses that it retains some spontaneity, and that while a person's habitus will typically direct them towards particular choices, it does not amount to obedience to rules. That is, the habitus generates the principles by which people are able to classify and organize encounters in the social and material world, and it is also structured or generated by them insofar as these encounters are the product of regular associations and shared conditions of existence.

One of Bourdieu's primary concerns in his work *Distinction* is the distributed nature of cultural tastes within societies, and how these tastes are actually important in reproducing social inequalities. In this sense, his account is radical and innovative. Could it be that things such as the music to which one listens, the books reads and the types of leisure practices one prefers are actually pointers to one's social location – and furthermore, actually play an active role in perpetuating one's social and economic position? Bourdieu calls the social aggregate of all these things an 'economy' of cultural consumption preferences, and he believes that such an economy can perpetuate social and economic inequalities. The economy of cultural goods refers to the particular combinations of cultural objects that classes of people consume. For example, Bourdieu's analysis of dominant tastes, presented in a two-dimensional plane diagram in his book *Distinction* (1984: 262), shows the particular distributions of preferences for musical works, composers, domestic interiors and cooking, plotted along with the degree of cultural and economic capital. Likewise, films seen in order of preference by Parisians are mapped to reveal the distribution of bundles of cinematic preferences held by secondary teachers, professions, and industrial and commercial employers (Bourdieu 1984: 271). The outcome of this cultural preference mapping is the plotting of a cultural consumption economy, which for Bourdieu is a step along the way to understanding the space of lifestyles and the role such patterns play in reproducing inequalities.

This economy of preferred cultural goods – a product of people's tastes – is also manifested in the ways in which people relate to culture. Thus, in Bourdieu's account, taste is not only something identifiable in *what* we consume, but also in the *way* we consume things. This performative element is certainly implied, but never strongly developed in Bourdieu's work. For example, he comments about the consumption strategies of the petite bourgeoisie that:

> The petit bourgeois do not know how to play the game of culture as a game. They take culture too seriously to go in for bluff or imposture or even for the distance and casualness which show true familiarity; too seriously to escape permanent fear or ignorance or blunders, or to side-step tests by responding with the indifference of those who are not competing or the serene detachment of those who feel entitled to confess or even flaunt their lacunae. Identifying culture with knowledge, they think that the cultivated man is one who possesses an immense fund of knowledge and refuse to believe him when he professes, in one of those impious jests allowed to a Cardinal, who can take liberties with the faith forbidden to the parish priest, that, brought down to its simplest and most sublime expression, it amounts to a *relation* to culture.
>
> (Bourdieu 1984: 330–1)

In Bourdieu's analysis, social classes relate to cultural objects in socially unique ways. This relationship to cultural forms such as films or music, manners or dress is referred to as **cultural capital**, and is one of Bourdieu's great insights. He insists on the existence of multiple forms of capital, apart from merely economic or financial capital, or social capital. Bourdieu's cultural capital can be defined as knowledge of arts and culture, the possession of particular cultural skills (such as being able to play a musical instrument), and the ability to enact one's cultural tastes and preferences in convincing and discriminating ways. Cultural capital is a product of the habitus, and is thus socially shaped, but it ultimately plays a part in reproducing one's social location. In Bourdieu's theory, dominant social classes are able to define what is culturally valuable, thus marginalizing the working-class habitus. For example, the bourgeois class's mode of consumption attempts to emphasize authenticity and naturalness in their relation to culture, as though it were made especially for them. In addition, bourgeois culture might be seen in popular terms as refined and learned, compared with the apparently brutish and base aspects of working-class culture. For example, in the realm of musical preferences heavy metal is associated with the working classes, while classical music and opera reflect the interests and bearing of the upper classes. While bourgeois consumption sometimes may be permitted to be eccentric, it is held together by a confidence that goes with a flair for cultivating culture as nature. The bourgeois classes typically cultivate an art to living so that, for example, meal preparation becomes as much an artistic endeavour as a biological necessity. The point of such everyday activities that are based in modes of 'artistic consumption' is that they demand 'pure, pointless expenditure' provided by the 'rarest and most precious thing of all . . . namely, time' (Bourdieu 1984: 281). On the other hand, the working-class aesthetic is dominated by a rejection of aestheticization and the cultivation of an art of living that is founded in modesty, pragmatism and simplicity:

> [O]ne sees examples in the behaviour of small craftsmen or businessmen who, as they themselves say, 'don't know how to spend the money they've earned', or of junior clerical workers, still attached to their peasant or working-class roots, who get as much satisfaction from calculating how much they have 'saved' by doing without a commodity or service (or 'doing it themselves') as they would have got from the thing itself, but who, equally, cannot ever purchase it without a painful sense of wasting money. Having a million does not in itself make one able to live like a millionaire.
>
> (Bourdieu 1984: 374)

Bourdieu's account of cultural tastes and their role in reproducing social structural inequalities is the most ambitious and thorough yet to be published. The strengths of his approach in *Distinction* are multifaceted. Fundamentally, its strength rests on the range of quantitative data available to Bourdieu through his survey material and the innovative techniques he employs in analysing the data. While Frow's (1987) deconstruction of Bourdieu's complicity in reproducing a regime of cultural tastes and value through his social scientific endeavours is compelling in terms of demonstrating the arbitrariness of his cultural categories, Bourdieu's analysis of social and cultural correspondences along dimensions of cultural and economic capital is the best empirical treatment of the social patterns of taste that is available. However, perhaps the most important reason for the work's substantial contribution to the study of taste is its application of an impressive theoretical basis that was developed by Bourdieu through a number of substantial prior works. Bourdieu advanced from a strong strand of structuralism in his earliest work to a more nuanced synthesis of objective and subjective principles in his middle period, writing on the logic of practice (Bourdieu 1977). This came to rest on his theories about the role of different forms of capital, the habitus and the dimensions of differentiated social space, impressively operationalized in *Distinction*.

Some researchers have raised questions about Bourdieu's central concept of the habitus. As pointed out above, habitus refers to the set of dispositions that are used in everyday practice to orient the choices made by individuals in their relations with people and objects in the social world. It is the sum of materials an individual possesses, which in Bourdieu's epistemological model serves the theoretical purpose of transcending the traditional theoretical division between social structure and the individual. A powerful critique of Bourdieu's concept of the habitus is that it is merely an apology for the incorporation of voluntarism and subjectivity. Because of Bourdieu's commitment to a materialist account in the last instance, a systematic investigation of tastes as autonomous cultural practices is neglected. Jeffrey Alexander's (1995) essay on Bourdieu is more acerbic than most on this issue:

> Despite Bourdieu's repeated claim that habitus is akin to Chomsky's generative grammar, it turns out to be more like a Trojan horse for determinism. Time and time again it is explained not as a site for voluntarism – for improvising within certain limits – but as the reflection and replication of exterior structures . . . Far from an alternative to social structural explanation, habitus merely operationalizes it.
>
> (Alexander 1995: 136)

Another core difficulty is that Bourdieu's account of taste overlooks the subjective and performative component of how and why these judgements are made. In his model, quotients of cultural capital and the habitus are deployed to explain tastes, but as an explanation they end up defaulting to ideas of social structure, cultural and economic dominance, and symbolic authority. Thus, for his critics, Bourdieu's theory of practice 'is nothing more than a theory of the determination of practice' (Alexander 1995: 140). The work of Michele Lamont (1992) makes a number of useful cultural criticisms of Bourdieu, but also suggests ways to move forward with a sensitivity to Bourdieu's vision. First, she suggests that his categories were not only based too much on Parisian attitudes and milieus, but that they sometimes relied on generalization from his own experiences (Lamont 1992: 186). In addition, Lamont argues convincingly that moral evaluations can operate both independently of and also strongly attached to people's possession of economic and cultural capital. Thus we might commonly think in terms of whether someone is a 'good person' apart from their wealth or education, or we might attach moral discourses to wealth and its symbolic expression through objects such as big cars or homes. Lamont's model thus explores non-economic forms of capital and cultural modes of social distinction in a discursive, non-reductive fashion.

Class as lived culture: culture as class opposition

On questions of the everyday texture and experiential nature of class, we need to look elsewhere. Work originating from within the British cultural studies tradition has been extremely influential in bringing aspects of everyday and working-class cultures into academic view. For example, Hoggart (1957) looked at working-class cultures and the way in which they were being changed due to emergent publishing and consumption industries of the time, such as magazines, newspapers, music and novels, which were mass cultural forms that slowly but surely intruded into the life-worlds and ideological worldviews of citizens. The result was a weakening of working-class culture and the development of a mass culture. The work of Williams (1958, 1961) and Hall (1973) built on Hoggart's insights, but Hall in particular introduced the important idea that readings of popular culture products, such as magazines, novels and television shows, are negotiated. While the ideological and class content of mass culture needed to be exposed, Hall's (1973) theory emphasized the interplay of ideology and agency. Much attention was paid to the way in which messages were constructed and coded within media forms, and how this disguised matters of class and power; however, there was also room for interpretation, autonomy and even oppositional readings in Hall's theory. Hall encapsulated this idea in his theory of how media texts were encoded and decoded, produced by media workers according to particular codes and textual norms and then consumed and read by everyday people who – at least in theory – had the capacity to generate ironic, oppositional readings of this content.

A common critique of the early British cultural studies models was that they had a certain air of sentimentality about them, which privileged traditional and entrenched cultural forms of the working classes. Young people, who had embraced popular media and music cultures, were to some extent seen to be contributing to the increased commercialization and growth of mass media forms that threatened to erode working-class values and solidarities. However, in the 1970s the ethnographic tradition expanded to consider what were seen as oppositional cultural forms that had emerged out of the youth cultures of the day, centred on new forms of music, dress and social values. In their book *Resistance Through Rituals*, Hall and Jefferson (1976) argue that youth subcultural practices should be considered as challenging and oppositional. Using the everyday resources of fashion, music and leisure practices, young people were seen to be using creative means for challenging accepted and traditional social practices and values.

Central here is the work of Dick Hebdige (1979). In this analysis, Hebdige addresses two questions. First, how is sense-making within subcultural groups enabled through various types of signifiers – for example, dress, self-presentation, musical preferences and various other accoutrements? Second, how can subcultures (particularly punk) cohere around a central belief in 'disorder' that is a symbolic challenge to mainstream culture? Hebdige (1979) pinpoints 'style' as a type of cultural weaponry of subcultural groups – conceptualizing it as a technique of 'intentional communication' that functions both for members within the group and for those in the general mass of 'straight' or conventional culture. 'Subcultural style' refers to the bundle of features that comprise one's self-presentation. For the subcultural groups Hebdige considered – principally youth subcultures centred around music and fashion – style is an 'emphatic combination' of dress, dance, argot, musical preference, hair colour and style, and accoutrements like hair combs, bracelets, earrings and watch chains.

Hebdige asserts that the key to understanding subcultural style is that it is intentionally, consciously *constructed* – in contrast to conventional style, which he sees as less consciously constructed. Punk style, for example, is assembled according to principles of drama and spectacle. 'Straight' or mass style is seen as drawing upon contrasting cultural codes and practices. In this sense, it too is a type of intentional communication, but the communicative intent is to be 'appropriate' and 'modest', and to 'fit in'. Dominant cultural discourses encourage us to identify straight or conventional style not so much in terms of a particular assemblage of ideological codes and symbols, but as something that is entirely natural and without 'history' in Barthes's (1967, 1968) sense – something that is without ideology. This view of straight style as *the* 'natural' way of presenting self is, of course, plainly wrong. The power of (sub)cultural communication comes from its ability to draw strategically upon the symbolic grammar of 'straight' style and to subvert it through various subtle, and not so subtle, ways.

Conclusion

This chapter has considered the concept of class through both traditional and contemporary sociological perspectives. The concept was introduced to the discipline by its founding figures, who used it as a central platform to understand the nature, form and durability of social inequalities in capitalist society. Like any scientific concept, class has a biography – or, to use sociological language, its own 'life-course trajectory'. Since the 1990s, sociologists and other social scientists have questioned whether class can and should retain its currency as the privileged concept of social explanations of inequality. The argument, considered in this chapter, is that in various important ways social differences and identities, politics and everyday life have become decoupled from a narrow, economically defined concept of class. The challenge of the cultural sociological approach is to show how class is culturally shaped, expressed and lived. Above all, it shows how cultural forms play a role in both reproducing and challenging structures and patterns of inequality.

Review questions

4.1 Distinguish between Marxist and Weberian accounts of class. Discuss the relative positions of cultural and economic factors in Marx's and Weber's explanations of class dynamics.

4.2 What is the distinction between 'social class' and 'class analysis'?

4.3 Outline the fundamental claims of the 'death of class' thesis. What does this thesis suggest about contemporary inequality?

4.4 What social and economic changes have made class a less salient concept in sociological explanation?

4.5 What is the 'post-materialist' orientation and how has it impacted on the contemporary salience of class analysis?

4.6 In what ways is 'life politics' different from class politics? Is life politics a viable form of political action?

4.7 What did Bourdieu mean by habitus? What can this term tell us about social class that was unavailable to traditional conceptions of social class?

4.8 What was so innovative in Bourdieu's book *Distinction* in terms of analysing social class?

Further reading

Bourdieu, P. (1984) *Distinction: A Social Critique of the Judgement of Taste*, Routledge, London.

Clark, T.N. and Lipset, S.M. (1991) Are social classes dying? *International Sociology*, 6 (4), 397–410.

Giddens, A. (1991) *Modernity and Self-Identity: Self and Society in the Late Modern Age*, Polity Press, Cambridge.

Hall, S. and Jefferson, T. (eds) (1976) *Resistance Through Rituals: Youth Subcultures in Post-War Britain*, Routledge, London.

Marshall, G. (1997) *Repositioning Class. Social Inequality in Industrial Societies*, Sage, London.

Pakulski, J. and Waters, M. (1996b) *The Death of Class*, Sage, London.

Skeggs, B. (2004) *Class, Self, Culture*, Routledge, London.

Wright, E.O. (1997) *Class Counts: Comparative Studies in Class Analysis*, Cambridge University Press, Cambridge.

5

Gender and Sexuality

Learning objectives

- To be aware of the various approaches to and debates in sociology and feminist literature on gender and sexuality.
- To understand how gender norms and heterosexuality are reinforced and contested in representational practices, media culture and laws.
- To learn about the symbolic dominance of the masculine heterosexual subject and male body.
- To be aware of the idea of an ethics of sexual difference.

Introduction

In cultural sociology, gender and sexuality are interpreted and researched as social processes and ways of being analysed through the prism of 'culture' broadly speaking. Specifically, this research focus is oriented towards understanding and investigating symbolic processes, that is, the construction and circulation of meaning, ideas and values through social interaction and everyday culture – clothing, objects, media entertainment, body practices and so on. Gender and sexuality remain important areas of contemporary sociological investigation, and the impact of cross-disciplinary theory and research – particularly feminist theory, politics and philosophy – informs sociology in general, and cultural sociology in particular. Everyday social interaction, imagery and discourse create assumptions and social expectations about gender and sexuality – for example, the assumption that everyone is heterosexual, or that embodying masculine and feminine styles of dress, mannerisms and deportment corresponds to, and is a reliable indicator

Cultural Sociology: An Introduction, First Edition. Les Back et al. © 2012 Les Back, Andy Bennett, Laura Desfor Edles, Margaret Gibson, David Inglis, Ronald Jacobs and Ian Woodward. Published 2012 by Blackwell Publishing Ltd.

of, sexual orientation or the sexed bodies underneath. These are, of course, tried and tested assumptions that have reliability – they are generally right because most people have internalized gender distinctions as part of their identity and corporeal way of being.

In liberal Western societies, individuals and groups also actively signify their gender style and sexual orientation(s) and this is particularly so in cosmopolitan, urban environments. Nevertheless, if we take assumptions for granted we fail to think consciously about how assumptions are, in themselves, a social practice. They are part of the way in which the normative and symbolic dominance of the sex–gender polarity and of heterosexuality is enacted, not only as what people generally *might be*, but what they *should be*. It is this second element – the moral force of the norm – that enables and underscores practices and institutional cultures of homophobia, gender and sexual discrimination. This chapter introduces key theoretical literature, particularly in relation to issues of gender and sexual ethics. It also focuses on the rise of greater gender flexibility and diversity of sexual identities and lifestyles in most democratic Western societies. Importantly, this chapter examines the relationship between the symbolic and representational process in relation to concrete lived histories and experience. In other words, it argues that how we live and relate to each other are ultimately intertwined with how identities are hierarchically ordered and constructed in both formal (legal and institutional) and informal (everyday interactions) social processes. This is a key argument in this chapter.

Understanding gender and sexuality

Gender is both a psychic (mental) and corporeal (bodily) process of becoming self-identified and identified by others as either masculine or feminine. Human beings become gendered through complex processes of adopting and learning the behaviours and traits that mark them as masculine or feminine according to degrees and styles of being either one or the other. This either/or structure can be strict in some cultures, and more fluid and permeable in others. Conformity to gender and to heterosexual orientation is an internalized and external social force. Gender is not simply a negative, enforced category of existence; it is also about the desire to be or not be a girl or boy and, by extension, a certain type of girl or boy. Of course, not wanting to or being unable to live the distinction is also a factor – **transgendering** exists in many societies (sometimes recognized as a third gender) and **intersexed** people also disrupt the sex-gender order as their bodies subvert the two-sexes body model and its either/or division.[1]

Gender identification is not necessarily fixed throughout an individual life, as *girly girls* may become feminine feminists and tough boys may become drag queens or sensitive social workers. The construction of gender on the basis of biological sex difference situates men and women in the world differently, and it inevitably shapes their consciousness in different ways. This is not to say that gender rigidly divides men and women, shaping distinctly separate consciousness along sex/gender lines. There is overlap, intermingling and cross-identifications of gender in sexes. Gender is not a discrete category – it is mediated by other identities and status positions such as race, ethnicity and class, which shape the kind of consciousness and experience of any individual person. However, an individual person cannot be reduced to these categories either – our individual lives are so biographically particular, and we are so singularly embodied as individuals, that we cannot be described or completely captured by these categories of gender, ethnicity, race and class. However, these categories are important sociologically because they recognize the constitution and location of individuals within status and identity groups. It is also important to note that in many Western societies, and especially among more privileged social groups and classes, people tend to see themselves as autonomous individuals transcending group identities.

Contemporary diversification in the configurations of gender and sexual biography were partly enabled by the identity movements of the 1960s and 1970s in Western democracies, and the subsequent transformation in political and state regulatory-legal cultures. The repeal of laws that once criminalized homosexuality, the transformation of divorce laws, abortion laws, human rights and anti-discrimination laws in countries such as Australia, Britain, the United States, France and Germany have created a larger sphere of personal autonomy, sanctioning more open identity and lifestyle diversity. Nevertheless, in many parts of the world personal freedom from religious and state control remains unrealized as laws against sodomy, same-sex relationships and adultery mean these are met with punishment – including death in some cases. For example, in Saudi Arabia male homosexuality can be punished by imprisonment and whipping, and in Uganda homosexual acts are punishable with anything from 14 years' to life imprisonment. In democracies governed by secular laws, questions of sexuality and issues of adultery are regarded as private concerns – not matters of law and state intervention. However, in countries governed by conservative religious law, sexual freedom, self-determination and privacy are often limited or non-existent, and women are generally subject to greater legal punishment and social shame in relation to adultery.

In secular, pluralistic societies, the institutional and cultural transformation in identity politics and representations revealed a way for both women and men to be conscious of gender *as a social construction*. This is an important point in this chapter – while **essentialist** gender politics and ways of thinking remain symbolically and institutionally powerful, they are also undercut by a deep archive of identity representations and stories that reveal to consciousness a recognition that change from socially constructed norms is both real and possible. Historical images and narratives tell us about change and diversity (as well as resistance and limits) in gendered and sexual ways of being, and this creates a distinctly modern consciousness influenced by the thesis of human agency and social constructionism.

Human agency refers to the idea that human beings construct their world through action and ideas, and therefore have the capacity to change how they live through reflection, group solidarity and social struggle. Identities become denaturalized or exposed as transformable through parody and other comedic activities in entertainment and advertising culture – for example, the representation of the decline of the serious, forbidding male through parodies of (mostly) working-class men/fathers in highly popular shows such as *The Simpsons*, *Married with Children* and *Family Guy* (Alberti 2004; Nathanson and Young 2001; Reese 2004).

In 2007, an Australian Heinz baked beans advertisement (available for viewing on YouTube) depicted two middle-aged ordinary men in a supermarket reaching for the same can of baked beans. They look at each other and realize that they know each other. As it turns out, they were at secondary school together, and were in fact boyfriend and girlfriend. The shock for one of the characters (and arguably the viewer) is thus that his high school girlfriend is now a middle-aged man. The punchline of the ad is about how it is good to know that some things never change – that is, baked beans. An American advertisement for Old Spice aftershave also reflexively plays with the questions of what it is to be a man. Current media-savvy generations are schooled in everyday practices of deconstruction as they unpack in their minds, or in conversation with others, representations and identity images in advertising. In so doing, they think and talk about the marketing strategy aiming to sell products to certain lifestyle and identity groups. Some advertising is quite sophisticated towards its audience, as it subverts/exposes its own game by showing that it is aware its audience knows what it is doing. This kind of reflexivity is part of postmodern cultural practice, and is a new form of consciousness. Furthermore, identifying, reading about and narrativizing 'types' (geek, butch, femme, jock, metrosexual) is also part of postmodern identity consciousness, and this brings essentialist identity politics into question. Contemporary generations live in an age of avatars and multiple identities, traversing virtual worlds and the real world (see Turkle 1995, 2009). Men adopt female avatars and women male avatars – invention and experimentation are part of contemporary self-performance and biography. However, one cannot assume that such playfulness inevitably translates into more open and inclusive gender and sexual politics in everyday face-to-face contexts.

Where people live in terms of nation-states, as well as environments such as cities, suburbs or rural areas, makes a significant difference to the opportunity for, acceptance of and even range of gender constructions and sexual diversity. Conformity to and regulation of gender and sexual norms remains powerful in face-to-face relationships, families and institutional settings. Nevertheless, in the twenty-first century, gender and sexuality have become more flexible – particularly in youth and adult life stages. To watch 1950s and 1960s American television shows such as *All in the Family*, *Father Knows Best*, *The Flintstones*, *I Dream of Jeannie* and *Bewitched*, or historical representations of these eras (such as *Mad Men*), provides a stark lesson in the transformation of gender identities and roles, and ways in which women and men might relate to each other and negotiate power and sexuality. However, as suggested, the relationship between representational culture and lived experience/contexts is complex and diverse, and there is an inevitable gap between the two. In cosmopolitan environments, diversity of sexuality and gender flexibility is a feature of everyday life, and therefore one might expect a concurrent representation within such a society's media.

Postmodern politics and culture are about recognizing the contradictions of political culture – that is, that subversive (or seemingly subversive) cultural products emerge from commercial or consumer values and markets. For example, while the American television programme *Queer Eye for the Straight Guy* might seem a positive representation of gay identity because its premise is that gay men can teach straight men about what women really want, it is also about white, middle-class consumer values, and is thus a conservative endorsement of capitalist consumer culture. So this television show – like many forms of popular culture – contains a mixture of political values: it is progressive in gender and sexual relations, while endorsing and encouraging the capitalist value of consumption.

Even since the 1950s, homosexual desire and relationships have been part of the narratives and characters of popular culture, particularly television. However, one would need to look closely at different genres, narratives and characters to fully explore the politics of such representations. In 1993, an episode of the American CBS comedy-drama *Picket Fences* had its lead character Kimberly Brock talking about her same-sex desire with her best friend, and they were shown kissing. This caused public debate, which in turn boosted ratings. In the 1990s, the absence of a gay kiss scene on the show *Melrose Place* was viewed as a sign of the continued conservative sway of advertising in dictating the limits of non-heterosexual erotic depiction. It was one thing to have homosexual characters as part of the show, but quite another at the time to show sexual body contact between men. There certainly exists generational change in the context of attitudes towards sexual desire and its depiction in the mainstream culture of liberal democratic countries.

The birth of the Internet, with its breaking down of the sexual censorship imposed by governments, corporations and religions, has transformed and rendered visible and accessible previously niche or underground sexual cultures and erotica outside of both mainstream heterosexuality and homosexuality. Online shows and the DIY culture of the Internet release cultural production from the corporate media sector and state control. At the same time, mainstream television productions such as *Glee, Nurse Jackie, Modern Family, Queer as Folk, The Lair, The Ellen Show, Will and Grace, Queer Eye for the Straight Guy, Queer Eye for the Straight Girl* and *Entourage*, and popular songs such as *I Kissed a Girl* by Katy Perry (while different in genre and political values), put homosexual desire, identities and relationships in mainstream media and consumer culture.

The sex–gender distinction

All societies recognize bodily sexed difference and organize their societies according to what these differences mean. By making distinctions, and thus creating categories, *social order* or *structure* is constructed. Through creating categories, the meanings of female and male are made and thereby lived. It is via this process that individuals come to know who they are – or rather, who and what they are *meant to be* in terms of self-understanding and the understanding and perception of others. This position in language is one aspect of what is termed social structure or social order. These terms include language and its use; architecture and the built environment; and institutions and their settings (schools, government, religions and their organizations, marriage and laws). Gender identity is 'learned and achieved at the interactional level, reified at the cultural level, and institutionally enforced via the family, law, religion, politics, economy, medicine, and the media' (Gagne *et al.* 1997: 479).

Sociologists generally make a distinction between **sex** – the biological differences between men and women – and **gender** – the learned differences. They argue that we are not born masculine or feminine, but rather acquire and learn to embody distinct gender attributes through processes of early **socialization**. Children in most cultures come to learn the expectations, patterns of behaviour, identification and biography associated with being a boy or a girl in their particular social, cultural or religious context. In other words, the distinction – that is, the either/or – becomes a social and psychological divide and a normative demand. Children, too, are the social-cultural agents of gender normalization at an early age, as they begin to police and repress within themselves, and in each other, inclusive gender characteristics and identifications. This is one of the pathological aspects of normative and particularly hegemonic masculinity, because it is defined in opposition to femininity and rejects any potentially feminine signs or behaviours in boys or men.

Cross-gender identification and embodiment are generally more acceptable for girls and women, as they represent identification with the positive, hierarchically centred gender – the masculine subject. Mainly within Western cultures, this gender order is deconstructed, critiqued and contested, but it remains a powerful ordering system that is supported institutionally and symbolically. Terms of derision – *sissy*, *girl*, *pussy* – signify and enact the policing and exclusion of the feminine as a negative value and characteristic. To desire to be a girl or *like* a girl, and to embody such identification in a male body, remains difficult for boys – who can risk violence, rejection and scorn. Indeed, to be like a girl puts into question the border between boy and girl, male and female, masculine and feminine. This is an important issue to consider – how much does cross-gender identification undo gender difference altogether? And does the absence of gender or the undoing of gender necessarily create more equality between men and women, boys and girls? These are difficult but important questions.

The sex–gender distinction begs the question of how to explain the relationship between the two. Does biological sex determine gender? In other words, is gender the natural, innate expression of biological sexed differences? Alternatively, is gender free-floating and not fixed or determined by people's sexed bodies? Can a biological female be masculine in the same way as a biological male? Or is it a question of a biological female being differently masculine when predominantly masculine in identification and style of embodiment? In other words, what difference does the body make in terms of formation, style and perception of gender? Gender is not like a piece of clothing that can be put on and taken off – it is a corpus: a body knowledge or way of *being* embodied. This idea becomes quite important in the lives of many transsexual or transgender people when they actively adopt a corporeal gender style in order to pass as categories of sex and gender from which they may be biologically excluded, but with which they identify and to which they seek to belong. The 'trans' can also refer to a form of living a sex-gender identity that is between and not reducible to, or captured by, categories of male and female, masculine and feminine. One of the difficulties of social constructionist positions is that they undermine the significance of sexed-bodily differences in relation to gender identity and gender body styles. The sexed body matters and cannot simply be assimilated into gender as if it is a neutral, blank slate without agency or an effect on how gender is experienced, embodied and interpreted (Gatens 1983; Edwards 1989).

Gender is not simply a question of embodied style; it also concerns attitudes and ideas about what men and women essentially are or should be. In other words, it concerns often essentialist ideas that men are naturally more aggressive and women naturally more intuitive. These kinds of clichéd gender essentialisms are often reinforced in popular culture and in therapeutic and self-help discourses (for example, the 1990s bestseller *Men are from Mars, Women are from Venus*). When an argument or theory is *essentialist*, it rests on the proposition or assumption of a unique female or male nature that is always already there as part of biology. So biological determinism often asserts these characteristics as innate to men and women as part of evolutionary inheritance. And biological determinist positions include scientific debate and research of the brain as itself sexed according to a division into (and effects of) male and female hormones.

Social constructionists question biological explanations for gender difference, asserting the importance of history, experience and cultural difference in creating diverse ways of being men and women, masculine and feminine (Kaplan and Rogers 2003). In other words, social constructionism is suspicious of particularly hard-line biological or evolutionary determinism, arguing that such theories and research are blind to the fact that biology has a history, and that language, culture, discourses and social organization are major factors constructing and producing gender differences. All men and all women do not constitute separate, homogenous (internally coherent) groups, just as all Australians, all Russians or all Anglicans are not specific homogenous groups. The recognition of historical and cultural diversity within the gender categories of man and woman puts into question biological determinism and its essentialist claims or aims.

Language and symbolic orders

The term 'woman' does not function as the universal or the generic term – that is, it is unable to represent both sexes and the concept of the human. Historically, 'man' has operated in speech and writing as the universal concept of the human, and woman has functioned as a particular of that universal. Imagine the term 'woman' operating as the universal, standing for the human subject in its diversity and representing both men and women. In social practice, the terms 'man' and 'woman' are not relativized in both directions – while 'man' can stand for just men but also women too, 'woman' cannot in turn stand for men and women as a practice that immediately makes sense or is common-sense usage. Early twentieth-century French feminist Simone de Beauvoir (1954) critically examined this structure of language as a part of the social/symbolic positioning of women as secondary to, and derivative of, man – who is positioned as and at the origin. She wrote about women's inequality, their status and positioning as *the second sex*, and the consequences in terms of how women are valued intellectually, economically (for example, the sexual division of labour and paid/unpaid nexus) and corporeally, as well as the kinds of biographies that women usually have or must struggle to achieve.

Since de Beauvoir wrote *The Second Sex*, French feminism has taken up the problem of the **symbolic order** and the absence of a feminine genealogy and origin. Indeed, feminist philosopher and cultural theorist Luce Irigaray argues that unless there are two subjects and two origins irreducible and asymmetrical to each other, the feminine/women will always be subjected to a logic assimilation under the sign and origin of the masculine subject and the male sexed body as the value standard and norm. To clarify, a sign is something that stands for something else, and in gender relations the masculine subject is able to take the position of the universal – as signifying or representing both genders. Similarly, this also means that the masculine is situated as the ground or origin from which the feminine arises. Indeed, the biblical story of Adam and Eve is an example of how the masculine becomes the origin of the feminine – her ground or source of being.

The same structure is played out in monotheism's God as Father – a figure miraculously prior to and independent of any supernatural mother figure. Monotheism's patriarchy is a structure of matricide (Gibson 2001). It would be necessary for the entire socio-economic system to be transformed to include the feminine subject-sexed-body on its own terms (its own genre) and its own value, both economically and reproductively. Some societies and economies have partly recognized this with the implementation of paid maternity leave and the protection of women's previous positions of employment, but it is done within an over-arching model based on the standard/norm of the male subject and body. In other words, women are accommodated within a system that does not include their difference in a positive, autonomous and foundational way. Systemically, across class-economic divisions, women's bodies are not regarded equally in their difference, and the capitalist-male identity-body system undervalues and appropriates the economic and social value that women's labour (as well as their bodies) produces through the paid/unpaid labour nexus.

In a different way from Irigaray, French feminist Monique Wittig (1935–2003) uses a structural strategy to displace the masculine subject as a single, assimilating origin. She deploys the term 'lesbian' as an origin or foundational term in its own right. Wittig argues that the term 'woman' is always already caught within the signifying/symbolic logic of both the masculine subject and heterosexism. In the collection *The Straight Mind and Other Essays* (1992) she uses the category 'lesbian' to subvert the categories man/woman. Indeed, Wittig contests the idea that women and men constitute 'natural groupings', and argues that binary categories in their essentialism are precisely essential for the founding/foundations of heterosexual societies. In Wittig's thought, men and women are political and economic categories and not natural givens. This means, in turn, that sexed bodies are not naturally given orders or divisions but are in fact culturally and socially constructed. Wittig is a linguistic materialist (like Judith Butler) in the sense that she sees an indivisible relationship between bodies, language and desire. Language embodies and constructs desiring subjects and objects.

The United Nations is one of a number of key organizations monitoring and seeking to practically address gender injustice at a global level. As the introduction to this chapter proposes, it is important to try to see the relationship between more theoretical understandings of gender and sexuality and lived realities. In other words, when we talk about the unequal symbolic valuing of women relative to men, this inevitably translates into how, and under what conditions, men and women live. Having explored the linguistic aspect of the gender debate, we can now consider how the symbolic valuing of different sexes compares in terms of global statistics. Let us take a moment to reflect upon gender disparities. A UN report titled *The World's Women 2010: Trends and Statistics* is one source that has collected data on the situation of women relative to men. The report includes these shocking facts:

- Two-thirds of the 774 million adult illiterates globally are women.
- Women own approximately 1 per cent of the world's land.
- Seventy per cent of the poorest people in the world are women.
- Some 72 million children of primary school age are not going to school, and 54 per cent of these are girls.
- Women are predominantly and increasingly employed in the service sector, and the gender pay gap (women being paid less than men) remains a problem globally.
- Two million women per year are victims of genital mutilation.
- Approximately 70 million women and children were subject to sex trafficking in Asia alone over the period 2000–10.

In democratic societies, particularly among middle-class populations, women fare much better than their counterparts in poorer, less democratic or non-democratic societies. Legal, economic and educational systems in democracies have transformed radically in the twentieth and twenty-first centuries to enable women to own property in their own right, to have independent bank accounts, to access state-based education as a right and social value, to initiate divorce, to gain custody and child support if divorced, to access birth control as a right and choice, and so on. While women across the globe can live such different lives economically, socially and politically, there are nevertheless structures or symbolic orders that they have in common. For example, Gayle Rubin's important essay 'The traffic in women: notes on the political economy of sex' (2006) examines how women across cultures are positioned as *objects of exchange* between men. There are many examples where this positioning is self-evident – particularly sex trafficking of women and girls globally. Boys, too, are part of this economy but statistically less so. Think about how the sexual objectification and exploitation of women and girls are considered more normal or less horrifying (partly because it conforms to male-served heterosexual desire) than cases of boys exploited by men (partly because it is male homosexuality). The social order – *a heterosexual order* – positions women/girls as objects of men's desire and sexual property, and this is considered more 'normal' even when the circumstances of this situation are exploitative and cruel.

The positioning of women as objects of property and exchange between men is also evident in the case of women and young girls ('child brides') offered for marriage between families where a dowry or bride price is part of the local/social economy. It can be difficult to change this economic position of women and young girls in poorer countries, particularly in rural communities where the local economy is entrenched within this gendered system for distributing wealth and property, and building alliances between families or village communities. In poorer communities, girls are often seen as an economic burden on the family, and early marriage is regarded as the solution. This gendered economy or structure is also symbolized in the Western marriage ritual, where a father gives his daughter away to his future son-in-law. This ritual might be experienced in a highly personal, even sentimental, way when women have the freedom to choose who they will love and marry, and at what stage in their life. One view of such an example is that in societies and social classes where women's inequality is less pronounced or worrying, traditions such as this are benign forms of patriarchy, and are seen through the lens of personal choice and emotion. Yet, regardless of how men and women in Western societies respond to this marriage ritual, the fact remains that it is a patriarchal gender structure that positions women, not men, in relationships of exchange. So while the lives of women and girls in various cultures and economies are inevitably different, with huge disparities in equality and autonomy between women, at the structural level and within the symbolic system of value, some things are common to all women.

We can take a moment to imagine or invent other symbolic economies or exchange relations between women and men: a wedding ceremony where mothers give their sons away and daughters receive the son in a ceremony, or boys/men requiring a dowry that goes to the mother as payment in the exchange. Imagine female genealogies, with mother–daughter family names passed on to both genders. In some relationships in Western societies, a husband takes on his wife's family name, even though this is usually still the father's name (the daughter's family name from her father's side).

As suggested already, feminism, broadly speaking, has critiqued the assumption that man can stand as the universal, representing women. The universal functions to assert the priority of men as figures of power and authority above and before that of women, and assumes the position of speaking for them. This structure is a form of assimilation, and continues in the political dominance of men within government, economics and religion. For example, is God a Woman? If it is claimed that God is neither male nor female (sex-gender neutral) then why should it matter if God is named as She? Why are religions in the main still resistant to such gender relativity in language use, even while proclaiming that God goes beyond sex-gender ascription? The symbolic order is an order of power, authority and representation, and religions are institutions grounded in the representation of God as Man, which reinforces and supports the dominance and authority of men in the non-spiritual world – the world of social, economic and political institutions. The spiritual foundation of most world religions is centred on God-the-Father figures and on father–son stories (Daly 1973). Women's symbolic positions in religious narratives, and their roles in religious institutions, are usually secondary – though not necessarily unrecognized or unvalued. Nevertheless, patriarchal religions are founded on the repression of the feminine and the displacement/erasure of the maternal as a cosmic and spiritual origin and creative force. Whether or not women belong to religions, whether they identify with and gain spiritual support from them, is separate to the structural and symbolic issue of religion's patriarchal symbolic and institutional structure. While some Christian churches in the late twenty-first century have moved towards greater gender and sexual orientation equality in the ordination of women, and of openly gay men and women, many religions condemn and actively resist such shifts in moral and identity orders.

Bodies, desires and sexualities

By making a distinction based on body sex difference, societies create social groups and status positions. Basically, in the case of sex difference, having one kind of sexed body (vagina, clitoris, breasts, XX chromosomes) puts you in *this* group rather than *that* group. The group within which you are placed (at the level of language – girl or boy) gives you more or less freedom of choice or more or less social or economic value (as well as different types of value). In a 'straight' heterosexual order, female sex corresponds to a primary or dominant feminine gender and sexual orientation is towards men. Likewise, a male sexed body primarily identifies with the masculine and sexual orientation is psychically mapped towards women. This mapping of the heterosexual social order is set out in Table 5.1.

Table 5.1   The heterosexual social map.

Sex	Gender	Sexual orientation
Female	Feminine	Male
Male	Masculine	Female

Table 5.2 Undoing the heterosexual map.

Sex	Female	Male	Transsexual (e.g. male to female)	Intersexed
Gender	Feminine	Feminine	Feminine	Masculine
Sexual orientation	Female	Female	Female (lesbian)	Intersexed

Table 5.2 reconfigures the heterosexist norms of construction around sex, gender and sexual orientation represented in Table 5.1. It opens up ways of rethinking and recognizing the matrices of desire and identity. It is important to consider the issue of what can or cannot be made sense of socially and politically at a given point in history – that is, what is intelligible and for whom. The heterosexual social order of gender and sexuality is a structure of intelligibility and common-sense thinking for many people. In other words, it seems perfectly 'normal', and normality in fact makes alternative genders and sexualities harder to recognize, to make sense of or to morally accept. Table 5.2 shows alternative, shifting links between identity, bodies and sexual orientation or desire. The table is limited in its representations, however, as the diversity of sexual and bodily ways of being is far more extensive, open-ended and arguably more fluid (unconsciously, that is) within the human psyche and in lived histories.

French philosopher and historian Michel Foucault (1926–84) suggests that something called *sexuality* comes into being through modern science, particularly through sexology, psychoanalysis and psychology.[2] Before the nineteenth century, homosexuality existed but 'the homosexual' as a subject or category of identity did not. Foucault also argues that modern Western culture is marked by the idea that each of us has a true sexuality, and that it is intrinsic to one's personal identity as something that can or should be known and explored. Of course, the rise of medicine has been important in creating not just a way of knowing the body but of changing it to suit the existing social order. Foucault writes about a modern kind of power, *biopower*, which is the way bodies are disciplined through ideologies and social and medical practices. Bio-chemistry is used to moderate hormones, which in turn moderate behaviour. Medical science has been important in controlling unruly bodies and identities (for example, intersexed people).

British sociologist Anthony Giddens (1994) argues that sexuality comes into being as something distinct, and as a property of each individual, when sexual behaviour is no longer necessarily bound up with reproduction. This raises a number of issues. First, birth control technologies, such as the contraceptive pill and other devices, have ushered in a contemporary attitude that procreation is a matter of individual choice and something that can be planned. Second, other forms of reproductive technologies, such as IVF, have made it possible to separate procreation from a procreative sexual act between a man and a woman. Third, the sexual revolution of the 1960s and 1970s, and the women's liberation movement of this era, both aimed to liberate sexuality from the institution, the moral authority of marriage and compulsory heterosexuality. This politics of liberation gave rise to a number of discourses concerned with exploring sexual pleasure, and rights to sexual pleasure – specifically orgasm for women.

Sexual desire and fantasy are not able to be policed at the level of the psyche, or indeed the unconscious – particularly in societies where access to sexual imagery is relatively uncensored. Indeed, the question of sexuality is rendered complex and problematic when it is taken out of the framework of identity and seen as a matter of desire or fantasy. For example, is a man who enjoys watching or reading male homosexual pornography but who only has sex with women gay, straight or bisexual? Does fantasy constitute one's sexuality or is the true sexuality about the sexed bodies with which one actually has sex? Foucault seeks a return to an understanding of sexuality that is about acts, desire and pleasures rather than sexuality as an identity. It would seem that sexuality is more fluid and less coherent than the identity categories to which we admit in conscious thought and by social recognition. The problem with identity categories is that they are containers creating the illusion of a unified, coherent self.

Conclusion

Categories, which are part of language and social ordering, divide and separate people into groups. From the time they are born, individuals are located within categories of identity – particularly sex-gender identity. The extent to which these categories constitute a sense of personal or individual *belonging* to a group identity is another question. For some people, the category to which they are assigned by birth does not correspond to the category to which they feel they belong. Transgender and transsexual identities contest the assumption of a neat fit between sexed bodies and how people think or feel about who are they are. Cultural feminists, particularly those from more philosophical and psychoanalytic areas, often prefer the term 'sexual difference' to that of the sex–gender coupling. Sexual difference is a concept that effectively undoes the awkwardness of a binary model of representation. Furthermore, writing/inscribing the terms as sex-gender rather than dichotomously as sex/gender also undermines the notion of an oppositional, either/or division between the two. The hyphen effectively inscribes the 'between-ness' of the two terms – their interrelationship. Finally, the critical or reflective position on seeking to explain the origin or cause of sexuality and gender lies not in seeking an answer but rather in questioning the desire to resolve gender and sexual difference through science or any other basis of knowledge, reasoning or research.

Review questions

5.1 Do you think that human beings are born with a pre-given sexual orientation or is sexuality more fluid than social structure, psychic life and moral orders permit us to know?

5.2 Do you think there would be greater social equality between men and men, women and women, and men and women if gender were less rigidly defined and heterosexuality de-institutionalized? Would you want to live in this kind of society? Why or why not?

5.3 Why should women give up their family name and take on their future husband's name? Would you, as a man, take on your future wife's name? Why or why not?

5.4 Do you think the symbolic order is an important feature of gender hierarchy and inequality? Discuss using particular examples.

5.5 What is necessary for an ethics of sexual difference according to Irigaray? Discuss the complex issues as they are explored in this chapter.

Notes

1 The cause of intersexuality can be chromosomal or hormonal. For example, some intersexed infants have a mosaic chromosome pattern of XY/XO while others have XY cells but cannot process testosterone. Hormonal imbalances can masculinize the genitals of XX children and an inherited condition called 5-alpha-reductase deficiency triggers an apparent female-to-male sex change at puberty. These biological-genetic factors challenge the model of two oppositional sexes, and also in turn contest a naive or overly deterministic social construction thesis.

2 Perhaps one of the major contributions of Foucault's thought within sociology is his interrogation of the politics and power of knowledge practices and discourses – the question of who or what is made the subject of research problems and investigation, and what purpose, ends or interests are served by this.

Further reading

Bleier, R. (1991) Science and gender, in *A Reader in Feminist Knowledge* (ed. S. Gunew), Routledge, London, pp. 249–56.

Gatens, M. (1991) A critique of the sex/gender distinction, in *A Reader in Feminist Knowledge* (ed. S. Gunew), Routledge, London, pp. 139–57.

Irigaray, L. (1996) *I Love to You: Sketch of a Possible Felicity in History* (trans. A. Martin), Routledge, New York.

Wearing, B. (1996) *Gender: The Pain and Pleasure of Difference*, Longman, Melbourne.

6

Racism, 'Race' and Difference

Learning objectives

- To plot the emergence of the idea of 'race'.
- To show how human beings were educated through science and philosophy to see race.
- To examine the relationship between race, chattel slavery and colonialism.
- To discuss the relationship between race, the state and modernity.
- To examine contemporary challenges for understanding racism today.

Introduction

African-American writer and activist W.E.B. Du Bois saw at the dawn of the last century racism's bloody climax, the culmination of a 200-year history in which Europeans ordered and ranked humankind through the mechanism of 'race' (see Du Bois 1989: xxvi). The idea of 'race' had been created over two centuries within science and philosophy to justify the supremacy of white Europeans. For Du Bois, the problem of the colour line not only included the experience of African-Americans who had been enslaved as chattel property and segregated by Jim Crow laws; it also included European forms of colonial domination and dispossession. Furthermore, it provided the mechanism through which to persecute Jews and gypsies – Europe's internal 'others' – and a means to justify the Third Reich's Final Solution. As George Fredrickson (2002) has pointed out, the twentieth century saw the emergence of 'overtly racist regimes' where racist ideas were codified into laws and forms of public policy in the American South, Nazi Germany and Apartheid South Africa (2002: 100). It also witnessed the fall of these regimes and a whole range of

Cultural Sociology: An Introduction, First Edition. Les Back et al. © 2012 Les Back, Andy Bennett, Laura Desfor Edles, Margaret Gibson, David Inglis, Ronald Jacobs and Ian Woodward. Published 2012 by Blackwell Publishing Ltd.

political movements that challenged racism in the law, in workplaces, on the streets, and in classrooms and universities.

With the election in 2008 of Barack Obama, American's first black president, many hoped that the problem of the colour line had at last been resolved, and that racism was in retreat. The world Du Bois knew had been transformed profoundly by the end of the twentieth century: Europe's colonies had won independence; Apartheid had ended in South Africa; and the civil rights movements in the United States had produced a situation where a black man could be president. Ideas of racial difference which developed in the eighteenth and nineteenth centuries had by now been largely discredited. However, racism has far from disappeared. In the twenty-first century, the human population is more mobile than at any other point, bringing the people of the world into more frequent and intense forms of contact. Xenophobia and anti-immigrant sentiment are on the rise in Europe, and in the European settler cultures of North America and Australia. Some 90 years after Du Bois' famous pronouncement on the colour line, the renowned writer and postcolonial critic Stuart Hall remarked – undoubtedly mindful of Du Bois – that: 'Diversity is, increasingly, the fate of the modern world . . . The capacity to live with difference is, in my view, the coming question of the twenty-first century' (Hall 1993: 361). The central argument of this chapter is that, in order to understand racism sociologically, we need to appreciate not only its history but also its ability to adapt to new circumstances.

The focus of the chapter is the emergence of ideas about racial difference and the ordering of humanity in Europe. This is not to say that racism is a uniquely European phenomenon. Racism is a form of power that reduces human beings to biological or cultural types, which in turn reduce human diversity to essential categories (black/white, Jew/Gentile), while at the same time justifying inequalities between them. Using such a definition, non-Western forms of prejudice and hatred might also apply. In particular, consider the forms of essentialist ideas about difference in Rwanda and Burundi that distinguished Tutsi herdsmen from agricultural Hutus, and that predated encounters with Europeans and German colonization (Lemarchand 1996). Equally, the relationship between racial thought in Japan and its envy of European modern nationalism and imperial power might also be characterized as racism (Arimoto 2010). However, it is argued by scholars that European forms of racism have had the greatest impact on world history (Fredrickson 2002: 11). It was in Europe that the logic of racism was fully worked out at the very same time that European nations claimed to be the bastions of civilization. Bearing this in mind, we will now turn to the emergence of racial ideas in Europe.

The idea of race, slavery and European expansion

Racial **difference** is not a product of nature but one of history. Part of the enduring power of the idea of **race** is that it seems natural and self-evident that human beings are different. Human beings have been educated to see race and organize the infinite range of human diversity into racial types. As the anti-colonial writer Franz Fanon points out, the idea of 'race' has moulded human difference through a process he called 'sociogeny' (Fanon 1986: 13). This, Paul Gilroy suggests, 'directs us to the costs, for both victim and perpetrators' of the racial straitjackets that inhibit the social and political environment 'where any common humanity is "amputated" and authentic interaction between people becomes almost impossible' (Gilroy 2010: 157). Gilroy's point is that the concepts of race and **racism** not only divide and discriminate between human beings, but also limit human potential and our capacity to relate to one another. Historians have shown that this was not always the case.

There is no equivalent to the idea of race in the ancient world. In his book *Before Color Prejudice*, Frank Snowden (1983) argues that there is no evidence of what we understand as racism among the Greeks, Romans and early Christians. It is important to suspend presumptions that race as we have come to understand it has existed throughout history. However, it would be wrong to suggest that antiquity was the equivalent of some kind of non-racist Eden. Historian George M. Fredrickson (2002) has argued that *supernaturalist racism* couched in religious terms emerged from antiquity into the medieval period. Fredrickson points to a series of key religious themes that shaped these early forms of proto-racism. The first is the idea that Jews were cursed by a collective responsibility for Christ's crucifixion. In the eyes of medieval Christians, the culpability of Jews as a group in this ultimate crime made them both 'less than human' and children of the Devil. Second, the idea of the 'curse of Ham' provided religious justification in the fourteenth and early fifteenth centuries for the association between blackness and slavery that anticipated anti-black racism, which later would be justified in scientific terms. Drawing on an ambiguous passage from the Book of Genesis, it claimed that sub-Saharan Africans were descendents of Ham and condemned to eternal bondage. Like the anti-Semitic guilt of Jews for Christ's crucifixion, Ham's descendants are doomed to servitude because he mistreated his father, Noah. Each of these forms of religious racism links a heinous crime with the origin and cause of, and justification for, a racial fate – be it enslavement or violent pogroms.

The emergence of discourses about race and the development of racist ideologies both need to be contextualized within the particular intellectual and philosophical environment of European societies during this period. Since the early Middle Ages, the practice of holding 'whites' as slaves had been in gradual decline. There were African slave merchants and rulers who were implicated in trading human beings (Thornton 1992). As European economic expansion and political domination took hold over large parts of the globe, the language of race took on another kind of meaning. The categorization of human beings into 'races' linked up to the development of new patterns of economic and social exploitation (Curtin 1964; Jordan 1968; Todorov 1984). This form of racism was an ideological response to *economic necessity*, providing a means to justify and legitimate servitude and economic exploitation. Eric Williams's (1964) book on *Capitalism and Slavery*, originally published in 1944, argues that slavery was essentially an economic phenomenon that arose because of the need to exploit labour through coercion. Similarly, Oliver Cox's (1970) classic *Caste, Class and Race*, which was originally published in 1948, locates the origins of 'race prejudice' in the period of European economic expansion at the end of the fifteenth and beginning of the sixteenth century. For Cox, 'race prejudice' justified the exploitation of the labour power: 'a social attitude propagated among the public by an exploiting class for the purpose of stigmatising some group as inferior in that the exploitation of either the group itself or its resources or both may be justified' (Cox 1970: 393). What Cox and Williams both argue is that it is a mistake to make race the key element of the explanation, because for them it conceals the underlying economic forms of exploitation at the core of the way capitalism works as an economic system.

Two fundamental criticisms of this perspective have been made: first, it has been argued that it is far too simple to see slavery as an economic phenomenon; and second, Williams and Cox have been attacked for viewing the development of racist ideologies in purely functionalist terms – that is, as serving simply as a justification for the exploitation of labour power. These criticisms have been backed up by historical research, which tends to question the usefulness of viewing either slavery or racist ideologies from a purely economic perspective. The point here is that racism takes on another kind of life beyond providing a kind of justification by the powerful for exploitation. Rather, it becomes a form of power that is not tied to either the economic base of the society or a specific historical moment, a point to which we will return later. The broader lesson in these controversies is the importance of historically contextualizing our understanding, and appreciating that racism itself is a form of power with many dimensions (economic, ideological and cultural) that changes and evolves over time.

Winthrop Jordan's (1968) classic study *White Over Black* showed that the white ideas about Africans evolved and hardened with the emergence of plantation slavery. In the sixteenth century Jordan documented that Europeans had complex and ambiguous views of Africans. These were transformed quite fundamentally by the experience of slavery in terms of economic domination and European expansion. Slavery in its various historical forms, and specifically the Atlantic slave trade, did not have a purely economic rationale; rather, it produced political structures as well as social representations of humanity that were ordered and ranked (Patterson 1982). These images did not remain fixed and unchanging across time and space, but during the seventeenth and eighteenth centuries the development of the slave trade was a defining moment in the formation of racial ideas. The legacy of this period endures today because it shaped the development of European images of Africans and other peoples.

Black slaves were treated as mere articles of commerce – as commodities – that were sub-human like animals that could be traded or disposed of with impunity. This was illustrated in 1781 by the notorious case of the slave ship *Zong*, whose captain threw 131 slaves into the sea to their deaths because the ship had run out of water. On returning to port the captain entered an insurance claim for the loss of his 'cargo'. At the trial, the issue was not about murder but whether the throwing overboard of the 131 slaves was a true act of jettison for which the insurance company would have to pay or a case of fraud. According to the Solicitor-General, John Lee, who defended the owners of the slaves, it would have been 'nothing less than madness' to have brought a murder charge since the slaves thrown overboard 'were property' (Walvin 1992: 16–21). Another example of the intertwining of the imagery of slavery and race during the late eighteenth and early nineteenth centuries can be found in the work of absentee Jamaican planter Edward Long. Long wrote his much-quoted *History of Jamaica* in 1774, and in it he defended not only the slave trade but the argument that Europeans and blacks belonged to different species. For Long, the slave trade was nothing but the 'healthy culling process' of an increasing African population. He saw the black slaves as not only lazy, but as lying, profligate, promiscuous, cowardly, savage, debased, ugly and demonstrably inferior to 'whites'. Plantation slavery in the Americas and the rest of the New World was held together and reproduced over time by vicious police laws designed to ensure the rights of those who dominated at every level of society.

It was not simply that these ideas provided a form of popular justification for enslavement or racial servitude. The late eighteenth and nineteenth centuries also witnessed the proliferation of scientific and pseudo-scientific theories of race. It is possible to date the emergence of race thinking through key figure like Swedish naturalist Carl Linnaeus, who in 1735 claimed that sub-varieties existed within humankind. Johann Friedrich Blumenbach claimed in his study *On the Natural Variety of Mankind*, published in 1776 – the year of the American Revolution – that human beings could be separated into five divisions: Caucasians, Mongolians, Ethiopians, Americans and Malays. Racial theories were to reach their high point in the nineteenth century; however, it is important to note that, in different forms, the use of scientific discourses in discussions about race continued to influence thinking about this issue well into the twentieth century and such discourses are being revived today in some areas of genetic science (Harding 1993; Reardon, Dunklee and Wentworth 2006).

By the early nineteenth century, an idea of 'race' had emerged which asserted first that physical appearance and the behaviour of individuals were expressions of a discrete biological type that was fixed in nature. These biological types could explain human patterns of culture and also conflicts between races/nations because of mutual incompatibility. These racial ideas espoused that some 'races' were inherently superior while others were inherently inferior. These arguments drew upon and developed the popular concept of the Great Chain of Being, which was to infuse the arguments of monogenists, polygenists and later social Darwinists alike (Lovejoy 1964). The concept was based on the metaphorical ladder from God to the lowest form of creation. Each 'race' represented a rung in the vertical construction, with black people somewhere near the bottom and whites somewhere near the top.

Comte Arthur de Gobineau's *Essay on the Inequality of the Human Races* was originally published in 1853. Although de Gobineau's work attracted little attention at the time, it is commonly seen as one of the classic texts of racist thought, and played a role in racial thinking well into the twentieth century. In practice, de Gobineau was essentially a synthesizer of ideas that were current in a broader social and political context (Biddiss 1970). He conceived of humanity as divided into three races – white, yellow and black – and began by stating that 'the race question dominates all other problems of history'. His analysis became famous in latter times because of both the way he saw the Aryan race as the creators of civilization and his view about the inevitability of racial degeneration through miscegenation. Such ideas were to prove an integral element of later racial thinking in a number of countries, including France and Germany. They also provided the basis of some key elements of the racial philosophy of the Nazis, though not always in ways he would have envisaged.

In the second half of the nineteenth century, the work of Charles Darwin began to play an important role in the development of thinking about race. This was evident, for example, in the popularity of social Darwinism and eugenics during this period (Mosse 1985). Arguments about 'natural selection' and the 'survival of the fittest' were simplified and adopted as part of racist thinking, and indeed they became an important theme in writings about race throughout this period (Stocking 1968; Jones 1980). Some cited Darwin's work as proof that Africans were doomed eventually to disappear in favour of the 'stronger' European 'race'. In other words, Darwin's notion of struggle for existence was reworked as a confrontation between so-called 'races' and natural selection was wedded to existing ideas about racial types. This was perhaps not surprising in the wider context of colonial expansion and imperial domination that characterized the late nineteenth and early twentieth centuries.

In summary, the emergence of race and racism in Europe was tied closely to internal differentiations that defined racial others within Europe (Jews, slaves, gypsies) and justification for external economic and political exploits and the expansion of Europe's imperial involvements. During this period, theological and scientific elements could be combined in the process of making racial categories and educating the human senses to see race and normalize white supremacy.

Imperialism, modernity and genocide

These emerging racial ideas also played a key role in justifying Europe's colonial exploits in South America, Africa and the Middle East. However, the interplay between racism, imperialism and colonialism is not straightforward. George Mosse (1985: x) argues that: 'Imperialism and racism . . . were never identical; their interrelationship was dependant upon time and place'. Images of the 'other' played a key role in the justification of colonial rule and the 'white man's burden'. Sander Gilman argues that:

> In the nineteenth century, in the age of expanding European colonies, the black became the primitive *per se*, a primitivism mirrored in the stultifying quality of his or her dominant sense, touch, as well as the absence of any aesthetic sensibility.
>
> (Gilman 1991: 20)

From this perspective, the linkage of colonized peoples with images of the 'primitive' took different forms in specific colonial situations. A case in point is the impact of the 'scramble for Africa' on images of the peoples of the 'dark continent', and the circulation of these images in metropolitan societies. However, Africa also became a place of exoticism and danger that was alluring, producing a form of Negrophilia.

In the British context, it seems clear that in the Victorian era the experience of colonialism and imperial expansion played an important role in shaping ideas about race, in relation to both Africa and India (Solomos and Back 1996). The linkages between colonialism and racism became evident throughout the late nineteenth and early twentieth centuries, in the form of the articulation between nationalism and patriotism in the construction of the definition of 'Englishness' and 'Britishness'. It would, however, be a mistake to see such racial images in isolation from the social and economic divisions and inequalities within capitalist societies. There are similarities during the nineteenth century between discourses about race and those about social class. This was evident in both Britain and the rest of the Empire. Douglas Lorimer's (1978) study of racial attitudes in Victorian society distinguishes the parallels between colour and the class prejudice of middle-class Victorians very clearly. He notes the similarities between the attitudes of those middle-class travellers whose tourism took them to India, Egypt and the East End of London, in order to view the strange, primitive and exotic creatures of the world.

However, it was in the twentieth century that racism saw its ultimate flowering into official policy, enshrined in overtly racist regimes. Racism became institutionalized, legalized and a matter of state policy. In the southern states of America between 1890 and 1950, **Jim Crow laws** enshrined the colour bar and segregation in law. The 'American dilemma', as Gunnar Myrdal (1944) calls it, was manifest in constitutional claims to freedom and equality, and at the same time the legal inequality that denied black people civil rights. From 1910, South Africa constructed a racist state in the form of the Apartheid regime that came to fruition in 1948 and systematically denied the equality of black Africans. In the midst of this emerged European fascism, the experience of the Holocaust and the genocidal policies of the Nazi state.

The term 'anti-Semitism' came into popular usage at the end of the nineteenth century, but it is widely accepted that it captures a long history of resentment and hatred of Jews. Anti-Semitism thus can be seen as referring to the conception of Jews as an alien, hostile and undesirable group, and the practices that derive from and support such a conception. As has already been suggested, the history of anti-Semitism is much more complex and of longer historical origin than the racial theories of the Nazis (Gilman and Katz 1991). In the British context, for example, there is evidence of anti-Semitism at different historical moments. But it is perhaps in the late nineteenth century that the arrival of sizeable numbers of Jewish migrants from Eastern Europe became a focus of political debate, leading to the development of a political anti-Semitism in particular localities. The political influence of anti-Semitism in France towards the end of the nineteenth century can also be seen as related to the changing political and social relations in French society at the time, which were dramatically brought to life in what came to be known as the Dreyfus affair. Captain Alfred Dreyfus, a young French artillery officer of Alsatian Jewish descent, was convicted of treason for allegedly passing French military secrets to the German Embassy in Paris. The Dreyfus affair brought French anti-Semitism out into public view, but notable intellectuals like Émile Zola and Émile Durkheim publicly opposed Dreyfus's public vilification (Wilson 1982).

The main focus of research on political anti-Semitism has been on the history of Germany. Although the history of anti-Semitism in Germany is by no means unique, it is certainly the case that in the aftermath of the Holocaust the German experience has been the focus of research and the key problem (Gilman 1991). The focus on the German experience has preoccupied scholars but it is important to stress that anti-Semitic ideas had currency throughout Europe. However, the German case shows both how a political movement made racist ideas a matter of state policy and the compatibility of racism with modernity itself.

Theodor Adorno and Max Horkheimer's (1986) *Dialectic of Enlightenment* provides a valuable early account of the role that anti-Semitism played in the politics of fascism. On the one hand, Adorno and Horkheimer sought to situate anti-Semitism in the broader context of class and political struggles in German society, and on the other to underline its specific and unique characteristics. Although they located anti-Semitism in the broader framework of capitalist society, they also highlighted the murderous consequences of the fascist construction of the Jews as a 'degenerate race': 'The fascists do not view the Jews as a minority but as an opposing race, the embodiment of the negative principle. They must be exterminated to secure the happiness of the world' (Adorno and Horkheimer 1986: 168). The use of racial theories by the Nazis thus provided not only a basis for the articulation of anti-Semitism but a means of justifying the 'final solution to the Jewish question' and the inevitable outcome of a 'race war'. Nazi theories made the maintenance of racial purity the paramount goal. Preserving the German race licensed genocide and provided the justifications for the extermination of Jews.

George Mosse's (1964) study *The Crisis of German Ideology* perhaps provides the best insight into the variety of factors that led to the emergence of anti-Semitism and racism in the period from the second half of the nineteenth century to the rise of Adolf Hitler. He also shows how latent anti-Semitism became institutionalized and accentuated through educational institutions, youth organizations and political parties. Mosse's rich account of Volkish thought during the nineteenth century provides a powerful insight into the social and political roots of German anti-Semitism. He highlights the contrast between German images of 'the uprootedness of the Jew' with those of the 'rootedness of the Volk' (Mosse 1964: 27–8). What we see here is the combination of racial mysticism with modern political techniques and bureaucracies. He also provides a detailed analysis of the linkages between the growth of anti-Semitism and the rise of national socialism as a mass political movement:

> That the Volkish ideology, wedded as it was to anti-modernity, could be absorbed by the modern mass movement techniques of National Socialism led to its final realisation. To be sure, if it had not been for very real grievances and frustrations, both on a personal level and on the national level, Germany's development in modern times might have taken a different turn. But the most important question is: Why did millions of people respond to the Volkish call?
>
> (Mosse 1964: 317)

The fact that the Nazis used racial ideas as a key plank of their platform is a vital part of the answer to Mosse's question. Race here provided a profoundly modern way to define who was a German, but also to establish those in the midst of the Volk who were not only other but also less than human.

In *Modernity and the Holocaust*, Zygmunt Bauman (1989) seeks to connect the Holocaust with some of the key aspects of modern culture and life. One of the ironies he notes is that anti-Semitism in Germany at the beginning of this century was weaker than it was in many other European countries. He points out that there were many more Jewish professionals and academics in Germany than in Britain, France and the United States. He also shows evidence that popular anti-Semitism was not very widespread in Germany, although it grew rapidly in the aftermath of World War I. Perhaps most controversially, Bauman contends that the Holocaust was not an aberration, but an integral feature of modernity:

> The Holocaust was born and executed in our modern society, at the high stage of our civilisation and at the peak of human cultural achievement, and for this reason it is a problem of that society, civilisation and culture.
>
> (Bauman 1989: 13)

From this perspective, he argues that a key feature of Nazism was its view of the need for 'social engineering' through its racial policies. Genocide for the Nazis was a means to construct the 'perfect society' (Bauman 1989: 91). In this sense, Bauman is agreeing with the arguments made by historians such as Mosse. The Nazi attempt to construct a 'racially pure' society, and to use state power to help bring this about, had a major influence on discussions about race and racism in the post-1945 period. In particular, it helped to emphasize and warn against the destructive and genocidal consequences of racist theorizing and political mobilization. By the end of the twentieth century, the terrible success of overtly racist regimes had both undermined racism's social legitimacy and cast a shadow over Europe's self-image as modern and civilized. In the form of the Nazi regime, Jim Crow racism and Apartheid's 'racial state' (Goldberg 2002), racism had reached what George Fredrickson (2002: 99) calls a 'horrendous climax'. Fredrickson comments:

> The Holocaust and decolonisation may have permanently discredited what I have called 'overtly racist regimes', but this good news should not be inflated into a belief that racism itself is dead or even dying.
>
> (Fredrickson 2002: 141)

In summary, there are a number of key issues illustrated within this literature with regard to the complexities of racism. First, the filtered perceptions produced within cultures of racism result in more than simply hatred. They can produce a complex web of exoticism, in which the 'other' can be attractive and alluring because of their difference. In this sense, through racism otherness is not merely repellent but can also be invested with a sense of desire that may be forbidden. This dimension of racist cultures can simply reproduce stereotypes; however, it can also form a basis for non-racist mobilizations and alliance to take hold – for example, the anti-colonial or anti-fascist movements. In addition, the regimes discussed in this section show how racism can take on an institutionalized form enshrined in both legislation and policy. Finally, what these regimes show is that racism is intrinsically tied to European modernity. Walter Benjamin, who was a refugee from Nazism, wrote: 'There is no document of civilization that is not at the same time a document of barbarism' (Benjamin 1999: 248).

From the colour line to the immigration line

At the start of the second decade of the twenty-first century, the human population is more mobile than it has been at any point in history. The United Nations estimates that the 'global stock' of migrants – that is, people living outside the country of their birth – is 200 million (see Vargas-Silva 2011). This is a conservative estimate, for it excludes temporary, irregular and undocumented migrants. During the colonial period, international mobility was largely channelled by colonial relationships. For example, West Indians came to Britain after World War II as citizen migrants, as subjects of British empire – although the racial discrimination they experienced denied them equal rights. The same is true of the relationship between France and Algeria, and we can see how colonial relations ordered the migration of Europeans to Australia, first through forced migration as convicts and then as white settlers and economic migrants. By the end of the twentieth century, those colonial relationships that provided the channels for international migration no longer existed. The new patterns of population mobility are more chaotic and unstable. As Jayati Ghosh (2009) points out, in the 'developed world' (excluding the former Soviet Union), the share of migrants in the total population more than doubled between 1960 and 2005.

In this context, racism has functioned as a means to create scapegoats – asylum seekers, refugees and 'illegal immigrants' – whose unwanted presence could both explain the source of social and political crisis and at the same time carry the blame for it. Here, racism provides a means to establish social solidarity through identifying enemies within and outside. The result is what Ghassan Hage (1998), in the context of Australia, calls a form of *paranoid nationalism*. In the aftermath of 9/11 and the ensuing 'war on terror', new dimensions have been added, which in Europe have led to concerns that multiculturalism has proved to be a historic mistake. The discourse of crisis is linked to what commentators on the left and right have referred to as the 'death of multiculturalism', in large part linked to the London transport system bombings of 7 July 2005.

The 'death of multiculturalism' does not relate to a situation that can be argued about or disproved empirically or factually. In the United Kingdom, Finney and Simpson (2009) lay bare the statistical myths at the base of allegations of 'sleepwalking to segregation' and 'too many migrants', and may help persuade some that social solidarity and 'diversity' are compatible. It is no longer 'tolerance' that mediates these patterns of differential inclusion; rather, it is fear and insecurity that give the racism of today its affective energy and force. As Benjamin Barber (2003: 215) comments, 'fear's empire colonises the imagination'. The insecurity that results is not only a personal state but also a battle to secure and defend society itself. The immigrant presence, acts of terrorism and the threat of multiculturalism require, so the argument goes, authoritarian monitoring and the policing of forms of diversity that are 'out of control'. Echoing Stuart Hall and colleagues' (1978) famous analysis of twentieth-century British racism, the 'crisis' is used to justify subjecting visible minorities to Draconian forms of policing and scrutiny, including the suspension of their rights through such policies as detention without trial, promoting an atmosphere of perpetual emergency and panic.

Scholars argue that in this new situation the old language of race is recoded in cultural terms. This has been referred to as the new **cultural racism** (Barker 1981; Gilroy 1987; Solomos and Back 1996), which was in fact identified by Franz Fanon in 1956 (Fanon 1980: 32). The central feature of these processes is that the qualities of social groups are fixed, made natural and confined within a pseudo-biologically defined culturalism. The 'immigrant' becomes the key figure and bearer of a cultural difference that is either incompatible or simply 'out of place'.

As has already been shown, the preoccupation with the 'immigrant' and the 'diversity' immigrants bring has distracted attention from the exclusive modes of national and European belonging that predate their arrival (Gilroy 2004). In this key sense, migrants do not produce or precipitate hatred; rather, they become the figure of its expression. Du Bois' 'colour line', mentioned at the beginning of this chapter, is no longer adequate when it comes to understanding the complexities of our current situation. It might be more accurate to say that the problem of the twenty-first century will involve the 'immigration line.' The immigration line is just as vexed politically, conceptually and practically as the line of colour or race. Indeed, it is deeply implicated in the legacy of racisms past and present, and in the foundational principles of citizenship and state-formation. The challenge relates to the way in which lines are drawn – the difference that makes a difference – and in which such lines mark the distinction between 'us and 'them'. This is not about the ethnic or cultural qualities of so-called 'immigrants'; rather, it concerns the ways in which the immigrant serves as a limiting figure in political life. The immigration line demarcates those lives that are endowed with the gift of citizenship and those that are cut short – often in transit, and with silent impunity. The life that is licensed by the work of the state is linked and implicated in the diminished lives of people caught – often fatally – at the border.

In order to meet the challenges of the present, it is necessary to include 'colour-coded' racism in a broader context of xenophobia that ranks and orders the relationship between European insiders and outsiders. Some analysts prefer the idea of 'xenoracism' or 'xenology' to address the limitations of the existing paradigms (Fekete 2009; Bhatt 2004, 2006). This shift opens attention to exclusions that operate through ideas of ethnic or cultural differences, which can be applied to the white strangers as well as the dark ones. From this point of view, it is possible to hold the plight of reviled Russians in Estonia who became 'immigrants' in 1991 after independence when the Soviet border receded in the same horizon of exclusion as the Muslim student in London who is seen as a potential terrorist and a dangerous 'enemy next door'.

In his essay 'Reflections on racism', Cornelius Castoriadis comments that hatred is best understood as having two sides. The first of these he calls the 'flipside of self-love' (Castoriadis 1992: 8). European power resulted in an inflation of self-worth and an arro-gant sense of being in the possession of superior moral values and civilization: affirming the value of white Europeans meant also affirming the non-value of non-white Euro-peans. The other side of this sense of superiority is what Castoriadis calls 'un-conscious self hatred'. The presence of the other becomes a cipher for self-doubt and ontological insecurity. Castoriadis (1992: 9) writes that 'in the deepest recesses of one's egocentric fortress a voice softly but tirelessly repeats "our walls are made of plastic, our acropolis of papier-mâché" '. The twentieth century saw not only decolonization in Latin America, Africa and the Indian sub-continent, and the collapse of the Soviet Empire, but also de-industrialization and the shift eastwards of productive power. The rise of xenophobia projects on to the body of the unwanted stranger the welter of other insecurities about the loss of power. Paul Gilroy (2004) refers to this as an inability to mourn the loss of empire that results in a kind of melancholia that is at once phobic and euphoric. The rising tide of anti-immigrant sentiment and the rise in the electoral success of the extremist in Europe today are part of this emerging situation. Increasingly elaborate forms of immigration control and border management are emerging as European governments strive to limit migration. In Australia between 2001 and 2007, the government's policy of transporting asylum seekers to detention camps on small island nations in the Pacific Ocean was referred to chillingly as the 'Pacific Solution'. The policy aimed to block migrants from reaching the Australian mainland.

For Paul Gilroy (2004: 165), 'the figure of the immigrant' provides a key political and intellectual mechanism through which our thinking is held hostage. Such categories of person become culpable in the creation of hierarchies of mobility through the im-migration structure. Colonial citizen migrants who came to Britain after World War II were transformed from 'citizens' into 'immigrants' on their arrival. From 1962, migra-tion from the Commonwealth was subject to increasing immigration control because of the assumption that 'immigrants' were very difficult to assimilate, or later 'integrate', and required limitation due to dangers of over-population and over-consumption of resources (Anthias and Yuval-Davies 1993). White migration from the old Commonwealth countries of Australia, Canada, New Zealand and South Africa was not policed, and both US and intra-European Union migration were not seen as problematic. In this sense, 'immigrants' are created through racially scripted forms of personhood that come to life at a particular conjuncture. While we argue that the 'immigrant' is imbued with racialized associations, the long history of Irish migration to Britain and the forms of racism experienced by such migrants further complicate the picture (Cohen and Bains 1988; Hickman *et al.* 2005). Some white migrants are invisible while others are marked out for distinction and differentiation. Who counts as an 'immigrant' is an effect of racism rather than the quality and history of patterns of population flows.

In summary, the nature of contemporary racism is shifting constantly. Racism no longer needs to have an ideology of race in order to continue to be socially active. To some degree, racism is able to endure in an epoch when the scientific value of 'race' as a way of describing human diversity has been discredited – that is, in post-racial times (Nayak 2006). This can work as the conception of human difference moves into the cultural terrain, and essentialist ideas about fixed cultural or religious traditions that are defined as incompatible with the 'host culture' can do the work that the idea of race once did. The shadow cast by the overtly racist regimes of the twentieth century means that racists today have to develop a greater degree of sophistication and cultural competence. The racist movements of today, from the British National Party to white supremacists in the United States, often profess that they do not hate anyone, but simply love their own people and their own identities. Even among extremist groups, there is an acknowledgement that any expression of open hatred is socially inappropriate. In everyday contexts, the predominant view of the social inappropriateness of racist talk results in unspoken forms of what Joel Kovel (1970: 31–2) calls 'aversive racism'. This takes the form of the social avoidance of difference or coded forms of racism that work through what appear to be non-racialized notions of 'immigrants', 'asylum seekers', 'welfare mums', 'gangsters', 'muggers', 'fanatics', 'terrorists', and so on. Yet while race is coded now, it is not necessarily dead as an idea. Despite the long tradition of work that has questioned the biological veracity of racial differences, genomics has made 'race . . . new again' (Reardon *et al.* 2006: 1). There is considerable scientific discussion over the appropriate use of racial terminology (Cooper, Kaufman and Ward 2003; Collins 2004), and the language of race as a way of describing human populations is reappearing at the dawn of the genome era, particularly in relation to medicine and congenital illness but also in claims that racial difference has a genetic underpinning.

Conclusion

The century that produced the first black president is different from the world that W.E.B. Du Bois knew. Racism has not disappeared; rather, it has changed, shifted and taken on new plural forms while adapting previous elements. In this sense, racism is a scavenger ideology that gains its power from its ability to pick out and utilize ideas and values from other sets of ideas and beliefs in specific sociohistorical contexts. A cultural sociology of racisms requires being attentive to the specificities of the current situation but also historical linkages through time. Race is a historically produced way of organizing our understanding of human diversity into categories that educate our senses to see race. Over time, racism has served very different purposes, but in all cases its role is to mystify and very often to justify discrimination, inequality and exploitation. In the case of slavery, racial ideas warranted the most extreme forms of human exploitation; in the imperial age, it legitimized theft, colonial rule and domination; in the era of Nazism, it justified the genocide of those defined as less than human; and in the age of migration, racism confers automatic rights and freedom to dominant white groups while denying civil and political rights to immigrant minorities.

Walter Benn Michaels (2007), reflecting on the historic election of President Barack Obama, comments that it would be correct to view his success as an indication that the United States is a less racist society than it was at the dawn of the twentieth century. However, it does not follow from this that the United States is a more equal society. Rather, American society is more unequal than it was in the days of institutionalized 'overt racism'. In 1969, the top 20 per cent of American wage-earners made 43 per cent of all the money earned in the United States while the bottom 20 per cent or quintile made just 4.1 per cent. Compared with the situation in 2007, the gap had actually widened, with the top quintile earning almost half of the total wages earned in the United States, and the bottom quintile just 3.4 per cent. Black Americans are under-represented in the top two quintiles and over-represented in the bottom two quintiles. Benn Michaels concludes:

> A society in which white people are proportionally represented in the bottom quintile (and black people proportionally represented in the top quintile) would not be more equal; it would be exactly as unequal. It would not be more just; it would be proportionally unjust.
>
> (Benn Michaels 2009: 12)

Having a black president does not change the plight of the black poor, and this brings us back to the importance linking the issue of race to the broader structure of social and economic life chances. In our time, racism is not needed to justify coercive economic relations as it did in the time of chattel slavery; nor are racist ideas about white superiority needed to justify colonial ambitions and expansion. Paul Gilroy (2000) points out that race thinking today is not only reproduced through ideas of racial inferiority or infra-humanity, but also through the image of super-human black athletes like Michael Jordan or Kobe Bryant. What links these extremes is the idea that the athletic multimillionaire superstar and the violent gangster are both a race apart.

Racism orders and ranks humankind into hierarchies, but it also limits and regulates our understanding of human culture and human difference. This is because racism reduces human diversity to essential types and uniform categories, defined in biological or cultural terms. Fundamentally, this has resulted in the infinite variety of humankind being reduced to a set of violent simplifications – blacks, whites, Orientals, Asians. A world without racism would not be one without human differences; rather, it would allow human difference to matter differently and not feature as a means to violate and regulate humanity itself. As Franz Fanon and Paul Gilroy argue, racism amputates our humanity and inhibits the realization of a truly global sense of humankind.

Review questions

6.1 In what sense is race a product of history?
6.2 Can racism be understood in economic terms?
6.3 Does having a black president in the White House mean that America is less racist?

Further reading

Anderson, E. (1990) *Streetwise. Race, Class and Change in an Urban Community*, University of Chicago Press, Chicago.
Back, L. and Solomos, J. (2009) *Theories of Race and Racism: A Reader*, Routledge, London.
Fredrickson, G.M. (2002) *Racism: A Short History*, Princeton University Press, Princeton, NJ.
Lentin, A. (2008) *Racism: A Beginner's Guide*, Oneworld, Oxford.

Acknowledgement

This chapter was developed out of a joint project between John Solomos and Les Back (Solomos and Back 1996). The authors would like to thank John Solomos for allowing us to reproduce some of his work and for his characteristic scholarly generosity.

7

Bodies and Identities

Learning objectives

- To explore sociological traditions and approaches to the body and identity.
- To understand the importance of the body in the development of individual and group identities.
- To understand how bodies materialize and signify social norms and values, as well as contest and resist prevailing norms and values.
- To learn how ideas and images shape the way we experience and understand our embodied existence.

Introduction

The body is central in the construction of individual and group identities, and in the production of social order. In the context of cultural sociology, the body is a key subject as it informs and engages with research on gender, sexuality, race and ethnicity as well as issues of subcultural styles, music, material culture and so on. The control, maintenance and appropriate presentation of the body are socially demanded and constantly achieved in everyday life through washing, grooming and dressing. Indeed, morally engaged citizenship and social inclusion are determined by how well or otherwise individuals appear to maintain or fall within the range of body size, shape/form, hygiene, grooming, clothing and dressing standards of their social world. Thus the homeless person in an urban Western middle-class environment is a particularly vulnerable figure in terms of how their body signifies disconnection and exclusion from productive labour, the money economy, non-property ownership, un-homed living, and the social and cultural

Cultural Sociology: An Introduction, First Edition. Les Back et al. © 2012 Les Back, Andy Bennett, Laura Desfor Edles, Margaret Gibson, David Inglis, Ronald Jacobs and Ian Woodward. Published 2012 by Blackwell Publishing Ltd.

settings (theatre, cinema, cafés, shopping centres) of economic citizenship. Social statuses, including categories of identity such as gender, sexuality, ethnicity, race and disability, are all lived and signified through the body. The body is both a symbolic system in the construction of social order and meaning, and an object through which the self is formed and recognized by others. This chapter will examine the position and place of the body, focusing on questions of identity, social order and human agency. Furthermore, the chapter will briefly consider the implicit and explicit ways in which sociology has rendered the body visible or invisible in social theory and analysis.

The chapter will begin with a brief discussion of the body in sociological traditions in order to distinguish between the body in sociology as an aspect of thinking and analysis, and sociology of the body – where the body becomes a subject and object of sociological knowledge. For example, in the 1980s the body emerged as a distinct subject of sociological knowledge, with Bryan Turner's *The Body and Society* (1984) and later Featherstone, Hepworth and Turner's book *The Body: Social Process and Cultural Theory* (1991), and the journal *Body and Society*. In other words, the sociology of the body emerged at this time as a distinct area of sociology orientated towards the analysis of culture. However, attention to the body in the social process had already been foregrounded quite explicitly by feminism, and by the influence of cultural historians such as Norbert Elias and Philippe Ariès (Cregan 2006), and the cultural anthropologists Marcel Mauss, Mary Douglas and Robert Hertz, to name a few. While this chapter is unable to deal specifically with each of these authors in turn, their respective work is worth some further reading, and some are taken up for discussion in the following sections, which are designed to give an overview of how the body figures, implicitly and explicitly, within various traditions or genealogies of sociology with a view to highlighting the 'cultural' elements within these traditions. The interdisciplinary nature of body research within cultural sociology is thus recognized and discussed in this chapter.

Sociology and the body

In the nineteenth- and early twentieth-century tradition of sociology, as well as in modern sociological thought (post-1950s), the body is often a symbolic or implicit presence in the formulation of social-historical analyses and critique. There are at least four traditions that can be differentiated in terms of how the body informs sociological theory and analysis, either explicitly or implicitly: the political economy of the body (Marx/Marxist tradition); the symbolic/representational body (Durkheim and cultural anthropology – Mauss, Douglas, Hertz); the bio-politics of the state and knowledge systems (Foucault/ criminology); and the self–body nexus (Freud/psychoanalysis, Mead/phenomenology, Goffman/symbolic interactionism). This schema, while open to additions or reconfigurations, allows us to explore different themes relating to the body in society, and to the nexus between bodies and identities. It is the Durkheimian tradition linked and embedded within anthropology and later symbolic interactionism that provides the main genealogical thread for grounding body research within cultural sociology. However, one can also approach other traditions within sociology – such as Marxism – in order to highlight the place of the body and its importance in the production of meaning, value and relations of power – key foci within cultural sociology.

Karl Marx's philosophical method of **historical materialism** articulates the importance of the body in the production of human existence. The labouring body – the body as both part of nature and as something that works upon and transforms nature through tools – is a central image in Marx's historical analysis of human evolution. The reproductive body is notably marginalized, positioned as ahistorical within nature. The relationship of the human to the natural world, and the mediation, control and transformation of nature through technology, are fundamental themes of modern Western thought and historical change. Both Marx and Max Weber analysed the rise of instrumental relationships, and the objectifying and calculating processes of capitalist modernity. This includes the regulation of labour and production through the growth of mechanization and the increasing surveillance and time-keeping structures of both white- and blue-collar workplaces. In the nineteenth century, the scientific management of workplaces emerged with the work of Charles Taylor. What became known as **Taylorism** is part of this history of the political economy of the body. Taylorism involved the development of time and motion studies, which closely documented the amount of time it took for workers to complete tasks in order to develop ways of increasing production and efficiency (Taylor 1911). In his 1844 manuscripts, Marx wrote about how the energies, drives and intellectual capacities of human beings are commodified and objectified as economic resources in the pursuit of profit. Indeed, both American industrialist Henry Ford's **Fordism** (assembly line production systems) and Taylorism are examples of modern objectification practices, as workers are reduced to their bodily and mental capacities. Workers become economic units with capacities and energies viewed as 'resources'.

Marx and the Marxist tradition (itself diverse) of social critique humanize the commodity – that is, goods produced for profit and exchange rather than immediate use – created through human labour. Marx wrote about the heart and soul of the worker as abstractly embodied in the commodity. Marxist thought maintains the nexus between production and consumption, and thus between differentiated economic, geographical and historical classes in what is today a global capitalist system. For example, people producing popular brand labels in factories in economically exploited developing countries invariably are producing goods for the construction and signification of identities and lifestyles that they themselves are unable to embody and live on a daily basis. In the system of global capitalism, one could speak broadly of classes and bodies of production servicing the consumption and identities of others.

Nineteenth-century sociologist Émile Durkheim (1995) uses the body to materialize and give form to his concept of society. The body is also part of his analysis of elementary aspects of religious classifications, particularly the division of and separation between the sacred and the profane. Like many writers on modernity, Durkheim explores the social complexity that comes with the increased division of labour, and the institutions and forms of government that emerged in modern life. In Durkheim's terminology, this whole social system – which he calls society – is like the human body, as it is made up of differentiated yet interconnected parts, each performing different roles or functions to support and maintain the health and welfare of the whole. Without this analogy, Durkheim's concept of society would remain abstract, disembodied and arguably unimaginable to students of sociology. Durkheim, whose work is traced through both sociology and anthropology, provides an important nodal point in the genealogy of cultural anthropology and its examination of the symbolic/representational body in the creation of social order. For example, *The Elementary Forms of the Religious Life* (Durkheim 1965) allows us to focus on the body as symbolic system in the construction of social order and classifications – for example, the distinction between sacred and profane and their separation through social rituals that include or exclude body contact.

Sociologist Norbert Elias (2000) is renowned for his study of changing attitudes and practices towards eating, sexual mores and standards of behaviour from the Middle Ages. His work represents an important genealogy of sociological thought about the body in society. Elias's work has been widely influential, particularly from the 1960s, informing the work of cultural theorists such as Pierre Bourdieu. The first volume of *The Civilizing Process* (2000) addresses such things as codes of sexual behaviour between men and women in court society, and the development of social manners in relation to eating and blowing one's nose. Elias traces the development of civil society, emanating originally from court society from the time of the Middle Ages in Europe. In Western cultures, the displacement of the hand and its mediation as a tool via the use of eating implements of knife and fork are features of the historical development of social manners that most people take for granted in their own personal histories of socialization. Most societies have body practices and rules around eating that may or may not use a hand directly in relation to contact with food. Regardless of cultural differences in relation to eating rules and practices, there is a moral, codified order of how to eat in relation to the body and the use of the hand as a tool. Along with Philippe Ariès, Elias has also been an important historian tracing the modern sequestration of death and the dead body from everyday spaces of community and ritual. Both Ariès and Elias examine the displacement of death as part of life, and the institutionalization of the dying process and dead body through the rise of medical institutions and medicalized ways of managing illness and mortality.

Robert Hertz (2007) – a student of Durkheim – is another cultural anthropologist who, like Mary Douglas, examines the importance of the body as a symbolic system in the construction of social order. It is important to note that the social order, which Durkheim and others conceptualize, is inherently a moral order. In *Purity and Danger: An Analysis of Concepts of Pollution and Taboo* (1966), Douglas examines how the body is a site of sexual and pollution taboos in relation to abject substances such as menstrual blood, urine and faeces. In *Natural Symbols* (1970), she examines how the body constitutes an entire symbolic system representing social ordering hierarchies – the head is the seat of reason, authority and sovereignty, while other parts of the body represent middle to lower social orders. Robert Hertz, in his famous essay 'The pre-eminence of the right hand: a study of religious polarity' (2007), examines the dichotomy between right and left hands in relation to the more fundamental religious division between the sacred and the profane. Hertz develops Durkheim's study of this division set out in *The Elementary Forms of the Religious Life* (1995), taking up his concept of **collective consciousness**.

Hertz argues that the dualisms found in the natural environment – between night and day, sky and earth – provide the conceptual schema for the construction of social order. Hertz discusses the cultural and historical punishment of left-handedness and the suppression of left-handed dexterity.

The right hand's moral superiority over the left is represented and embodied in language, as right means dexterity and superiority. This hierarchical division between the two hands is symbolized in modern politics – the division between the right and left. Hertz also gives examples of how the right hand as a symbol of rightness and morality is embedded in rituals – couples joined in marriage through their right hands, the right hand taking the oath in court, and the joining of two right hands in the handshake. The left hand, in contrast, symbolizes perjury, treachery and fraud. This social division and ordering form part of collective consciousness, and while individuals today may regard this ordering as arbitrary and biased, it nevertheless persists in social rituals, in the design of tools and in the architecture of everyday life.

The subject matter of modern sociology (post-1950s) has been shaped profoundly by the identity-based social movements of Western democracies. Through his examination of sexuality, madness, medicine and punishment regimes, Michel Foucault (1926–84) mapped the rise of modern epistemologies disciplining, deciphering and codifying bodies in the creation of modern forms of subjection and subjectivity, that is, types of identities and social statuses. Foucault is perhaps one of the most influential historians of ideas in sociology since the 1980s. His work crosses disciplinary divides and has been particularly influential in sociology. Some key works include *The Birth of the Clinic* (1963), *Madness and Civilisation* (1964), *The History of Sexuality* (three volumes, 1976–84) and *Discipline and Punish* (1975). In terms of the concerns of this chapter, Foucault argues that there is no pre-given subject or essential self outside or prior to discourse. The concept of the subject has two senses in his work. First, it is the idea of being subject to someone else's control, and second, it is the idea of being subjected to your own identity by moral consciousness (conscience) and self-knowledge (the ways we act upon ourselves, mediated by the prevailing ideas and values of our time and place). We are largely the product of discourses (and discursive practices) that constitute ways of being, thinking and understanding ourselves and others in the world at a given point in history. The fundamental argument for Foucault is that we are constituted by discourses. In other words, in the Foucauldian way of thinking sociologically, it is meaningless to ask a question such as 'Who am I really?' or 'What is my true self?' Such questioning will have different answers, depending on the historical period in which we live, and the culture and discourses that give rise to such questions in the first place, then provide ways of answering such questions. In Western societies where psychology has existed as a culturally pervasive knowledge system for more than a century, psychological ways of thinking are now part of common-sense interpretations of self and society (Furedi 2004). We are always framed by discourses that 'think through us', even as we try to think through them – questioning or rejecting them as we go.

The rise of the culture of experts and their positioning within state-sponsored and commercial media is the way in which modern subjectivity is both individualized and generalized. Medical, psychological and sociological discourses (rather than religious discourse) are the locus of modern morality and social control. Everyday discourses about what we should eat, how much we should exercise, how we should bring up children, the moral dangers of television, computer games and pornography, safe levels of alcohol consumption, and so on morally codify and discipline the behaviours and bodies of individuals, families and identity groups. In her Foucauldian analysis of the focus on obesity as an example of modern disciplinary culture, Markula argues that:

> in contemporary society, fitness centres can be classified as disciplinary places where, ac-
> cording to governmental campaigns for 'healthy lifestyle', an individual is to spend a set
> amount of time each week. Foucault developed the idea of power relations further through
> his concept of governmentality [which] is a complex form of power that takes the welfare of
> the 'population' . . . 'the improvement of its condition, the increase of its wealth, longevity,
> health' . . . as its purpose.
>
> (Markula 2008: 55)

The good citizen is one who appears to be actively engaged with the advice of experts and lifestyle gurus, just as the recalcitrant citizen fails to adapt to and adopt the identity and lifestyle moralities of psychology, health and medicine. However, even if we reject dominant ways of thinking, even if we reject standard, everyday psychological ways of thinking or the demands or requests of 'experts' to change how we live and our bodies via behaviours, we are still 'within' discourses of one kind or another – even if they are radical or non-mainstream, or hark back to earlier histories of thinking or forms of therapy. There are always alternatives, but these need to be seen within a historical framework in order to understand the conditions under which they are marginalized or have less cachet. For Foucault, it is always a matter of competing discourses.

Pierre Bourdieu (a student of Foucault) also introduces into sociology an embodied account of social class and status through his concept of **habitus**.[1] Accordingly, individuals embody their access to, as well as their knowledge and deployment of, cultural capital. Class is reproduced through the body and the incorporation and signification of 'tastes'. Thus how someone eats and drinks, what they eat and drink, what they read, what they value as knowledge or as worth knowing, their body size, their demeanour, how they walk, sit, speak and gesture – many of these are corporeal dispositions articulating and reiterating class position or habitus.[2] In a broader, global context, the conspicuous consumption of the body marks the availability and affordability of food to the average consumer in developed economies. Obesity and medical conditions arising from this condition are health problems and identity issues in developed economies among largely disadvantaged socio-economic groups. In other words, in developing societies socio-economic class is signified and differentiated by larger or smaller body size:weight ratios (BMI – an example of biometrics) in the context of food abundance rather than scarcity. In contrast, in developing countries where majorities are often socio-economically deprived, a larger body size:weight ratio signifies greater wealth and consumer status, while a small body size:weight ratio signifies a position and relationship to food scarcity or a lifestyle of basic needs consumption. The relationship to over-eating in a developing society is morally and discursively codified as a matter of discipline, self-care, health and welfare. This type of moral discourse is irrelevant in geographical contexts where it has no lived reality. In other words, the Foucauldian approach to questions of body and identity in relation to modern discourses emanating from science and medicine needs to be modified and contextualized for relevance in a global framework of body-identity politics.

Embodied subjectivity: becoming a social body

Human beings are first and foremost bodily beings, and the relationship between self, mind and body is never entirely unified and seamless. This section addresses the body–self nexus, and looks at the types of sociological theory and research that explore this relationship. Writers like Mead, Goffman and Garfinkel, and the traditions of symbolic interactionism and ethnomethodology, while not explicitly engaging with the body as an object of study, certainly bring the body to sociology in the micro-practices and performances that create social patterns and structures of interaction. Our bodies react – flinch, sneeze, pulsate – with or without intentionality or an act of self-will. Bodies betray or articulate states of mind, feeling, health and well-being. For example, when someone anticipates or over-thinks a potentially frightening or challenging situation, they may find themselves breaking into a sweat, or twitching or shaking uncontrollably. Indeed, the intersubjective space of social relationship is where we are acutely aware of our embodiment as formative in the social process.

The symbolic interactionist tradition of sociology explicitly brings to image the body as part of the work of thinking and doing sociology. The concept of face-to-face interaction is in itself an embodied concept. Symbolic interactionist Irving Goffman is one of the key modern sociologists to explicitly write about the body in his scenarios of various performances of self-identity within social settings of interaction. One of his most sociologically embodied accounts is his essay 'Embarrassment and social organization', which begins:

> An individual may recognise extreme embarrassment in others and even in himself by the objective signs of emotional disturbance: blushing, fumbling, stuttering, an unusually low- or high-pitched voice, quavering speech or break of the voice, sweating, blanching, blinking tremor of the hand, hesitating or vacillating movement . . .
>
> (Goffman 1972: 97)

Human beings are not born with an existing self-perceiving consciousness, but must learn through social interaction and bodily experience to form a self-concept. Imitation, will and desire are all aspects of the human psyche motivated in early childhood development through significant core relationships. Infants strive to walk, to talk, to be like and please the people around them, who in turn encourage and cajole – this is the profoundly interactive sphere of self-formation. Representations, signs and symbols are important in producing identities, and in signalling the group identity and belonging. George Herbert Mead (1932, 1934) argues that people take on the attitude of others towards themselves. As such, people look at themselves as if through the eyes of others, and this is how we adjust, conform and successfully act in the world (become social actors).

Psychoanalytic theory provides some of the most compelling social psychological analysis of the development of the ego or self as bodily. Freud argues that self-consciousness does not arrive or 'spring up' in the brain in some automatic way. The self comes into existence only via relationship to others and the physical world. Indeed, self-awareness develops both in and out of the dynamic interaction between internal stimuli and external stimuli. For example, hunger is an internal stimulus, and when a child is hungry it usually cries out in need. The caregiver – for example, the child's father – attends to the child's hunger by feeding – an external response and stimulus: the father and the food. This in turn maps back on to the child's sensory, mental and organic processes. This is a complex interplay, which lays the foundation for an emerging bodily ego or self.

The self as bodily or embodied is also formed through its relationship to the physical world, according to Freud (1986). As an infant starts to explore the world, they invariably put objects into the mouth (the oral stage). In so doing, the child learns about the world through oral processing. When the infant starts to roll around on the floor, and bumps into objects, again the child starts to feel its own bodily surface against the surface of other objects in the world. The knock, the bruise, the object or surface that refuses to budge – these all map the body, and the mental processing of these bodily experiences is articulated through the emotional and explanatory responses of others (parents, siblings), who also lay the foundations for the embodied self. All these types of sensory impressions map the body–mind nexus, creating the possibility for a sense of self to emerge as a mental concept that is fundamentally intertwined with the body. It takes time for a human infant to know and feel that they begin and end at the skin – that 'I begin here and end there', 'this is part of me and this is not' or 'I am here and this object is over there'. These mental constructs are rudimentary to the development of the self or ego. For Freud, the ego or self is essentially a bodily ego – it is not just a surface; it is *the projection of a surface*. This means that we, as human beings, have to psychically or mentally imagine the self into being as a unified form contained by the surface of the skin. We then become 'housed' or contained, so to speak, by our skin. Human beings have to feel both separate and contained to really have something akin to an ego or self. This is a very complex process where the psychical (mental) and the somatic (body) are indivisible.

Bodies and identities

Modernity is characterized by features of fragmentation, increased social complexity, abstract systems, objectification and simulation. Some of these features have been discussed in earlier sections of this chapter. Examples include the fragmentation of labour – and indeed of the body according to distinct tasks and specializations – as well as the complexity of identity as individuals become socialized and/or marked by a range of statuses and classifications, many pertaining to their embodiment. Individual lives and bodies, as well as group identities, are objectified and abstracted through bureaucratic systems of classification, documentation and record-keeping. In these systems of social organization and control, individuals are identified through social security numbers, DNA profiling and biometrics. Furthermore, we live in a technological era of virtual interactions and communications, enabling a creative reconfiguring of the relationship between bodies and identities. The face-to-face relationship of embodied interaction, while not devoid of practices of 'passing' for identities that may not correspond to past knowledge or formally recorded identities, is nevertheless a more direct relationship to the body–identity nexus. In contrast, the virtual, simulated world of online communication allows for bodies and identities to be mapped in new ways, and for individuals to explore forms of identity in virtual spaces of living and community via avatars.

Identity categories are mediated by the perception, interpretation and valuing of bodily attributes within cultural and historical contexts. In an epoch of image saturation built around advertising, consumption and entertainment industries, cultural sociology recognizes that gender, ethnicity, and so on are grafted by other systems of bodily representation and social evaluation. In other words, size, beauty and youth, in conjunction with gender, race, ethnicity and disability, combine to produce differentiated symbolic and economic capital that shapes individuals' life chances. Indeed, it is often through beauty, physical or 'sporting' talent and creative ability that an individual can gain symbolic and economic capital that might otherwise be scarce within a socially disadvantaged group identity. The individual from a disadvantaged background or social group who has 'made good' is a popular discourse, which supports the status quo of social inequality while offering the illusion that change is possible for anyone who *really* tries, regardless of background or circumstances.

Most individuals in modern consumer societies are actively engaged in taking up and working on their identities. However, there is a lot of social control and group regulation towards norms that constrain or delimit individual agency. Social identity theory focuses on the extent to which individuals identify themselves in terms of group memberships. The central thesis or proposition of this theory is that individuals define their identities along two dimensions or axes: social (defined by membership in various groups) and personal (idiosyncratic attributes that distinguish one individual from others). There is necessarily an interplay or interrelationship between the two. At the same time, the culture of individualism tends to disconnect the relationship between personal life and identity on the one hand and group histories and social statuses on the other. Indeed, individualism as a cultural force can make people blind to the fact that they constantly perform group identification and location in the minute details of interaction, conversation and embodiment. While individuals are always positioned within categories of identity that mediate the emotional, intellectual and physical experience of the social world, there is inevitably a gap between the subjective sense of self and externally constructed categories of social positions and recognition. The gap between the subjective sense of self-identity and the externally constructed constructions of one's identity is inevitable. However, the lower the status of one's identity configurations, or the more negatively valued they are, the greater discrimination and prejudice there will be, and the more difficult and painful that gap is. Those who experience racism or other forms of hatred and prejudice profoundly and painfully struggle with this divide. Those with greater identity normativity, as well as symbolic and material power, can never know at a personal and subjective level the mental and physical impact of identity-based prejudice and discrimination. There is a tension between individuals forming their own identity and groups assigning identity. Sociologists often use the word 'self' and 'identity' interchangeably. However, in some senses there is identity without a self and the two are separable. You can have a stable sense of self while having a fluid and contingent social identity. For example, individuals can look at a photograph or look in the mirror and realize that they have changed over the years. But in this action they realize that they are still 'me' – albeit an older me. Thus there is identity change through ageing, but the self ultimately coheres as a stable ground of self-recognition through time. However, psychiatric or neurological disorders open up for sociological thought the relationship between the body and the stability of the self. For example, the later stages of dementia create complex processes of forgetting and remembering of both self and others – particularly significant others, such as children, partners, and so on. While there are clearly neurological and even psychiatric causes involved in the onset of dementia, how people explain and respond to this disease is social and cultural. Neurological and other biological conditions remind us of the nexus between self and body – differences and changes in bodies inevitably impact on self-identity and the self–other relationship. The self is an embodied intersubjective formation and process, and a transformation in one person changes the intersubjective space of mutual recognition and the negotiation of identity (who I am in relation to you and vice versa).

Gender and bodies

There are cultural and historical frameworks shaping the content or meaning of identity categories (as well as the categories themselves) at a given point in time. As children grow up and become social actors, they learn to apply these identifications to themselves and others. At the same time, young adults in particular may alter or try to change how they are socially or peer identified through adopting particular clothing styles and other body practices. A key idea in social theory of the body–identity nexus is that language does not simply represent bodies, but fundamentally shapes and contours how individuals experience or do not experience their embodied selves. At the same time, how bodies are experienced may be in conflict or contradiction with the metaphors and representations that constitute the dominant cultural imagery of sex-gender, race and/or ethnic identities. Chapter 5 of this book offers an extensive discussion of the gender, sexuality and body nexus. It provides additional and supporting material on the issues addressed in this section.

There are often complex conjunctions and disjunctions between metaphors of bodies and the experience of embodiment. For example, Susan Bordo (1999) writes about the overly determined construction of the male body as hard and tough – the phallic male body that renders invisible and outside normative representation a more complex and vulnerable lived experience of male embodiment. While bodies are informed by language and representations, they do not exactly mirror or match the terms and images that define and inform how they are experienced and contoured. This gap, then, allows us to know otherwise and to subvert normative culture through representation, humour and other cultural activities.

Cultural sociologist David Morgan (1993) comments that male authority is sustained or produced either through making the body invisible or by heightening its visibility. Whether or not men's bodies are visible or invisible, and how a bodily form appears to be hidden or revealed, depends upon – among other things – context. There are many examples in which this is evident. Where physical strength and virility are essential for representing power or authority, thereby inciting responses of awe or fear, a muscled male body (or muscled female body) may be rendered highly visible to the eye. What we see and how we see bodies is constructed through representations that have pre-existing codes or cues, which direct our interpretations and responses – mostly unconsciously. Morgan suggests that the division between mental and physical labour also mediates the extent to which the body is seen and how it is seen (if it is indeed seen). For example, he writes:

> [P]ictures of stockbrokers, bishops or dons might not seem as embodied as images of sportsmen or warriors, but if we fail to see their bodies in these cases this may be because of a prior framework of understanding that links men, bodies and action.
>
> (Morgan 1993: 71)

Morgan is interested not only in the question of how men's bodies are seen, but when and why they are visible and invisible because of 'existing frameworks of understanding'.

Both men and women are also subject to divisions between mental and physical labour, and the codifications and normative expectations of dress, deportment and demeanour around such divisions. For example, women who are stockbrokers, priests, teachers or librarians may have to appear less embodied – particularly sexually embodied – than women who are television newsreaders, shop assistants or waitresses. However, as David Morgan and Elizabeth Grosz (1994) have pointed out, women tend to be constructed as more embodied than men. In occupying positions of intellectual authority, men's bodies generally are less subject to scrutiny – including self-scrutiny – than are women's bodies. Men in Western society have more easily been able to transcend, and thereby repress or hide, their embodiment as sex-gender subjects because they are associated with and stand in the place of the unmarked universal subject, while women are less able to occupy such a subject position inside and outside language, and positions of status and authority. This often means that women are subject to scrutiny about their objectivity or lack of bias when they are in positions of authority. For example, women teaching feminism and gender studies invariably are perceived and judged by their students (men and women) differently compared with men who teach in these areas. This difference in treatment by or the attitude of students is worth further exploration and discussion.

In her groundbreaking book *The Speculum of the Other Woman* (1985), Luce Irigaray closely and critically re-read Freud's essays on sexuality and femininity, taking issue with the male bodily bias and masculine perspective of Freud's theories of sexuality and gender difference. (For further discussion of Irigaray, see Chapter 5.) For many feminists, psychoanalysis (including the modern Freudian doyen Lacan) is regarded as repressing sexual difference, in particular the specificities of women's sexed bodies through the privilege accorded to the penis as the symbolic marker of the difference between the sexes. Thus having or not having a penis – a structure of presence or absence – organizes sexual difference through privileging the male sexed body. These ideas are illustrated in Table 7.1.

Table 7.1 The privilege of the penis.

Penis	*Clitoris*
+ positive sign and marker of value	– negative sign and already marked/signified through the value of the penis (male sexed body). Similarly, the vagina becomes signified through terms such as lack, hole – signs of absence rather than presence, of passivity rather than activity.

How can we reality check the truth-value of this construction in our everyday life, particularly in ways of speaking and writing? Well, when a woman is seen as aggressive and strong (that is, masculine), she might be said to 'have balls'. If she is seen as challenging male phallic authority, she is called 'a real ball breaker' (in other words, she is castrating). On the other hand, a man who is perceived as being passive and weak (that is, feminine) might be called a 'pussy'. While Irigaray (1985) critiques psychoanalysis as a discursive system that claims universality, she – along with Jacqueline Rose and others – recognizes that psychoanalysis is also identifying/representing the social reality of a male sexed symbolic order. As discussed in Chapter 5, for Irigaray two subjects irreducible to each other (having their own foundations) represent the only way to build a symbolic order based on equality and difference (non-assimilation).

These symbolic constructions are material because they inscribe bodies and demarcate sexed body parts, giving them meaning. Language is itself material – it marks, values, divides, names and orders the material world, including the flesh. Language both orders and organizes our bodies – though not completely or seamlessly. Furthermore, we can think about how little girls and boys are not taught to know or name female sexed body parts in their specificity. The word 'vagina', if it is used at all in the context of families and formal education, is usually the catch-all word that conceals recognition of the clitoris and by extension a sexed body part that is not reducible to the activity of reproduction. Again, this accords with Irigaray's (1985) important argument that what is unsaid and unnamed within dominant discourses and systems of representation perpetuates the assimilation of the feminine sexed body as symmetrical with the male sexed body and subject (assimilation into the One, unity). Sexual difference (as well as an ethics of sexual difference) is thus excluded by not recognizing the asymmetry between the two and by refusing to collapse the difference.

Conclusion

In late modernity, minds and bodies increasingly are coming under the management and control of scientific discourses and practices – that is, medicine, psychology, psychiatry and drug companies. This transformation in the ways we experience our mental, emotional and physical being has ushered in terms such as 'Prozac culture'. Sociologists have questioned the increasingly pharmacological processes through which behaviour, emotions and identities are managed, largely in the interests of the capitalist economy (sustaining a productive labour force) and to maintain the stability of institutions that support it (families and schools). We live in an age of technological responses and solutions to the human conditions of birth and death. This, in turn, has created counter-cultural movements seeking to reclaim the body from its denaturalization and alienation from culturally alternative or less mainstream forms of experience and sensation. Thus the natural birth movement, the rise of anti-anti-depressant alternatives in natural therapies and the reclaiming of death as natural to life are part of this cultural turn. The risk society[3] has created a kind of precautionary culture that circumvents possible experiences already deemed to be dangerous to mental or physical well-being. Indeed, the rise of body-modification practices and subcultures embracing and ritualizing pain is partly a reaction to the deadening of the body by flattening out of experience within a risk-averse society. The modern primitive movement embraces and ritualizes pain as legitimate for fully embodied human experience in the cultivation and transformation of identity. However, nothing in itself is either liberating or repressive, radical or conservative. A claim of non-mainstream body modifiers to be liberating repressed sexuality or primal urges is only meaningful in the context of normative body cultures and regimes of sexuality.

Bodies are the vehicles through which identities and social statuses are constructed and signified. The project of identity in late modernity is mediated by body practices such as diets, exercise and a wide range of beauty and health regimes. However, the project of identity through the body fails to recognize the limits of individual self-manipulation as genetic and biological differences, socio-economic status and lifestyle, gender, race and other realities of embodied existence delimit and organize how and under what conditions bodies are socially situated, identified and transformable. Furthermore, despite the extensive medical-technological construction of and intervention in bodies in late modernity, bodies and identities continue to age and die. The bodies of economically elite individuals and groups are able to signify via Botox injections, facelifts and other medico-technological interventions that they have agency and the economic ability to act upon the body and its biological temporality. The elite bodies of modern technological and consumer cultures are atemporal in their orientation and idealization. In other words, they are body-identities that strive to look unmarked by the effects of time and lived experience (Gibson 2006). Thus, in contemporary celebrity and media culture, post-pregnant bodies are monitored and valued according to the ability of women to return to their pre-pregnant body size and image without a trace. The body that appears to be unmarked by time is then idealized as a project, with its attendant disciplinary ethic of exercise and eating. Body-identity projects striving to look unmarked by experience and ageing are the new fantasy of consumer capitalism.

Review questions

7.1 Should sexed bodies that do not fit the classifications of either male or female be altered by medical technologies to fit into socially and medically dominant models of sexed-gender identity?

7.2 Bordo and others argue that the way we experience our bodies and understand them is powerfully shaped by the kinds of cultural metaphors (for example, hard and soft) that are available to us. What do you understand by this idea?

7.3 Do you think it is too simple to say, 'Well, if it makes people feel better about themselves what is wrong with cosmetic surgery, Botox and other interventions?'

7.4 Is it really sufficient to accept or indeed promote the value of a body-modification practice on the basis that it apparently improves individual self-esteem? In other words, how do individualistic approaches to assessing social practices elide or exclude consideration of the social and cultural impact of body modification practices and their normalization?

7.5 In what ways are identities signified and attached to bodies? Can there be identities without bodies?

Notes

1 The concept of habitus resonates with Marcel Mauss's earlier work on the analysis of bodily dispositions in the largely unconscious processes of early childhood socialization.

2 The concept of habitus can be illustrated through the example of George Bernard Shaw's play *Pygmalion*. Set in the Victorian era, the play (and later the film *My Fair Lady*) directly engages with the politics of class in British society. It is a story about acquiring cultural capital. A young cockney woman (Eliza Doolittle) is trained by a Professor of Linguistics (Henry Higgins) to *pass* as a duchess in high society. All the markers of her lower-class background are thus systematically stripped and exposed as she is retrained in dress, speech, conversation and manners towards the habits and style of a woman of upper-class descent.

3 A concept developed in the work of Anthony Giddens and Ulrich Beck.

Further reading

Balsamo, A. (1996) On the cutting edge: cosmetic surgery and new imaging technologies, in A. Balsamo, *Technologies of the Gendered Body*, Duke University Press, Durham, NC, pp. 56–79.

Bordo, S. (1993) 'Material girl': the effacements of postmodern culture, in *Unbearable Weight*, University of California Press, Berkeley, CA, pp. 245–76.

Grosz, E. (1994) *Volatile Bodies: Toward a Corporeal Feminism*, Allen & Unwin, Sydney.

Welton, D. (ed.) (1998) *Body and Flesh: A Philosophical Reader*, Blackwell, Oxford.

Part III

Fragmented Ideology

8

Politics and Culture

Learning objectives

- To understand why politicians use symbols and rhetoric instead of debating the merits of competing policy proposals.
- To realize the difference between coercion and legitimate authority, and look at how rituals and performances help to increase the legitimate authority of political leaders.
- To discover how British cultural studies focuses on politics, and examine the strengths and weaknesses of this approach.
- To find out what it means to say that the state is an analytically autonomous political bureaucracy.
- To explore how the autonomy of the state influences politics, and examine the kinds of skills and resources necessary for someone to be successful in politics.
- To understand the mediatization of public life, and look at how it has changed politics.

Introduction

Towards the end of the 2008 US presidential campaign, candidate Barack Obama was approached while campaigning by Joe Wurzelbacher, a plumber in Ohio. Wurzelbacher told Obama that he was planning to buy into his partner's plumbing business, and he was concerned about how Obama's tax plan would affect him. The two men had a short conversation about taxes and public policy, with news cameras filming the entire

Cultural Sociology: An Introduction, First Edition. Les Back et al. © 2012 Les Back, Andy Bennett, Laura Desfor Edles, Margaret Gibson, David Inglis, Ronald Jacobs and Ian Woodward. Published 2012 by Blackwell Publishing Ltd.

discussion. It was a fairly typical encounter, even if it was slightly less scripted than most campaign events.

Three days later, during the final presidential debate, Obama's opponent John McCain brought up 'Joe the Plumber' within the first five minutes of the debate, and went on to mention him on 22 separate occasions during the course of the evening. 'Joe the Plumber' became a central theme in the final push for the McCain campaign, as a **symbol** of why Obama's presidency would be bad for America. Indeed, McCain and his running mate would go on to mention 'Joe the Plumber' at virtually every campaign appearance. Wurzelbacher appeared with McCain at two campaign stops in Ohio, and McCain proclaimed to the audience at one Ohio event that 'You're all Joe the Plumber'. A series of McCain campaign commercials criticizing Obama's economic proposals continued the theme, with a variety of different 'ordinary Americans' proclaiming to the camera that 'I'm Joe the Plumber'.

But the meaning of Joe the Plumber was not controlled solely by the McCain campaign. News outlets around the country delved into the background of Wurzelbacher, reporting among other things that he owed back taxes and that he was not actually a licensed plumber. More analytical news stories pointed out that Wurzelbacher would not actually owe more taxes under Obama's plan, and in fact he would probably be eligible for a tax cut. McCain's references to 'Joe the Plumber' were lampooned on political comedy shows such as *Saturday Night Live*, *The Colbert Report* and *The Daily Show with Jon Stewart*. Wurzelbacher himself also proved to be beyond the control of the McCain campaign. Promoting his book, *Joe the Plumber: Fighting for the American Dream*, Wurzelbacher revealed that he had not wanted McCain to be the Republican Party's presidential nominee, and that he considered McCain to be 'the lesser of two evils'. Wurzelbacher continued his criticisms of McCain throughout 2009 in a series of appearances at conservative political conferences, even announcing at one point that he was quitting the Republican Party.

How are we to understand this sequence of events? Why did McCain believe that it was more effective to use Joe the Plumber as a symbol for what was wrong with Obama, rather than engaging in a rational discussion about the strengths of his own proposals and the weaknesses of his opponent's? Why was he unable to control the meaning of his own campaign rhetoric? In general, why did this campaign strategy fail?

This chapter outlines the different ways in which politics and culture are intertwined in contemporary society. We begin by introducing three basic concepts that cultural sociologists use to study politics. Political actors use symbols in order to link their arguments and policy proposals to the broad, over-arching codes and narratives that hold a society together. By doing so, they hope to infuse a particular issue with a layer of extra meaning and connotations, in a way that will resonate with specific identities of their target audience. They put these meanings into action through rituals, which charge the symbols they use with emotional energy. Finally, they try to insert themselves into these rituals and symbolic actions by attempting to produce effective cultural performances, in which they try to present themselves as authentic actors motivated by the public good. At the same time, they try to cast their adversaries as cynical, self-interested and inauthentic politicians, who are motivated only by the quest for power.

After introducing these basic concepts, we go on to identify the key differences between a cultural sociology of politics and two alternative approaches to studying political life: political sociology and cultural studies. Political sociology emphasizes the organizational capacity of the state, and the way in which non-state actors need to mobilize organizational resources in order to compete effectively for political power and influence. Cultural studies emphasizes the struggle for influence, or **hegemony**, that takes place between a society's dominant and dominated groups. Both of these approaches make important contributions to an understanding of political life, but they need additional tools in order to explain incidents like Joe the Plumber. Accordingly, we try to show how cultural sociology can provide these tools.

In the last part of the chapter, we explore why events like the Joe the Plumber incident are becoming more prevalent in political life, and why they are so difficult to control. In other words, we want to make an argument about the increasing prominence of culture as a central feature of politics. Here, there are two key changes that need to be explored. The first is the rise of media, and the fact that politics tends to occur within mediated publics and mediated forms of deliberation. This means that politics needs to be choreographed carefully for a variety of overlapping audiences that have their own standards and practices for interpretation. The second change is the rise of **cultural politics**, in which political conflict occurs over values, meanings and lifestyles, rather than public policy proposals.

Symbols, rituals and performances in political life

On 20 January 2009, Barack Obama was inaugurated into office as US president. The administration of the oath of office took less than a minute, but the inaugural ceremony took about an hour, and included prayers, processionals, a poem and music. More than a million people, stretching over 3 kilometres, crammed into the National Mall to watch the ceremony at first hand. Millions more watched on television or online at work or at home, not only in the United States but throughout the world. Of course, in addition to the actual inauguration, there were some thirteen galas and multiple VIP dinners planned by the Presidential Inauguration Committee at a total cost of well over US$30 million, involving over two million people. Some US$5 million was spent on salaries alone. Around 25,000 law enforcement officers from 58 federal, state and local law enforcement agencies provided security for the events. The obvious question is: why all the hoopla? Indeed, why an inaugural event at all? Why not proceed directly to actualizing Obama's political goals, such as revitalizing the economy or health care reform?

While at first glance elaborate inaugural events might seem like a waste of money, from a cultural sociological point of view such rituals are a vital aspect of social and political life. **Rituals** are episodes of repeated and simplified cultural communication (Alexander 2006: 29). Weddings, funerals, graduations, bar mitzvahs – and presidential inaugurations – are all liminal or transitional ritual events. They succinctly communicate a new beginning: 'out with the old [social state], in with the new'. Given their similar transitional function, it should come as no surprise that all these ritual events tend to be composed of the same basic elements – processionals, prayers, music and oaths. Each component helps affirm the new reality for all concerned. The ritual climax in both presidential inaugurations and weddings is the oath. The oath of office (or recitation of marital vows) is the pivotal sacred moment in which the celebrants commit to their new role (president or vice-president, husband or wife). In the receptions (or galas and balls) that follow, witnesses not only celebrate but demonstrate their support for the acclaimed ritual subjects as they take on their challenging new roles.

However, in addition to being an important transitional ritual event, presidential in-augurations are also a **performance** of democracy. They not only celebrate but actualize democracy – that is, the official, peaceful transfer of power. Elections in which 'the people' decide who will govern, and democratic inaugurations in which power is officially trans-ferred, are ritual moments through which rational-legal *legitimacy* is sustained (Weber 1958). Such performances help *legitimate* the new leaders and the new administration. In almost every close election, in fact, the public commentary surrounding the ritual of inauguration will emphasize how amazing it is that a non-violent transition of power is taking place. This is one of the key meanings of democracy, and a central function of the inauguration ritual itself.

In sum, while power refers to the ability to carry out one's will regardless of resistance, authoritative power is sustained through respect rather than coercion (Weber 1958). In fact, global political history is full of moments in which electoral results are *not* recognized and/or 'former' leaders refuse to leave office. In both cases, it is through violence or the threat of violence that power is then cohered. By contrast, in a democracy, leaders, former leaders and the public all come together not necessarily to celebrate the victory of the newly elected, but to unanimously affirm their authority to lead – that is, to affirm the democratic rules of the game. Inaugural rituals affirm that, no matter what our political differences might be, we are a democratic nation and, whether we voted for him or not, we accept the new leader. As one anonymous commentator stated, 'the symbolism is actually substance'.

If cultural sociology can help us to understand pre-planned public rituals such as inaugurations, how can it help to explain more contingent events such as the Joe the Plumber incident? First, it is no accident that the incident took place during a scheduled campaign appearance – in other words, during a ritual event where the attention of the media and the public was already concentrated. During this ritual, the symbolic meaning that Obama was trying to convey was that he was 'a man of the people' – that he was interested in the ideas and the concerns of everyday Americans. In order to perform such a ritual effectively, of course, Obama actually had to engage in casual, unscripted discussion with everyday Americans. But there is a risk to these kinds of media events – namely, that the meaning can be hijacked by those who have other symbolic agendas (Dayan and Katz 1992).

Wurzelbacher recognized the cultural goals of the campaign stop, and used them in order to put forth a different set of meanings that he wanted people to associate with Obama. For Wurzelbacher, the goal was to transform the meaning of the event by suggesting that Obama's proposed economic policies would hurt small business – that he did not really understand the concerns and the values of blue-collar workers in the United States. This alternative narrative had a basis in other failed performances by Obama that had taken place earlier in the campaign. For example, when Obama bowled a 37 in a campaign event earlier in the year, critics used this event as evidence that he was 'out of touch' with ordinary Americans. This alternative narrative was reinforced during a speech Obama made in San Francisco, in which he criticized the bitterness of small-town workers in states like Pennsylvania and Ohio, whom he described as 'cling[ing] to guns and religion' rather than facing their situation rationally or pragmatically. In other words, Wurzelbacher did not need to create this alternative meaning about Obama from scratch; it was already in place, as a result of the jockeying to define how the public should interpret the various associated events that formed the tableau of the larger political campaign.

If politics usually involves a struggle over meaning, however, this does not mean that culture is the only thing that matters in politics. Money, social contacts, media access and other material resources also matter. Leaders of government, corporations, elites and other dominant groups all have access to immense resources that are not available to ordinary people. Those in power use the material resources at their disposal in order to implement their decisions and to ensure the obedience of the public. There are also elements of exclusion involved in the exercise of power, as decision-making is often restricted to a small group of other powerful individuals. Closed-door strategy sessions are common, as are clubs and networks that are open only to the powerful. Once decisions have been made, they are reinforced by the presence of police, security personnel and other mechanisms put in place to force obedience if it is not readily forthcoming.

Still, while those in power have recourse to the use of coercion in order to realize their will, they prefer to exercise power through the creation of **legitimate authority**. With legitimate authority, members of society agree that the decision being made is in the public interest, or that the individuals carrying out the decision have the authority to do so, or both. Power attached to legitimate authority is much more effective and efficient than power exercised solely through coercion, because it reduces the cost of enforcement, and it produces much less resentment or resistance (both of which increase enforcement costs). And the production of legitimate authority is always a matter of culture.

How political sociology and cultural studies view politics

As we have argued above, political activities are infused with meaning. Political actors make heavy use of symbols, rituals and cultural performances as part of their quest for power. Indeed, this attention to the cultural dimensions of politics has become increasingly important in political sociology today, leading Kate Nash (2007) to speak of a 'new political sociology' that is above all concerned with culture and cultural politics.

Still, while there is clearly a new and more cultural political sociology on the rise, the dominant approaches in political sociology still focus on material resources and the organizational capacity of the state. In other words, not all political sociologists are studying cultural processes. Furthermore, the new political sociology about which Nash is speaking is not the first attempt to think about how cultural identities shape political conflicts and political processes. Scholars associated with British cultural studies, influenced by Gramsci's theories about hegemony and group conflict, were studying the struggle for influence between dominant and dominated groups as early as the 1970s. Before turning to a consideration of why culture is becoming more important than ever in political life, then, we first want to consider these two alternative approaches to studying politics. It is important to highlight the significant contributions that these perspectives have made; however, we also want to demonstrate why they are not well equipped to explain the kinds of cultural politics illustrated by incidents like Joe the Plumber.

British cultural studies: culture, hegemony and the struggle over meaning

One fruitful way to think about politics and culture has been to emphasize how different groups compete to define the social. Gramsci described this competition as a process of *hegemony*, which involves the attempt by dominant groups to make their worldview seem like 'common sense' to the rest of the population. To the extent that they can do this effectively, dominant groups have an easier time establishing public policies that reinforce their interests and privileges. For example, if business owners can get people to believe that higher taxes lead to more unemployment, then they have achieved hegemony over economic policy. If those in the automobile industry can get people to think about cars as an expression of their individual freedom and their personal identity, then they have an easier time achieving hegemony in the area of transportation policy. If people can be made to believe that a woman's place is in the home, then it is easier to create a male hegemony in the areas of work, politics and public life.

Rather than being a one-sided understanding of political influence, the concept of hegemony emphasizes group struggle. In other words, while dominant groups try to impose their own vision of the world on the rest of society, their attempts are contested by competing groups. Gramsci emphasized how every group had its own **organic intellectuals**, whose purpose was to articulate the publicly held worldview of that group, and to criticize the competing worldviews being put forth by other groups.

The battle for cultural influence takes place on an unequal playing field. The organic intellectuals who express the worldviews of the dominant groups have better credentials and more broad-based authority than the organic intellectuals of other groups. This makes it much easier for privileged groups to dominate the official debates about social issues and public policies. Furthermore, the dominant groups have better control over the means of public communication, particularly in the era of mass media. This makes it easier for dominant groups to use the media in order to create **moral panics**, scandals and other public events that tip the balance of influence more in favour of their own particular interests.

Where the study of media and politics is concerned, the battle for hegemony was explored most fully by Stuart Hall and his colleagues, who in the 1960s and 1970s developed a distinct approach to studying politics and culture that has come to be known as British cultural studies. In *Policing the Crisis* (1978), Hall and his colleagues explored the British media's growing obsession during the 1970s with the 'mugging crisis'. The term 'mugging' was not a legal concept, nor was it a descriptive term that had much of a history in England. Rather, it was a term that was imported from the United States, where it had been used by politicians and journalists to describe urban crime in a context where cities were becoming racial ghettos and where drugs were increasingly a part of the urban landscape. British journalists initially used the concept in stories about American crime waves, but they eventually began to apply the label to Britain as well, and they did so before any concrete instances of 'mugging' ever appeared in the United Kingdom (Hall *et al.* 1978: 23).

Hall and his colleagues argued that the introduction of these mugging stories served to naturalize racial fears, creating a moral panic about urban crime that had significant political consequences. In the press, the attention paid to dramatic and violent events focused on the most extreme cases of urban crime. At the same time, the news practices of privileging official voices allowed police, judges, politicians and crime experts to define what the events meant. Discussions of causes were largely avoided, as the emphasis shifted to what needed to be done to stop the crisis. The emphasis on the urban ghetto as a space of inadequate socialization encouraged moral condemnation that equated 'black' with 'insufficiently British'. This cultural achievement prevented cross-racial working-class alliances from forming around the common problem of worklessness. The resulting racialization of urban crime and poverty created a hegemonic situation, which naturalized middle-class sensibilities as the best way to deal with the economic and political challenges facing the United Kingdom at the time. In other words, the mugging crisis allowed the dominant groups in the United Kingdom to shift attention away from the failure of the British state to protect its citizens from economic crisis, and to focus instead on the moral threat posed by racial minorities in poor neighbourhoods. In the end, this process of hegemony produced a new form of conservative populism, which allowed the Thatcher government to maintain power for more than a decade.

There are two key advantages of using British cultural studies to study politics. The first is the recognition of how much cultural work is necessary in order to create legitimate authority. States and other powerful actors cannot assume that their interpretation of the situation will prevail, or that their authority to respond to a situation will be accepted unproblematically. Instead, they need to intervene actively in the collective interpretation of public events, and they need to do so in a way that will derail potentially powerful alliances from forming against them. Furthermore, cultural studies recognizes that hegemony is always temporary, and it is always under challenge by competing interpretations being made by the organic intellectuals of out-of-power groups. Hegemony always creates its own counter-hegemony, and both processes need to be a part of the research agenda of political sociology.

The second advantage that British cultural studies offers is the recognition of how much coordination between different types of groups is necessary to create the conditions for hegemony. Politicians, lawyers, experts, judges and journalists were all involved in the creation of the 'mugging crisis'. To create a hegemonic interpretation that could derail an effective political challenge, the interpretations of all these groups needed to be combined into a single narrative, with each element reinforcing rather than contradicting the others. The challenge of this kind of coordination was compounded by the fact that there was no conscious conspiracy by the powerful to dominate the powerless. Rather, the coordination of cultural strategies was shaped by the over-arching values and standard operating practices of the different professional groups involved. Showing how hegemony is a product of shared professional values rather than back-door conspiratorial dealings is a major contribution of cultural studies.

While providing a very influential analysis of the rise of conservative politics in the United Kingdom, Hall's account was not without its critics. First, Hall tended to over-emphasize the ideological consistency of dominant groups, underplaying the political and intellectual conflicts that took place among elites and their organic intellectuals (see Jessop *et al.* 1988). Hall also overstated the degree to which the state was able to control media representations. In general, Hall assumed a level of elite and state integration that failed to account for how politicians, academics and journalists compete to establish a legitimate vision of society (see Bourdieu 2005). In other words, there is much more conflict and contestation in the process of hegemony than Hall's empirical account suggests.

In order for a theory of hegemony to explain incidents like Joe the Plumber, it would need to have a more robust understanding of social conflicts, elite divisions and cultural agency. It would also need to clarify the relationship between the state and the more extended hegemonic field, in a way that recognizes that the state's interests will not always mirror the interests of the dominant class. This more nuanced understanding of state and political power can be aided immeasurably by paying attention to key contributions of political sociology, and its focus on the organizational capacities of the state.

Political sociology and the organizational capacities of the state

Most political sociology begins from the work of Max Weber, and the recognition that modern societies tend to concentrate the means of administration within the nation-state. Taking advantage of the organizational features and technical superiority of bureaucracy, modern states have increased their administrative capacity immensely. As a result, they are able to coordinate the activities of increasingly large territories, to extract resources from those territories, and to do so in a way that is more effective and efficient than had been possible before. This political coordination was backed by the possibility of force, as the state has managed to secure for itself a monopoly over the legitimate use of coercion (Weber 1958). However, in its everyday operations, the state has generally avoided the use of coercive techniques, relying instead on the technical superiority of its administrative practices, and the legitimate authority of the official rules and procedures that the bureaucratic state was carrying out (Weber 1958).

As the bureaucratic state has grown, politics has been organized into political parties in a way that places a premium on the organizational capacity that can be mobilized by a given group. Because of this, many sociologists have emphasized how the growing organizational complexity of politics and political parties has led to the inevitable development of political elites; these elites control the key bureaucracies, and they compete among each other to capture the votes of a relatively quiescent public (Mills 1956).

Yet the modern state does not simply reflect elite interests. As a bureaucratic organization that organizes interests of its own, the state forces political actors to modify their interests and their strategies whenever they enter the state arena. As Weber (1946) noted long ago, there are two basic factors that regulate this process: (i) a normative commitment to the principle of office; and (ii) an administrative commitment to the protection (and potential expansion) of jurisdictional authority. For this reason, the interests of the modern state do not simply mirror the concerns of those seeking its control (Skocpol 1979, 1985; Skocpol and Amenta 1986; Evans, Ruechemeyer and Skocpol 1985). It is a relatively easy exercise to identify examples of the state acting in ways that are contrary to the interests of economic elites (for example, anti-trust measures), interest groups (for example, campaign finance reform) and citizens (for example, raising taxes). Further, state managers have their own interests and often act on their own behalf (which may be defined at any given moment in terms of individual needs, party needs and/or needs of the state).

In order to provide an adequate account of public policy, then, it is necessary to understand the state as an analytically autonomous political bureaucracy. For Skocpol (1985), the state bureaucracy consists of a set of administrative, policing and military organizations coordinated by an executive authority. In its different bureaucratic embodiments, the state competes with other powerful groups to extract resources from society and to control these resources, as a basis for maintaining a variety of administrative and coercive organizations. To be sure, the state uses many of its resources to maintain order and to defend its position in relation to other nation-states. But the elected officials and bureaucratic managers of the state apparatus also use the resources available to them in order to guarantee their administrative autonomy, and to try to expand the scope of their jurisdictional authority. Two important ways in which state actors seek to maintain and expand their authority are (i) through increasing revenues for initiatives, programmes and institutions to which they and their constituents are tied (for example, military and social programmes – see Amenta *et al.* 2001); and (ii) through identifying new areas in need of regulation (such as health care – see Skocpol 1996).

From this understanding of the modern state, what kinds of political actions are likely to be the most effective? Political sociologists have tended to approach this question by looking for activities where individuals and groups are successful in attracting the attention of state bureaucrats and political party leaders. Lots of attention has been paid to lobbying efforts, social networks and getting media publicity. What all three of these activities have in common is that they require lots of organizational resources. Money, influential contacts, bureaucratic skills and marketing savvy are all useful resources that groups need to mobilize if they wish to be successful in politics.

However, while it is clear that groups need organizational skills and resources if they want to be successful in politics, this is not the whole story. There are lots of groups with ample skills and overflowing resources that never manage to capture the attention of state actors or of the public (Jacobs and Glass 2002). In order to be successful at attracting this kind of attention, political groups need a lot of cultural skills – or a lot of cultural luck. Cultural sociology can help us to understand both of these processes.

Cultural skills are related to a political organization's ability to convince state actors that their goals are based on an authentic commitment to the public good, rather than a cynical pursuit of their own self-interest. Representing themselves as agents of the people and as protectors of democracy, politicians and journalists are on the lookout for secret dealings and influence that 'shady' groups are having on the political process (Jacobs and Sobieraj 2007). Journalists are particularly active in this respect, withholding publicity from those groups whose members seem inauthentic, and incapable of saying anything other than the organization's official 'talking points' (Sobieraj 2011). The point is that success in politics requires the skilful and flexible use of rituals, symbols and cultural performances in order to convey an authentic commitment to the public interest.

Cultural luck is related to the chance that an organization's symbolic activities will be connected to the 'issues of the moment'. Political sociologists tend to talk about this in terms of a **frame alignment** process, in which a group will be successful if it can manage to frame its concerns in a way that connects to the public agenda and the attention space that exists at a given moment in time. The element of luck is related to the fact that political organizations do not really have control of the public attention space, but must continually respond to it.

What cultural sociology adds to an understanding of frame alignment processes is the recognition that the public agenda is itself a space that is shaped by symbols, rituals and performances. Issues do not rise and fall at random, but rather are connected to the representational activities of the two most powerful groups in the public sphere: politicians and journalists.

The case of Joe the Plumber is a perfect example of how cultural luck is connected to the over-arching symbols, performances and representations that are taking place in the political realm. Journalists and political strategists both recognized that the unscripted interaction between Obama and Wurzelbacher was more authentic and dramatic than the highly scripted moments that define most campaign activities. In other words, journalists were drawn to the image of Joe the Plumber not because of a desire to aid the cause of political hegemony, but rather because of their general suspicion that political campaign events were deeply inauthentic. Because of this, they gave a lot of attention to this encounter, attempting to define its general meaning and significance as a symbol of concerns that people had about the current state of the economy and the different proposals that the candidates had for fixing the economic crisis.

The intense media attention that journalists and political strategists gave to Joe the Plumber created new opportunities for other groups that could effectively align their own representations with the new symbolic climate. This was particularly true for groups that had an affinity with Wurzelbacher's belief system. Because Wurzelbacher was enjoying his unexpected fame, there were new opportunities for political groups to make alliances with him, allowing him to extend his fame by encouraging him to speak as their public representative. In fact, Wurzelbacher made regular appearances at conservative political rallies around the country, arguing against taxes, against labour unions and in favour of conservative 'family values'. At the same time, groups who opposed these policies were quick to mobilize anti-Wurzelbacher performances, frequently enlisting the voices of 'real plumbers' to ridicule Wurzelbacher and the groups inviting him to appear at their rallies. Plumbers had probably never been so politically relevant in American public life.

The point is that the ability for groups to attract the attention of political elites and other state actors is highly dependent on their abilities to respond quickly and skilfully to the ever-changing public attention space. The element of skill is connected to their ability to create public rituals and performances that connect to the changing symbolic environment, with its characters and its stories of the moment. There is also an element of luck involved, as they must wait until the cultural environment is right for them to go forward with their own public rituals and performances. This cultural activity occurs primarily in and through the media.

Media, politics and culture

One of the reasons why politicians are less able to control the meanings of their political symbols and their public performances is that public life – including politics – is organized in and through the media. As Thompson (2005) argues, this mediatization of public life has fundamentally reordered the way in which power operates.

Before the mediatization of politics, there was a sharp distinction between public and private, which had important consequences for the exercise of power. 'The public' was associated with politics, while 'the private' denoted everything else, including family, leisure and domestic life. Furthermore, while public life was open and available for discussion, private life was supposed to be hidden from view and closed from discussion. This set of distinctions made it much easier for those in power to control and orchestrate public events. Essentially, powerful groups could coordinate their actions in private, hidden from public view, and then emerge periodically through spectacular ritual displays of authority, in which they represented their power to the public.

With the increasing mediatization of public life, however, the distinctions that regulated public and private began to break down. Public life increasingly came to be witnessed in private, through the media. At the same time, the private lives of public figures increasingly came into public view, so that nothing was hidden from the media gaze. As the 'back stage' of political life came into public view, it became much more difficult for powerful actors to orchestrate their political performances, as their scripted actions were undone by unscripted outbursts, gaffes and scandals (Thompson 2005: 134–49).

The rise of cultural politics

This brings us directly to how and why culture is essential in politics: respect is grounded in symbols and meaning. Thus it is not only transitional ritual events such as presidential inaugurations, but politics in general, that are saturated with symbols, rituals and performance. Political life is inherently symbolic – it is mired in meaning.

This is why some social issues (such as abortion or gay marriage) carry political weight far beyond their actual policy ramifications. They are *symbolic* of a whole range of ideas. The stance a political leader takes in regards to these hot-button issues is seen as 'speaking volumes' about *them* as politicians and people. They are a 'litmus test'. Thus, for instance, a conservative politician might vote against the decriminalization of marijuana for fear of appearing 'soft on crime', even though pharmaceutically speaking the same politician considers marijuana more analogous to alcohol than heroin, and believes in 'less government' in the private lives of individuals. The *representation* of her vote is more important than the vote itself. These are prime examples of cultural politics, in which conflict occurs over values and meanings rather than actual policy.

Once we understand that *meaning* often trumps actual policy implications, we can see why *language* is so central in politics today. Getting your initiative passed or your politician elected follows the same logic as creating memorable rituals of transition (whether weddings or presidential inaugurations): the goal is succinct, effective communication. It is framing and representation that are key. Thus, for instance, advocates in such volatile contemporary debates as abortion label themselves 'pro-choice' and 'pro-life' (rather than 'pro-abortion' or 'anti-choice') respectively, for good reason. Each side names itself in accordance with how it wants the issue to be framed (around 'choice' or 'life'). Time and again, the phrasing of propositions impacts upon whether or not voters will approve them.

Yet contemporary cultural sociologists not only underscore how symbols are strategically manipulated by political actors, but also that symbols often *cannot* be completely controlled. Postmodern society is a mass-mediated society, such that images, codes and narratives often spin out of control. Symbols are nested in narratives and events that have a life of their own.

For instance, a political actor who lines him or herself up on the 'right' side of the symbolic binary of 'good' and 'evil' at one point in time might find him or herself on the wrong side later, as meaning changes. This is exactly what happened to Hillary Clinton in the 2008 US presidential campaign. She was plagued by her 'error' in voting to authorize the US-led invasion of Iraq in 2002. Of course, at the time of the vote in 2002 the minority of legislators who opposed the invasion were deemed 'anti-American' (and worse), but by 2008 the *meaning* of the vote – and the war – had changed significantly. Clinton attempted to circumvent criticism by insisting that she was misled by false intelligence on Iraq's weapons of mass destruction presented by the Bush administration, but in fact she found herself in a political and symbolic quagmire (since admitting that she was bamboozled by the Bush administration was seen as representing weak statesmanship). The point is that Clinton's image and political future were significantly affected by connotations in meaning over which she had little or no control. Similar shifts in political fortune occurred in the United Kingdom and Australia, where politicians who had supported the invasion of Iraq found themselves increasingly on the defensive once the meaning of the war changed. Such is life in the postmodern world.

This brings us to a final point about cultural politics in our mass-mediated postmodern society. Max Weber pointed out long ago how the non-rational, magical qualities of charisma can significantly undergird political authority. Weber (1958: 295) used the term charisma to refer to 'the *extraordinary* quality of a person [regardless of] whether this quality is actual, alleged or presumed'. Philip Smith (2000: 103) has since maintained that the love of the charismatic leader is actually rooted not so much in the leader's *own* sacred qualities but rather in the binary codes and salvation narratives to which the charismatic leader is attached – for instance, 'a hatred of the evil against which they fight'. Thus those who struggle for power must strive to project powerful symbolic images on the public stage.

This is precisely why, despite having little or no actual political expertise, celebrities are in such a good position to excel in the political arena today. The television era advantages celebrities because these individuals are adept at using the medium, are photogenic and are very good at attracting media coverage. In addition, of course, they have not only wealth but the ability to fund-raise due to their star power; consequently, they are able to adroitly plaster their mediated image and message far and wide. Celebrity actors, comedians and novelists made regular appearances on the campaign trail in the most recent British elections, as they have done for years in the United States. In other instances, celebrities such as Ronald Reagan and Arnold Schwarzenegger have become elected politicians themselves, blurring the boundaries between media, politics and celebrity.

In fact, as the growing mediatization of politics continues, many politicians are deciding to avoid the electoral arena altogether, choosing instead to limit their activities to the media arena. In the nineteenth century, if someone wanted to get into electoral politics, the best way to do this was to start a newspaper (Schudson 1978). Today, many media figures feel that they can achieve more political power as hosts of political television programmes, and they are completely uninterested in campaigning for political office on their own (see Jacobs and Townsley 2011). As media politics eclipses electoral politics, we can expect many more incidents like Joe the Plumber, and we can expect to see the political process become even more saturated with symbols, rituals and cultural performances.

Conclusion

As we have argued, politicians rely on symbols, rituals and rhetoric to build support for themselves and their policies. Rather than simply debating the merits of competing policies, political actors organize elaborately staged events and produce skilled performances as a way to build and enhance their legitimate authority. In this sense, politics is theatre, and it is becoming increasingly so because of the growing importance of mass media.

The cultural dimensions of politics operate alongside other kinds of resources that political actors rely upon – things such as money, social contacts, media access or access to the state bureaucracy. Those who have more access to material resources are more easily able to produce effective rituals and performances that attract public attention. But even the most privileged and powerful need to attend to the cultural dimensions of politics, and they need to do so in a way that is both compelling and responsive to the contingencies of any cultural performance. Furthermore, as we have argued, the cultural aspects of politics provide openings for those who are further away from the centre of power, provided that those individuals and groups can develop cultural skills, and use those skills when the cultural environment is right.

Today, the cultural aspects of politics are more important than ever. Developments in media have erased the distinction between public and private, turning the private lives of political actors into 'character issues' that have a large impact on their political fortunes. The same is true of cultural politics, in which a political actor's stand on such 'hot-button issues' as abortion, same-sex marriage or media violence offers a 'litmus test' for their true nature, and an essential clue about what kind of political leader they will be. All of this makes it more challenging for politicians to control their public standing, making it more likely that cultural events like Joe the Plumber will continue to have a large impact on political life.

Review questions

8.1 Why did John McCain use 'Joe the Plumber' in his campaign ads, rather than simply criticizing the policies of his political opponent? Did the 'Joe the Plumber' ads succeed or fail?

8.2 How do those in power use culture in order to reinforce their authority?

8.3 What are some similarities and differences between the ways in which politics is studied by British cultural studies and by cultural sociology?

8.4 Why is cultural politics more important today than it was in the past?

Further reading

Hall, S., Critcher, C., Jefferson, T., Clarke, J. and Roberts, B. (1978) *Policing the Crisis: Mugging, the State and Law and Order*, Palgrave Macmillan, New York.
Thompson, J. (2005) *The Media and Modernity*, Stanford University Press, Stanford, CA.
Weber, M. (1958) *The Protestant Ethic and the Spirit of Capitalism*, Scribner, New York.

9

Globalization

Learning objectives

- To comprehend various definitions of what globalization is, what it involves and its effects.
- To understand the different dimensions of globalization processes: economic, political, social and especially cultural.
- To evaluate arguments about the benefits and drawbacks of globalization processes.
- To assess the strength of arguments about cultural imperialism and global cultural homogenization.
- To consider how globalization processes may promote cultural complexity and localized forms of cultural resistance.

Introduction

Talk about **globalization** is everywhere around us today. It seems increasingly impossible to ignore world-level forces, movements and structures when thinking about contemporary social life. If you want to understand how you and other people around the planet live today, you have to understand what globalization is and what its effects on all aspects of human life may be.

Globalization is a controversial term. Different types of scholars mean rather different things by it. The simplest meaning, one that would be accepted by most people, is that globalization involves a worldwide social condition whereby what happens in any one part of the world can have huge, and generally unintended, consequences for many – or even all – other parts of the planet. Every part of the world is connected to every other part in myriad complex ways. In such a situation, every single person's life becomes bound up with everyone else's on the planet, sometimes in ways that are obvious, but often in complicated ways that remain largely hidden or difficult to see fully (Albrow 1996).

An example of more obvious and easily visible globalization is the current world financial crisis: it is not difficult to see how the economic well-being and livelihoods of people all across the world are affected, in different sorts of ways, by crises in banking, finance and industry. An example of more hidden globalization involves the food you buy and the clothes you wear. These are very much influenced by complicated globalization processes, ranging from many everyday foodstuffs you find in the supermarket being transported very large distances across the planet, to most clothes worn by people in Western countries (the developed world) being made in factories in the developing world (what used to be called the Third World) by workers who are paid next to nothing for their efforts. In all sorts of ways of which most people are not fully aware, our everyday lives are structured and made possible by planet-spanning social, political and economic processes. The shorthand way to describe the sum total of all these processes is globalization. The term 'globalization' therefore refers to the way in which the whole planet and all the people on it are connected to, and dependent upon, each other in multiple and increasingly complex ways.

What can cultural sociology say about globalization that other forms of analysis are less well placed to see? Cultural sociology is particularly able to look at the culturally highly complex nature of globalization processes and their effects on people's lives. Cultural sociology at its best insists on viewing globalization not as a simple process that has uniform effects (as cruder forms of globalization analysis do), but instead as a set of multiple, complicated and often contradictory processes leading to ever greater levels of cultural complexity across the planet. This places cultural sociology at odds with some other kinds of analysis, which regard globalization primarily as an economic and political process, with effects that are seen to be leading to a single, uniform 'global culture' that is exactly the same in every part of the world. This new global culture is said to be characterized by Western-style consumerist attitudes, reinforced by Western-produced mass media, and embodied in the consumption by tens of millions of people of the goods marketed under the great global capitalist brands available almost everywhere across the world – such as Coca-Cola, Nike and Gap.

Cultural sociology sees this vision of globalization as being far too simplistic, stressing instead the uneven and complicated nature of both globalization processes and their social and cultural consequences. Cultural sociology does not deny that there is some truth in claims as to global **cultural homogenization** – that is, the whole world becoming culturally similar in some ways. But this is only in *some* ways and is not the whole story, for forms of **cultural heterogenization** – things becoming more culturally complex – are also part of, and are produced by, globalization processes. Cultural sociology also insists that trends towards cultural homogenization (such as the spread of McDonald's and similar fast-food chains to many countries) can have unintended consequences, not the least of which is their capacity to produce various types of resistance to themselves, as will be seen below. Cultural sociology stresses that globalization often has contradictory and unpredictable social and cultural consequences. Cultural sociology thus lays a strong emphasis on the highly culturally complex nature of the world today. How cultural sociology can understand a world characterized by powerful globalization processes is the central theme of this chapter.

Understanding globalization

'Globalization' is a word that means different things to different people. Both the politically right-wing supporters of 'global capitalism' and its radical left-wing critics tend towards the view that 'globalization' is a fundamentally economic phenomenon, involving the creation of world-spanning free markets and the global reach of capitalist systems of production and consumption. Whether one believes – as do the right-wingers – that global capitalism brings with it jobs, opportunities, increasing wealth and higher standards of living across the world, or whether one thinks – as do left-wing critics – that it leaves in its wake a trail of social and environmental disaster, the shared belief among both left and right is that globalization is essentially a product and expression of a world-level capitalist economy. On this view, globalization involves:

> the inexorable integration of markets, nation-states, and technologies to a degree never witnessed before ... in a way that is enabling individuals, corporations and nation-states to reach around the world farther, faster, deeper and cheaper than ever before ... [The end result is] the spread of free-market capitalism to virtually every country in the world.
>
> (Friedman 1999: 7–8)

From this viewpoint, capitalist markets are nowadays not just *inter*national but in fact *trans*national in nature – they move across and beyond national borders without respecting the territorial power of governments.

Economically driven globalization is also widely seen to have certain political consequences. This involves a debate about the degree to which national governments remain in control of their economic and other affairs, and whether economic globalization has profoundly undermined the power of national governments. The idea of a state with unquestioned control over its own 'national' territory – a condition political scientists call 'sovereignty' – was invented only as recently as the seventeenth century. Over the last several hundred years, individual states have (at least in theory) had the power to run affairs within their own borders, without interference from other states. According to many observers, what capitalist-driven globalization does above all is to undermine the power of the state within its own territory. If **transnational corporations** (TNCs) such as Coca-Cola and Toyota can pick and choose the countries within which they situate their businesses, if capital and resources are geographically highly mobile, and if all national economies are thoroughly bound up with each other, then it would seem to be the case that the capacity of the state to control its own economic affairs is undermined – perhaps very seriously. So, while economists tend to understand globalization as the worldwide spread of capitalism, political scientists tend to define it as the undermining of each government's power to control events in its own territory. However, the actual extent to which states have lost power and authority due to globalization processes is a matter of great controversy (Held and McGrew 2000).

There are also other views of globalization beyond those we have just mentioned, which focus on the social and cultural dimensions of globalization processes. In terms of the specifically *social* dimensions of globalization, British social theorist Anthony Giddens (1990: 64) views globalization as involving 'the intensification of worldwide social relations which link distant localities in such a way that local happenings are shaped by events occurring many miles away and vice versa'. In other words, what happens in one place can have effects in a number of others that are very far away in geographical terms, and this often occurs in unexpected ways. Similarly, for the British sociologist Martin Albrow (1996: 88), globalization in part means a situation where 'global practices . . . exercise an increasing influence over people's lives', where 'global practices' could mean various things, from a big corporation closing down a factory in one country and moving it to another where costs are lower to a non-governmental organization such as Friends of the Earth campaigning in national or local media. The central point is that, under conditions of globalization, what happens *here* is influenced not just by what happens *there* but in a whole series of *theres*.

In a similar vein, the British political scientist David Held and his colleagues (1999: 16) see globalization as involving profound transformations in social relationships. These are no longer primarily tied to 'local' areas and contained within the boundaries of states. The people with whom you work and do business, the friends you have, the acquaintances you know – all of these could be in geographically distant locations. Our relationships and forms of interaction increasingly have become unconstrained by geography and are no longer necessarily 'local' or 'national' in nature. This sort of situation involves what Giddens (1990) refers to as **disembedding** processes. Individuals and their social relations with others are no longer embedded in particular spatial locales, but potentially can be expanded infinitely across the world.

Giddens (1990) also highlights the changing nature of time and space through globalization. When a jet aircraft can transport you a vast geographical distance from Australia to Europe in a fraction of the time it used to take by boat, then the connections that used to hold between time and space are shattered and new connections are put in place. This alteration in time and space can fundamentally change people's understanding of their most important social ties. If your relatives live four weeks away by boat, then they will seem very far away. But if they are only a few hours away by aircraft, they might not seem so far away at all. If they can be contacted almost immediately by telephone or via the Internet, they may seem very much present even if they live on the other side of the world. The 'stretching' and 'disembedding' of social relations greatly transforms what counts as 'here' and 'there', and alters what people perceive to be close to them or far away.

This is why Australian sociologist Malcolm Waters (1995: 3) defines globalization as a 'social process in which the constraints of geography on social and cultural arrangements recede and in which people become increasingly aware that they are receding'. This definition usefully highlights the possibility that 'globalization' is not just about the 'world becoming smaller', but that people's actions and beliefs are affected and changed precisely because *they believe* that this is indeed the case.

The understandings of globalization processes just mentioned were coined by sociologists who do not see themselves as cultural sociologists. They tend to understand globalization processes as being as much cultural in nature as they are economic, political or social. One of the pioneering cultural sociological analysts of globalization was British sociologist Roland Robertson (1992), who in fact was one of the first people to use the term 'cultural sociology' in general. He insists that globalization involves not just changes in economic, political and social circumstances, but also alterations in culture, especially in terms of how people think.

Robertson defines globalization as 'the compression of the world and the intensification of consciousness of the world as a whole' (1992: 8). Concomitant with economic, political and social aspects of globalization, there is also a key cultural development, namely the construction of **globality**. This comprises different ways of thinking, all of which regard the whole earth as 'one place' (Beck 2000). Feelings of globality are dramatized in, for example, self-consciously 'global' affairs like the Olympic Games, media events televised around the globe such as Live Aid and other charity concerts, and the appropriately named soccer *World* Cup.

On Robertson's view, such 'global' imaginings have come more and more to shape how everyone across the planet thinks, feels and responds to things. Everyone comes to see their lives as being thoroughly connected to, and dependent on, events and affairs that encompass everyone and everything on the planet. Robertson is emphatic that this does not mean that everyone comes to think in exactly the same ways. Instead, everyone on the planet thinks and feels in light of the culture of the group(s) to which they belong and with which they identify. However, all such groups are forced to frame their thinking – especially thinking about themselves and who they are – within global frames of reference. They are compelled to see themselves as just one part of a much greater global whole. That global whole is not a homogeneous mass for Robertson, but rather a very complicated mixture of differing cultural dispositions and mentalities. So today there are multiple ways of thinking and acting that exist across the planet, but they are all forced to understand themselves as part of a world where everything is connected to everything else in increasingly complicated ways. Everybody is compelled to think about themselves as inevitably a member of the 'whole world', but how precisely they think about that situation depends on their particular social circumstances.

The one thing that people who may otherwise be as different as a Taliban fighter in Afghanistan and a teenage rocker in Sydney or Chicago have in common is that they have to recognize that their individual existences and their future prospects are very much tied up with everyone else's on the planet. When such a situation is seen by a person as a positive thing, to be embraced for the opportunities it affords for understanding people from other cultures and interacting with them in positive ways, rather than be rejected as a source of fear and uncertainty, that person is engaging in **cosmopolitan** attitudes and practices. Globalization processes inevitably are ambivalent: they can either encourage a cosmopolitan and open attitude towards the wider world and all the different cultures and groups within it, or they can be involved in the creation of negative feelings towards people from other cultures, involving racist and ethnocentric attitudes. Globalization can foster situations where people either warmly embrace cultural differences or violently reject them. In many cases, sociologists have found that particular individuals and groups today exhibit a mixture of both positive and negative feelings towards those in other cultures (Skrbis and Woodward 2007). What this shows is that globalization processes are unlikely ever to have simple, uniform effects, but generally involve ambivalent, mixed and contradictory outcomes.

Globalization as cultural imperialism

In both right-wing and left-wing political discourses, globalization is seen to be primarily an economic issue, involving the global spread of the capitalist economy, especially over the last two decades since the demise of communism. For right-wingers, the global expansion of the capitalist economy has a number of beneficial effects, such as what they regard as the increasingly free flow of information across the world. They can highlight the important role played by Western media organizations in disseminating news and information across the planet. The owner of the cable and satellite news channel CNN, Ted Turner, famously declared that 'with CNN, information circulates throughout the world, and no-one wants to look like an idiot. So they make peace, because that's smart' (Mattelart 2000: 95).

His point was that CNN's potentially planet-spanning news coverage of world affairs would encourage peaceful relations between states, because the 'whole world' could see when a particular regime was acting unreasonably or dangerously. The threat of being condemned in the eyes of global public opinion would be enough to force potentially rogue states to give up their eccentric policies. On this view, the development of communication media like satellite television, digital radio and the Internet is a great boon for freedom of information and human rights, as these technologies can transcend national borders. People living within a particular state's territory can at least potentially receive information from outside the borders of that country, even if the authorities do not wish them to have access to such information. While highly repressive national states – such as the current regimes in Burma and North Korea – strongly seek to control such access, it is nowadays probably more difficult than ever before for states to control precisely what information flows into their territory. So media globalization can be seen as a good thing, because it promotes freedom and democracy across the world.

A much less positive view of media-related globalization processes is put forward by left-wing critics, who understand the globalization of culture as primarily about **cultural imperialism**. For them, Western-based mass media companies are Trojan horses of Western consumerist values, spreading ideas and encouraging ways of life that undermine local cultures, which are 'battered out of existence by the indiscriminate dumping of large quantities of slick commercial media products, mainly from the United States' (Tunstall 1977: 57). The primarily US mass media are on this view purveyors of 'cultural imperialism', which involves the imposition of the set of values of one country or region (the United States or the 'West') on to all other parts of the world.

It is alleged by left-wing critics of globalization that the TV programmes, films, music recordings, magazines and so on of Hollywood and other Western media corporations spread across the world, contaminating and then destroying local cultures as they go. An early expression of this view was offered in the 1930s by US cultural critic Clement Greenberg:

> [Western media have not] shown any regard for geographical and national-cultural boundaries. [They have] gone on a triumphal tour of the world, crowding out and defacing native cultures in one . . . country after another, so that [they are now creating] a universal culture, the first universal culture ever . . . Today the native of China, no less than the South American Indian, the Hindu, no less than the Polynesian, have come to prefer to the products of their native art, magazine covers . . . and calendar girls.
>
> (Greenberg 1986: 13–14)

The argument can be updated easily. The global exportation by Western media corporations of pop idols like Lady Gaga, of films with stars such as Jennifer Aniston, and of television programmes like *Friends* and *Lost* can be seen as thoroughly marginalizing locally produced acts and programmes in a range of different countries.

The alleged 'triumph' of US, and more generally 'Western', culture around the world today is regarded by left-wing critics as particularly involving the unavoidable global presence of certain brands and labels (Wolff 2002). Brands recognizable by people in most parts of the world today include those of American corporations such as McDonald's, Coca-Cola, Pepsi, Disney and Levi's. Some Europe- and Japan-based brands, like Benetton, Motorola and Sony, are also globally present.

The worldwide presence of these labels is certainly a key cultural feature of the early twenty-first century. As the German sociologist Ulrich Beck (2000: 42) puts it, in 'the villages of Lower Bavaria, just as in Calcutta, Singapore or the *favelas* of Rio de Janeiro, people watch *Dallas* on TV, wear blue jeans and smoke Marlboro'. Some authors view this collection of symbols, products and ideas as the constituent elements of a 'new world culture' (Cvetkovich and Kellner 1997: 7), the 'first universal culture ever' that Clement Greenberg spoke about in the 1930s.

For left-wing critics of cultural globalization, it seems that 'the world is becoming more uniform and standardized, through a technological, commercial and cultural system emanating from the West' (Nederveen Pieterse 1995: 45). The main culprit behind these processes is seen to be the United States. The perceived threat to local and national cultures is 'of an American economic and political hegemony, with its cultural consequence being a homogenized world resembling a sort of . . . [global] Disneyland' (Berger 2002: 2). As one of the leading left-wing critics of globalization, Jeremy Seabrook (2004: 4), puts it, 'globalization has declared war upon all other cultures . . . It imposes its own culture, which profoundly influences the lives of people everywhere'.

People in all parts of the world start to become ever more 'American', wearing Nike trainers and tops from Gap, eating at McDonald's and watching films like *Independence Day* and *Pearl Harbor*. In this way, national cultures are eroded, if not totally obliterated. At the same time, simplified and phoney versions of these national cultures are sold to Western consumers. Thus supposedly 'authentic' Indonesian cuisine is served up to middle-class consumers in places like Melbourne and Manchester, at the very same time as actual Indonesian culture is eroded by the invasion of Western media and consumer brands. For left-wing critics, cultural globalization can only ever lead to the destruction of local and national cultures outside the West, and packaging of fake versions of these for consumption in the West itself.

Local and global cultures

Left-wing critics' condemnations of cultural imperialism and global consumerism certainly identify some real and troubling aspects of globalization. But for the cultural sociologist, such analyses must be handled with some caution, and not accepted uncritically. This is because some of the more extreme views about cultural imperialism can be founded on serious over-simplifications of a much more complex reality. They can be based on 'superficial and anecdotal examples' rather than on serious, in-depth empirical investigations of particular places and situations (Schuerkens 2003: 214). We cannot just state baldly that globalization only ever simply involves cultural imperialism and the construction of a single, homogeneous global culture of consumerism. There are other, more complicated processes involved too, and other ways of thinking about them.

Ideas that define cultural globalization simply as cultural imperialism sometimes rely on stereotypical definitions of what constitutes both 'Western culture' and 'American culture'. It is in fact quite difficult to pin down what these actually are. For example, someone from Eastern Europe:

> looking West for cultural inspiration, comes on free market ideology versus environmentalism, freedom of speech versus 'politically correct' speech codes [and we might add, Christian fundamentalism], Hollywood machismo versus feminism, American junk food versus American health food, and so on . . . 'the West' is hardly a homogeneous cultural entity.
>
> (Berger 2002: 15)

In other words, there is no simple thing called 'the West' or 'Western values' that can then easily be exported to the rest of the world. The same applies to 'American culture': it is made up of different sorts of ideas and activities (for example, feminism and Christian fundamentalism) that are contradictory and do not fit together in one neat, coherent package that can then be shipped overseas. Here we see one of the main claims of cultural sociology – that cultural phenomena are always complex, and it is one of the jobs of the cultural sociologist to point out that complexity, challenging simplifications that do not stand up to closer scrutiny.

Another problem with cultural imperialism arguments is that they do not take into account the possibility that media images and consumer goods are received by people living in everyday socio-cultural contexts. Those contexts cannot necessarily be regarded as being wholly changed by such goods and images. Instead, these may be incorporated into the ongoing flow of everyday activities. Eric Hobsbawm phrases this point thus:

> somewhere on the road between the globally uniform coke-can and the roadside refreshment stand in Ukraine or Bangladesh, the supermarket in Athens or in Djkarta, globalization stops being uniform and adjusts to local differences, such as language, local culture or . . . local politics.
>
> (Hobsbawm 1998: 2)

So the cultural sociologist cannot ever simply assume that 'globalization' is wholly destroying 'local' cultures. This is a matter for sensitive empirical investigation, and cannot be based on strong prior assumptions.

Everyday social situations need not be understood as wholly colonized and dominated by the products of global media and consumer systems. The consumption of some 'global' product, like a Big Mac, can have different meanings for different people living in different places. In a situation where McDonald's has become a routine and ordinary feature of a person's everyday activities, eating there may not 'mean' very much at all, and certainly would not indicate that that person has somehow picked up 'American' habits, as the cultural imperialism arguments would imply (Caldwell 2004).

Many cultural sociologists would argue that we cannot assume that the content of a particular message must necessarily have a direct and unmediated effect on the receiver of that message (Morley 1992). In a much-cited study, the Israeli authors Katz and Liebes (1985) argue that the 1980s American television soap opera *Dallas* was received very differently among different social groups in Israel because the cultural values of each group strongly impinged upon individuals' responses to the show. Those people recently arrived in Israel from Russia – which was a communist state at the time – regarded the show as a criticism, rather than as a celebration, of US consumerist values. Another group, Israeli Arabs, meanwhile tended to see it as a warning against the negative effects of Western culture. Similarly, anthropologist Daniel Miller (1992) found that the reception in Trinidad of the US daytime soap opera *The Young and the Restless* involved understanding the programme through a mesh of local cultural concerns, with Trinidadians relating the programme to situations in their own day-to-day lives.

The point made by authors like Katz, Liebes and Miller is that cultural imperialism arguments assume that 'texts' (media products like TV programmes and films) shape 'contexts' (people's everyday cultural worlds). So US or Western texts are assumed to change the contexts of people in other parts of the world radically when they are exposed to those texts. However, for cultural sociologists the process actually is equally likely to work the other way around: it is not just that texts change contexts, it is also that contexts *receive and appropriate* texts. In other words, people use and interpret media products in light of their local and national cultural contexts, reinterpreting those texts through the lens of their own cultural dispositions and orientations.

So, while globalized cultural goods like US soap operas can spread to all parts of the world, these texts cannot ever fully dictate how people in particular places will respond to and engage with them. A text is always received and made use of in contexts. That means that contexts can change texts at least as much as texts can change contexts. The texts of globalized media culture may be able to change local contexts in some ways, but local cultural contexts also have the capacity to take those texts, and to receive them and interpret them in more 'local' ways. People around the world do not become 'American' or 'Western' just because they watch or read media products originating from those places. For the cultural sociologist, how people interpret and make use of global media texts is more complicated than the cultural imperialism arguments often suggest.

This leads to another cultural sociological criticism of simplistic models of cultural imperialism and global cultural homogenization. They assume that the cultural processes of globalization are wholly in tune with political and economic developments. It is presumed that *because* Western governments hold most of the political power in the world, and *because* Western economic interests are the dominant ones in the global capitalist economy, then it *must* be the case that the West is dominant in cultural terms too. But this assumes far too much, for it asserts a complete and perfect fit between economics, politics and culture. The real world is more complicated than that. Cultural globalization is of course connected to economic and political globalization processes, but it is not purely produced or controlled by them. We have to take account both of situations where Western economic and political power strongly structures cultural processes, and of situations where it does so only indirectly or marginally (Appadurai 1996).

Cultural complexity

Rather than being simply swept away by the onslaught of 'global culture', as the cultural imperialism arguments suggest, most people's cultural experience today can be seen as a complex mixture of interactions between the *more* (but never purely) 'local' and the *more* (but never totally) 'global' (Cvetkovich and Kellner 1997). Sometimes, in certain contexts and in certain ways, the 'global' may be predominant. But at other times and in other contexts, the 'local' may be the more dominant feature of people's experience. Often the interpenetration of the 'local' and the 'global' can produce new and unique cultural forms. This is the condition of **glocalization**, to use Robertson's (1992) phrase, a situation where the more local and global facets of culture are complexly intertwined and constantly mutating.

These novel cultural combinations can be described as hybrid or creole cultural forms. Processes of **hybridization** and **creolization** involve the interweaving of previously separate – or relatively separate – cultural patterns, ideas, tastes, styles and attitudes (Bhabha 1994). A situation of cultural mixing and mingling – where, for example, Western traditions are fused with Asian and African influences – can be seen as the real nature of 'global culture' today. This is a very different understanding of global culture than one emphasizing its purely Western and consumerist roots (Nederveen Pieterse 1995). A focus on 'hybrid' and 'creole' cultures allows us to look at how different cultural worlds can come together today, and then mesh, combine and mutate, producing novel forms and styles. Globalization on this view promotes cultural complexity, not global cultural similarity. As one of the main advocates of a focus on cultural hybridization, Jan Nederveen Pieterse (2001: 223), puts it, it seems that 'nowadays there's no end to the travel and spread of hybridity'.

Today's world may exhibit high levels of cultural hybridization and creolization. However, it would be misleading simply to think that in the past different ethnically or geographically based cultural traditions were wholly separate from each other, whereas now in a globalizing world they have suddenly collided. Throughout human history, different groups have encountered each other, in the process learning new ways of think-ing and doing things. Often this has been through the means of warfare, conquest and empire-building, but even violent clashes between different groups do not necessarily imply that the culture of the 'losers' gets totally wiped out by the culture of the 'winners'. Certainly this was pretty much the case in terms of the European colonization of North America in the 1800s, where native American culture was almost totally destroyed by the invaders. But even in the equally notorious case of the Spanish conquest of South America from the 1500s onwards, when the cultures of the indigenous populations were severely disrupted by the activities of the conquerors, the flame of 'local culture' was not entirely extinguished. Instead, in some cases native cultures mutated and took on new, disguised forms. Although the Spanish 'converted' the natives to Christianity, lo-cal religions survived by adapting to, and taking on the external form of, Christianity. Local religious cults of saints and saints' days, for example, were in fact survivals of pre-Spanish conquest religious beliefs, covered over with a layer of Christian iconog-raphy (de Certeau 1984). Local cultures can survive in all sorts of subterranean ways, even when they apparently have been obliterated by seemingly more powerful external cultural forces.

Beyond seeing globalization as involving complex cultural hybridization processes, another way of thinking beyond simplistic claims to encroaching global cultural homogeneity involves arguing that globalization processes in fact are productive of trends towards cultural heterogenization and the assertion and proliferation of new forms of cultural complexities. On this view, we live in a world where, rather than cultural matters becoming ever more the 'same' on a planetary scale, increasing cultural differentiation and multiplicity are the norm. It is precisely because of the fact that (relatively) different 'cultures' have become more interconnected with each other that a situation has come about where each 'culture' becomes even more 'distinctive' than before. This is because each culture is held up by its proponents as being highly distinctive. These proponents want to assert their own apparent uniqueness in a global condition they perceive to be highly homogeneous and uniform. So it is the *perception* or *imagining* of encroaching global cultural homogeneity that produces trends towards the more or less conscious and deliberate assertion of cultural difference by particular social groups.

Sociologist of religion Peter Beyer (1994: 62) argues that 'individuals seek to orient themselves in our impersonal, global society through identification with a particular group and its specific culture' in order to strengthen their feelings of security and mental well-being. Likewise, leading Spanish social theorist Manuel Castells (1997: 2) argues that as people in different parts of the world feel threatened by what they imagine to be globalization – involving, for example, the loss of economic security and a strong sense of 'who we are' – they turn towards 'expressions of collective identity that challenge globalization . . . on behalf of cultural singularity and people's control over their lives and environment'. Asserting one's local and national identity – as a New Zealander, a Catalan, a Scot, a Mexican, or whatever – involves a 'turning in the direction of traditional symbols, customs, images and behaviour', which stand as potent symbolic challenges to what is regarded as the threat of cultural homogenization promoted by globalization forces (Macleod 1991: 11).

So, paradoxically, globalization does not just unsettle local and national cultures; it can also stimulate the reassertion of these by people who feel threatened by the contemporary global cultural condition. This involves 'the search for a refuge from the unsettling confusion[s] of the larger world' by the assertion of cultural particularity, locality and uniqueness (Strassoldo 1992: 46). Consequently, globalization can 'actually encourage the proliferation of smaller competing entities, rather than wip[ing] them off the map' (Nairn 1993: 168–9). How these dynamics of local and national resistance to globalization have played out in one highly symbolically and emotionally charged cultural domain – namely the realm of food consumption – is examined in Chapter 13.

Conclusion

In this chapter, we have seen that cultural globalization can be viewed as being thoroughly Western/American and consumerist in nature, involving processes that erode local cultural particularities and specificities. On an extreme version of this view, daily life in many parts of the world is seen as being restructured along the lines of the typical US shopping mall and cinema arcade. Clearly there are elements of truth in this view. One only has to go to a multiplex cinema in practically any country to see how patterned it is on a US model: most of the films are from Hollywood, the foods offered are snacks like hot dogs, popcorn and cola which are standardized on American lines, and when you stand in the ticket queue the surroundings and general ambience are exactly like those in thousands of similar places across both North America and the wider world.

But for the cultural sociologist, it is a vast over-simplification to assert that, in all parts of the planet today, people are simply gobbling up Hollywood film and television, and existing only on a diet of Coke, burgers and fries. Cultural sociology has the power to go beyond simplistic claims about globalization from both right-wing and left-wing authors, to discern the many complexities of culture in a globalized world. Far from leading to complete cultural homogenization across the planet, cultural sociology emphasizes that globalization has multiple dimensions and cannot be reduced to economic and political factors alone; nor can these factors be seen as simply shaping cultural forms and processes in a direct and straightforward fashion. Cultural sociology highlights how the cultural dimensions of globalization are as much about complexification and heterogenization of culture as they are about global cultural sameness. Cultural sociology's focus on the meaningful and symbolic facets of human life allows it to see that meanings and symbols across the world today are marked by variety and contradiction, and not simply similarity and the power of powerful groups located in the West. Cultural sociology opens up new possibilities for understanding globalization. The main point that cultural sociology can make about globalization is that the world is unlikely ever to become dominated by a single global capitalist and consumerist monoculture. Where left-wing critics often despair about the cultural conditions of the world today, cultural sociology can bring to the discussion a hard-headed form of guarded hope and cautious optimism about the cultural consequences of globalization.

Review questions

9.1 In what ways is your life affected by globalization forces and processes?
9.2 Does globalization inevitably destroy local cultures?
9.3 In what ways might globalization make cultural life more complex?

Further reading

Beck, U. (2000) *What is Globalization?* Polity Press, Cambridge, MA.
Featherstone, M. (ed.) (1990b) *Global Culture: Nationalism, Globalization and Modernity*, Sage, London.
Howes, D. (ed.) (1996) *Cross-Cultural Consumption: Global Markets, Local Realities*, Routledge, London.

10

Culture and Religion

Learning objectives

- To learn about the classic sociological definitions of religion.
- To understand the relationship between religion and spirituality.
- To study seminal critiques of religion.
- To explore the significance of religion in the postmodern world.

Introduction

One of the most startling global developments of the late twentieth century was the rise of religious fundamentalism (Armstrong 2000: ix). For over a decade, US politics has revolved around fear that Islamic fundamentalism is spawning a new age of terrorism, and since the dawn of the twenty-first century, Islamic fundamentalism has become even more pronounced. However, it is not only Islamic fundamentalism but Christian fundamentalism and Orthodox Judaism that have been burgeoning. Biblical laws are being interpreted more stringently than ever (Armstrong 2000; Davidman 1997).

Yet in the late nineteenth century, prominent social thinkers predicted not a resurgence but a decline in religion in the United States as well as across the globe. For Max Weber (1958), the increasing rationalization of society – that is, an increasing reliance on formal, calculative methods and rules, and demands for efficiency, productivity, predictability and particularly the establishment of highly rational bureaucracies – meant that the structure of society would be sustained by bureaucratic rather than religious legitimation. Public culture would be secular rather than religious. Other social scientists expected increasing religious pluralism, as well as the expansion of science as a means for explaining

Cultural Sociology: An Introduction, First Edition. Les Back et al. © 2012 Les Back, Andy Bennett, Laura Desfor Edles, Margaret Gibson, David Inglis, Ronald Jacobs and Ian Woodward. Published 2012 by Blackwell Publishing Ltd.

the world, to result in a decline in religious affiliation. Their thinking was that exposure to both scientific explanations and attitudes towards the world, as well as exposure to people holding religious explanations of the world quite different from their own, might cause individuals to question and challenge the plausibility of one tradition. As Peter Berger (1967: 156) puts it, the fundamental problem of modern religious institutions is 'how to keep going in a milieu that no longer takes for granted their definitions of reality'.

Certainly, our world *is* becoming increasingly modernized and secularized. Today, most people look to scientists rather than the clergy to explain natural phenomena such as earthquakes, meteor showers and floods. Our religious knowledge and literacy are in sharp decline, and the number of people who consider themselves 'atheist' or 'agnostic' is increasing (Prothero 2008; Hout and Fischer 2002). In fact, for the year 2000, David B. Barrett (World Christian Encyclopedia 2001) classified 150,089,508 people (2.5 per cent of world's population) as atheists, and 768,158,954 people (12.7 per cent of the world's population) as 'nonreligious' for a total of 918,248,462 (15.2 per cent of the world's population). Of course, today it is Europe that is most well-known for being secularized. For instance, while 50 years ago Spain was an officially 'Catholic' country, today nearly a quarter of Spaniards are either atheist or agnostic (Froese 2001). Similarly, non-believers outnumber believers by two to one in Great Britain, where some 63 per cent of the population describe themselves as 'nonreligious'. Two of the most acclaimed contemporary 'new atheists' (discussed shortly) – Christopher Hitchens, author of the 2007 bestseller *God is Not Great: How Religion Poisons Everything*, and Richard Dawkins, who famously compares religion to child abuse, are British – and according to one *Guardian* poll, 82 per cent of British people contend that religion 'does more harm than good' (http://www.guardian.co.uk./uk/2006/dec/23/religion.topstories3). In fact, it is not Great Britain, but France, that is undoubtedly the most militantly secularized European nation today. Since the state officially separated itself from the Catholic Church in 1905, France has vigorously sought to keep religion out the public sphere. In the last decade, France has garnered considerable attention for defending 'the French tradition of secularism' (instigated most famously by French Enlightenment figures such as Voltaire, Diderot and Montesquieu) by banning headscarves in state schools in 2004, and outlawing full face veils in public in 2010. Even in the most 'religious' of all post-industrial nations – the United States – the number of people who profess to have 'no religion' is rising (see Figure 10.1).

Yet, interestingly, even a majority of the increasing number of Americans who classify themselves as 'non-religious' say that they *do* believe in God or a higher power, and that they *do* believe in life after death (Zuckerman 2003; Hout and Fischer 2002). Apparently, American 'religious dissenters are distancing themselves from the church and not from God' (http://www.eurekalert.org/pub_releases/2002-05/asa-sri051002.php). The sale of religious and spiritual books, media and paraphernalia is on the rise, and there is a renewed interest in both New Age and premodern spiritual symbols and practices, such as yoga, Kabbalah, paganism, crystals, angels, walking meditation and pilgrimages. For instance, while in the 1980s only a few pilgrims arrived at the Cathedral of Santiago de Compostela in Spain annually, the route now attracts millions of pilgrims from around the world.

Put in another way, since the dawn of the twenty-first century, not only religious fundamentalism but progressive and synthetic forms of religion and spirituality have been

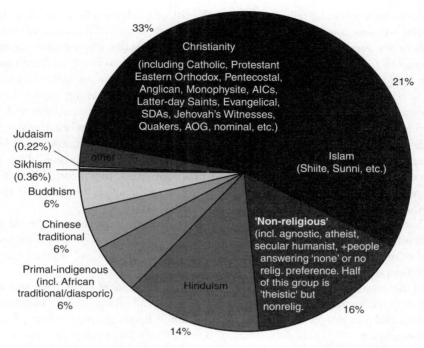

33%

Christianity

(including Catholic, Protestant
Eastern Orthodox, Pentecostal,
Anglican, Monophysite, AICs,
Latter-day Saints, Evangelical,
SDAs, Jehovah's Witnesses,
Quakers, AOG, nominal, etc.)

21%

Judaism
(0.22%)

Sikhism
(0.36%)

Buddhism
6%

Chinese
traditional
6%

Primal-indigenous
(incl. African
traditional/diasporic)
6%

other

Islam
(Shiite, Sunni, etc.)

'Non-religious'
(incl. agnostic, atheist,
secular humanist, +people
answering 'none' or no
relig. preference. Half
of this group is
'theistic' but
nonrelig.

Hinduism

16%

14%

Note: Total adds up to more than 100% due to rounding and because upper bound
estimates were used for each group.

© 2005 www.adherents.com

Figure 10.1   Religious affiliation in the world.
Source: http://www.adherents.com/Religions_By_Adherents.html (accessed 16th August
2011).

thriving. Spurred to action by the theological distortions of their conservative brothers
and sisters and the vulgar penetration of conservative economics, politics and religion,
many religious progressives have not abandoned spirituality altogether, but rather joined
forces to combat the exclusivist and violent message of religious fundamentalisms (see
www.spiritualprogressives.org). Religious progressives who 'came out of the closet' in
the aftermath of what they perceived to be the disastrous 2004 US national elections were
grandly rewarded for their efforts in 2008, when one of the most esteemed and eloquent
role models and spokespersons for progressive Christianity, Barack Obama, was elected
president of the United States.[1]

The point is that, despite modernization and secularization, and despite increasing
religious pluralism, spirituality and religion have *not* fallen by the wayside. The imperative
sociological questions concern why and how this is so. Why do millions of people across
the globe join in religious pilgrimages, buy spiritual self-help books and partake in
religious services each week? What is the appeal of religion and spirituality in the modern
and postmodern world?

Of course, one market-oriented answer to this question is that religion and spirituality
are big business. According to the so-called 'new paradigm' in the sociology of religion,
it is competition between 'religious firms' that keeps them thriving: 'In a competitive

environment, a particular religious firm will flourish only if it provides a product at least as attractive as its competitors' (Finke and Iannaccone 1993: 28). Of course, nowhere is the spirit of competition more apparent than in the United States, where multimillionaire televangelists (television preachers) use the latest technology to bombard the airwaves with their appeals. The Trinity Broadcasting Network (TBN) is not only the world's largest religious network; it is one of the world's largest broadcasting groups, whose broadcast signals are carried by 48 satellites and cover every major continent with the exception of Antarctica. In light of the power and influence of Christian media and marketing (for example, the bumper stickers, angels, plastic Jesus figures, gold-plated crosses on necklaces, Christian video games and rock music, religious publishing and even a religious theme park – the Holyland Experience), one might conclude that the reason religion remains so pervasive throughout the world is that it is not really about religion at all. It is about the selling of religion (Edles 2002).

There is no question that religion is big business. For instance, whereas in the old days route information about the pilgrimage to Santiago de Compostela was passed on by word of mouth (from pilgrim to pilgrim), today tour companies and websites provide exact itineraries, and accommodation reservations are a must.

Yet the question remains: what exactly is being marketed here? What is the appeal of religion in our increasingly modernized, industrialized and rationalized 'secular' world? Are 'spiritual pilgrimages' really about religion? Are 'religious' people just being duped? Or does religion (still) speak to essential concerns? This chapter attempts to answer these (and other) issues, paying particular attention to:

1. the social functions of religion, as first outlined by Émile Durkheim;
2. the substantive issues that all religions address, as first delineated by Max Weber;
3. provocative critiques of religion, such as those of Karl Marx and Sigmund Freud;
4. spirituality and the individual, as set forth by William James;
5. religion and social change, and the continued prevalence of religion in the postmodern world.

Religion in a post-industrial age: Émile Durkheim and functionalist approaches to religion

Sociologists have long maintained that religion fulfils important personal as well as social functions. At the level of the collective, religious rituals and beliefs help create and maintain social solidarity. As Émile Durkheim (1965: 262) famously states: 'It is by uttering the same cry, pronouncing the same word, or performing the same gesture in regard to some object that they become and feel themselves to be in unison'. At the level of the individual, religion often provides emotional sustenance. Especially (but not only) in times of crisis, people find tremendous comfort in religion.

In his now-classic book, *The Sacred Canopy*, Peter Berger (1967) maintains that the single most fundamental function of religion is to provide symbolic and moral order. Human beings are 'congenitally' compelled to impose a meaningful order (or *nomos*) upon reality – in other words, the human craving for meaning is as powerful as instinct. Social solidarity and emotional sustenance can be accrued only because of the existence of a meaningful symbolic order or pattern. According to Berger (1967: 3–5), this is the primary distinction between non-human animals and human animals: the former are endowed biologically with highly developed ordering mechanisms (instincts), but the latter are 'unfinished' at birth. Lacking the 'highly specialized and firmly directed drives' of non-human animals, human beings must create their own world. As Berger states:

> Man invents a language and then finds that both his speaking and his thinking are dominated by its grammar. Man produces values and discovers that he feels guilt when he contravenes them. Man concocts institutions, which come to confront him as powerfully controlling and even menacing constellations of the external world.
>
> (Berger 1967: 9)

Berger (1967: 27–8) goes on to insist that religion occupies a distinctive place in this enterprise of 'world-building'. Religion is the 'infusion of reality with his [man's] own meanings . . . religion is the audacious attempt to conceive of the entire universe as being humanly significant'. As Berger maintains:

> Every *nomos* is an area of meaning carved out of a vast mass of meaninglessness, a small clearing of lucidity in a formless, dark, always ominous jungle . . . every *nomos* is an edifice erected in the face of the potent and alien forces of chaos. This chaos must be kept at bay at all cost . . . [for instance] Death presents society with a formidable problem not only because of its obvious threat to the continuity of human relationships, but because it threatens the basic assumptions of order on which society rests.
>
> (Berger 1967: 22–8)

The point is that the human need for emotional sustenance, social solidarity and meaning has not fallen by the wayside – but may well be increasing (rather than decreasing) in this post-industrial age. Divorce and remarriage, the geographical dispersion of families in search of employment and sustenance, war, poverty, drug and alcohol addictions, domestic and global violence – to name a few rampant postmodern social conditions – mean that finding and maintaining emotional, psychological and communal sustenance and stability may be even more difficult than in 'premodern' days. Regardless of the monumental changes in our global world, our basic psychological and communal needs are no different from those of our premodern forebears.

From this perspective, religious fundamentalism is not an archaic throwback to an earlier era, but part and parcel of modern and postmodern society. The relationship between modernity and fundamentalism is symbiotic, not paradoxical. Moreover, 'there have always been people, in every age and in each tradition, who have fought the modernity of their day' (Armstrong 2000: xi). Wherever they are found, religious fundamentalisms are rooted in a sense of moral decadence. Fundamentalists see the world dualistically and perceive themselves to be in a clash of good against evil (Patterson 2004).

In addition, it is not only frustration and angst about liberalizing trends in society as a whole, but within their own faith, that helps explain why religious fundamentalisms are continual and thriving. Whether European counter-reformers in the sixteenth century, American Christian fundamentalists in the 1920s or Islamic fundamentalists in the Middle East in the 1980s, in all the major religions throughout history, fundamentalists have been propelled into action by what they perceive as intolerable internal as well as external change. The plea 'back to the well-springs!' is one and the same for them all (Armstrong 2000: 5). Thus, for instance, today protracted battles over gender and sexual orientation are dividing churches and temples right and left (pun intended). In 2008, conservative Anglicans and Episcopalians split off from the world-wide Anglican Communion and formed a new body, called the Fellowship of Confessing Anglicans, in direct response to the appointment of Gene Robinson, an openly gay man, as bishop. Similarly, 'irreconcilable differences concerning the roles and rights of men and women in the synagogue' led to a split in one Jewish temple studied by sociologist Phil Zuckerman (2003: 88). Paralleling the conservative Episcopalians who could not tolerate a gay man as bishop, those in the more Orthodox group left the synagogue because they could not stomach the inclusion of women in every aspect of the syna-gogue rituals. Both conservative groups found refuge in traditional patriarchal religion. Both progressive camps found strength in a revitalized, 'living' religion (rather than archaic forms).

In summary, from a functionalist point of view religion is 'alive and well' today because as individuals and social groups attempt to navigate modern and postmodern realities, religion is more fundamental than ever. Not only does it provide beliefs and practices at the level of the individual and membership in specific social groups, it provides a meaningful order (or *nomos*) that shields human beings against terror.

In addition, of course, both religious identity and experience are firmly rooted not only in tradition but in habit. Most Christians are raised in Christian households, and the same holds true for Muslims, Hindus, Buddhists and Jews – as well as non-believers. To be sure, some children raised as Christians do grow up and become Buddhists (and vice versa). However, sociology is about 'life chances' or odds, and researchers consistently find that most of us stay in the religion in which we are brought up. For instance, more than 90 per cent of people born Jewish stay Jewish, and more than 90 per cent born Protestant stay Protestant (Greeley 1991, cited in Zuckerman 2003: 45). Moreover, even when individuals do convert, they are most likely to do so in order to align themselves with the religion of significant others, most commonly their spouse (Stark and Finke 2000).

Religion and the post-industrial world: Durkheimian vs Weberian approaches to religion

This functionalist emphasis on order and meaning brings us back to basic definitional issues. Sociology was born in the context of, and in order to explain, profound processes of social order and change – and from the start religion was perceived as a fundamental piece of this equation. Founding figures such as Durkheim considered religion an 'elementary form' or building block in *all* societies, and both Durkheim and Weber maintained that in order to understand any particular society, we must understand the religion therein. Meanwhile, such analysts as Karl Marx, who preceded the discipline of sociology historically but contributed significantly to it, and psychologists such as William James and Sigmund Freud, provided entirely distinct conceptualizations of what religion is and how religion works.

Though Durkheim and Weber both considered religion pivotal to comprehending human societies, they defined and conceptualized religion in quite different ways. These two distinct definitions of religion, which sociologists often label 'functionalist' and 'substantive', continue to be the theoretical scaffolding for the sociological study of religion today.

Thus far we have examined the 'functionalist' view of religion as a basic requisite to social life. Durkheim defined religion in a very broad way, and maintained that wherever there is human society there is religion. Specifically, Durkheim defined religion as a system of symbols and rituals about the sacred, involving a community of believers. Thus, rather than focusing on the substantive content of religion (such as whether or not there was a belief in 'God' or gods – as did Weber – to be discussed below), Durkheim underscored how collective sentiments held a group together. Specifically, for Durkheim, a symbol is something that stands for something else. A **sacred** symbol (such as the Christian cross, or the wine/wafer in the Christian communion rite) is one that is 'above and beyond the everyday world'; the symbolic opposite of the sacred is the **profane**, or everyday, mundane world. In Durkheim's terminology, sacred ritual acts (highly routinized acts such as lighting a candle as part of a religious ceremony, or taking communion) are quite unlike profane acts (such as lighting a candle because the electricity is turned off, or drinking a soda to quench thirst) because only the former are 'set apart' and revered. It is both the relative immutability of sacred symbols and ritual acts, as well as the fact that they are shared, that is key.

By contrast, though he never set out a single, explicit definition of religion, in practice Weber conceived of religion as dealing with three substantive issues: (i) **soteriology** – a 'right' relationship with a higher power; (ii) **theology** – an explanation for evil; and (iii) **ethics** – notions of right and wrong. He set out to sort out the 'practical impulses for action which are found in the psychological and pragmatic contexts of religion' (Weber 1946: 267), or religious 'worldviews' – that is, how a specific religious *perspective* (or worldview) shapes specific human actions.

Weber was most intrigued by the process of the **rationalization of society** – that is, the increasing reliance on methodical procedures and calculable rules rather than tradition and emotion not only in attitudes, but also in interactions and institutions in human society. Weber (1958: 130) maintained that while the rationalization of society would result in greater efficiency in obtaining designated ends, it would also lead to the 'disenchantment of the world' where 'there are no mysterious incalculable forces that come into play, but rather that one can, in principle, master all things by calculation'. In other words, Weber perceived the process of rationalization to be inescapable as the empirical world became increasingly complex. Weber maintained that the growing dominance of an instrumental and scientific orientation to life would necessarily result in the disenchantment of the world – that is, a loss of ultimate meaning. For while science and engineering can provide technological advances that enable us to address more efficiently how to do things, it cannot provide us with answers to the more fundamental philosophical and existential questions.

Despite their distinct conceptual frameworks, Durkheimian and Weberian approaches to religion reflect a similar symbolic dichotomy. Weber's concepts of enchantment and disenchantment parallel Durkheim's concepts of the 'sacred' and the 'profane'. Weber conceptualized a **disenchanted world** as lacking in ultimate transcendence, that is, one in which 'nothing' is held 'sacred' in Durkheim's terms. For instance, the scientific method (as an ideal type) epitomizes disenchantment. The hallmark of the scientific method is that data alone – not emotion, opinion or tradition – determine 'the facts' (that is, what we 'know' about the world), and that new and better data can and should up-end old theories and 'facts' without consternation. In contrast to 'religion', which is rooted in tradition and sacred ideas (that is, that are not to be 'touched', that are symbolically set apart and revered for all eternity), scientific theories are supposed to be mutable rather than immutable – that is, continually open to testing and, if disproven, replaced with new theories and ideas. Interestingly, so-called 'new atheists', such as Richard Dawkins, share Weber's view about the symbolic dichotomy between 'religion' and 'science'. In his recent book *The God Delusion*, Dawkins insists that science is 'rational' while religion is not, and that human societies would be better off if they abandoned religion and embraced science as a means of explaining and navigating the world. For both Weber and Dawkins, the basic difference between science and religion is that one epitomizes *rationality* and the other does not (and many religious fundamentalists would concur with this point). While science rests on ('objective') formal rules and impersonal procedures (such as the scientific method) to ascertain 'truth', religion rests on ('subjective') tradition, beliefs and values.

However, from a Durkheimian point of view, the distinction between 'religion' and 'science' may not be as great as Dawkins and Weber assume, and the scientific world may not be quite as 'disenchanted' as it seems. First, Durkheimians might point out that, despite their distinct worldviews, new atheists such as Dawkins and his religious fundamentalist adversaries both discount contrary perspectives and attempt to convert others because they see their view as replete with tremendous benefits to humanity and the alternative as replete with extraordinary costs. In addition, of course, both use science and religion respectively to impose order and meaning on a chaotic world. Most importantly, however, Durkheimians might point out that the 'scientific' worldview is not as 'rational' as scientists claim, for scientists actually imbue the scientific method itself with sacrality. For the scientific community, it is the scientific method that sets the boundaries of science; the scientific method is the 'ultimate truth' that scientists hold most dear. In order to call yourself a scientist, you must accept the scientific method as the ultimate means for attaining 'truth'; you must not forsake it (if you want to call yourself a scientist), for it defines the scientific approach to the world.

Contemporary 'culture war' incidents between religious fundamentalists and atheists also reflect that while 'atheism' and 'religion' are substantively quite different, they perform similar social functions. For instance, in January 2009, 800 buses rolled out of depots across Britain plastered with advertisements informing people that 'there's probably no God. Now stop worrying and enjoy your life.' The ad campaign, sponsored by the British Humanist Association, was a direct response to the Christian messages on buses and websites that warn non-believers they are destined to go to hell (Chu 2009). The important point here is that, despite their contrary content, both messages assert meaning and are concrete directives concerning the proverbial (religious) question: 'How shall we act and live?'

For cultural sociologists, the central point is not whether or not we consider atheism or science a 'religion'. It is that the human condition is bound up in the search for *meaning*. At the dawn of the twentieth century, Weber pessimistically imagined that rational and bureaucratic structures would render the religious spirit obsolete. But what we have seen throughout the twentieth century and now in the twenty-first is that the human search for meaning cannot so easily be eradicated.

This is precisely what Frank Schaeffer, the son of the famous evangelical theologian Francis Schaeffer, stated in a recent compelling interview with National Public Radio's Terry Gross. Schaeffer explained that he cannot help being religious simply because it is in his bones:

Terry Gross: 'You converted to Greek Orthodox in 1990 . . . why did you feel the need to convert . . . if you were unhappy with your faith why didn't you leave faith altogether?'

Frank Schaeffer: 'The reason I didn't leave faith altogether is one that I'll never know. Because I don't where my conditioning as a person of faith begins and where my choices begin and where they end. All I can tell you is that if I wanted to become an atheist the first thing I would do is pray to God to help me. And that probably tells you that I'm stuck. I'm stuck because faith is just a part of my life. I don't know whether it is because faith is real or because that's just the way I was brought up. But a day that doesn't begin with prayer feels empty to me even when I'm questioning the existence of God. And that's just who I am. And so for me I had to wash up in some sort of a faith community or feel that a limb was missing.

'And why I'm in the Greek Orthodox Church is because I found refuge in a liturgical tradition that is not centred around a local guru. Our priests are interchangeable, they face the altar not the people, they lead the people in a liturgy that was set in the fourth or fifth centuries and has nothing to do with clever ideas or what is fashionable or politic . . . I find refuge in a changeless liturgical tradition that gives me religious food, spiritual food without the twenty-first century spin that I got so caught up in. It's just where I feel comfortable and that's why I'm in the Greek Orthodox Church'.

(Schaeffer 2008)

Schaeffer's eloquent insight – that he does not know where 'his conditioning ends and his choices begin' – is also the crux of cultural sociology. Cultural sociology focuses precisely on that remarkable intersection between the individual and the collective, and the rational and non-rational realms. Schaeffer and cultural sociology both underscore the depth and penetration of the cultural and social into our psyche, but also show that we still have 'choices'. Schaeffer made a conscious choice to convert to Greek Orthodox from evangelical Protestantism, but this choice was a direct result of his childhood witnessing of the 'cult-like' status of his father – whom he knew to be simply a human being. Schaeffer's comments reflect that as we go about our daily lives, we are a tangled amalgamation of individual and biographical and social and cultural conditions and realities – not just one or the other.

Two pivotal critics of religion: Karl Marx and Sigmund Freud

Karl Marx and Sigmund Freud are two classical thinkers who would probably perceive Schaeffer's experience quite differently. In conjunction with prominent atheists such as Dawkins, Marx and Freud both viewed religion as a powerful *illusion* and a psychological crutch for weak people.

In accordance with Durkheim, Karl Marx perceived religion as fulfilling a significant social function. However, in stark contrast to Durkheim, Marx maintained that religion functioned not to hold the society together for the good of the whole. Rather, he believed religion was an ideology that – like other ideologies – was simply a tool of the ruling class, used to maintain and legitimize their power. As Marx and Engels (1978) famously state, 'the ideas of the ruling class, are in every epoch, the ruling ideas, the class which is the ruling *material* force of society is at the same time its ruling intellectual force'. From a Marxist point of view, it is typical of hierarchies – whether political or religious – to create and institutionalize systems of ideas that grant specific prerogatives to *their* group while denying them to others. Thus, for instance, the all-male hierarchy of the Catholic Church (among others) continues to issue proclamations that support denying the priesthood to women. In a parallel way, the Hindu caste system continues to legitimate and solidify prevailing inequalities.

To be sure, Marx also realized that religion was a comfort for the working class. As Marx (1978) famously states:

> *Religious* suffering is at the same time an *expression* of real suffering and a *protest* against real suffering. Religion is the sigh of the oppressed creature, the sentiment of a heartless world, and the soul of soulless conditions. It is the *opium* of the people.
>
> (in Tucker 1978: 54, emphasis in original)

This passage is even more meaningful when one learns that the upper class really did use opium as a means of escape: Marx considered religion the low-budget alternative for those who could not afford opium. Both opium and religion enable individuals to cope with the misery of the everyday world. While opium makes one oblivious to pain and suffering, religion 'makes sense' of it, and religion provides hope as individuals set their sights on the next world.

At this point, one might wonder what is wrong with oppressed people finding comfort in religion. (After all, religion does not have the disastrous physical consequences of drug addiction.) According to Marx, the problem is that religious illusions prevent the working class from both seeing and changing the conditions that create and perpetuate their suffering. Religion is not at all innocuous because it helps ensure the maintenance of the status quo. This helps explain not only Marx's antipathy towards religion but why he advocated abolishing it. Marx imagined that under the proper conditions – that is, in a communist world – religion would no longer be necessary. Marx perceived workers' distress to be entirely man-made, and in communism religion would no longer be needed. As Marx states:

> To abolish religion as the illusory happiness of the people is to demand their real happiness. The demand to give up illusions about the existing state of affairs is the demand to give up a state of affairs which needs illusions . . . Thus the criticism of heaven turns into the criticism of earth, the *criticism of religion* into the *criticism of law* and the *criticism of theology* into the *criticism of politics*.
>
> (in Tucker 1978: 54, emphasis in original)

Of course, Marx is not at all alone in his perception of religion as an illusion. Sigmund Freud (1961) also famously argued that religion is a delusion – a function of human beings' inability to deal with the inevitability of suffering and death. Freud saw religion as a childlike craving for a Father God who assures victory over every hardship, even death itself. For Freud, religion is nothing more than a neurosis that impedes psychological maturity and health.

As we have seen, contemporary 'new atheists' such as Richard Dawkins continue to portray religion as nothing more than a psychological crutch for weak people. They also similarly contend that the harm, destruction and divisiveness caused by religion far outweigh its psychological and social benefits. They view the illusiveness and the falsity of religion as problematic, and they insist that religion is not a necessary component of human societies.

There can be no doubt that, as Marx maintained, those in the ruling class often use religion to maintain and legitimize their power, while ironically, at the same time, those in the oppressed class find great comfort in that same ideology – which, according to Marx, impedes their interests. Thus, for instance, women are often devoted practitioners of extraordinarily patriarchal religions that deny their basic civil rights. Nor can we refute that a wellspring of religious entrepreneurs and organizations throughout history manufacture religious creeds, and recruit and exploit 'believers', solely for their own gain. For example, Christian fundamentalists sell books and tapes and hold workshops for parents on how to turn their gay children 'straight', while gay Christians themselves spend thousands of dollars on programmes in an attempt to become 'ex-gay'. Overwhelmed parents of chronically sick children pour huge amounts of money into dubious ministries and faith healers, clearly out of desperation.

Yet, as we shift from a modern to a postmodern world, it seems clear that the relationship of human strife to the system of production is more complex than Marx let on. And while Freud astutely assessed the psychological complexity behind and within the human pursuit of religion, the question remains: is the powerful, persistent quest for meaning as 'childlike' and psychologically unhealthy as Freud portends? Is it as caustic for human societies as Dawkins and Marx and Freud maintain? After all, studies consistently show that religious practitioners evince better psychological health than non-believers. Perhaps, despite the 'illusiveness' of the psychological security of a 'Father figure' and their not insignificant material sacrifices (such as paying tithes, that is, 10 per cent of one's income), religious adherents *are* acting in accordance with their own interests.

Religion, spirituality and the individual: William James

William James (1936) was among the most important analysts to take the *nature* of religious experience seriously. As a psychologist, James was most interested in the internal 'intimate communion with the divine', rather than in the social function and effects of religion (as were Marx and Durkheim). Indeed, in polar opposition to Durkheim, James defined religion as 'the feelings, acts, and experiences of individual men *in their solitude*, so far as they apprehend themselves in relation to whatever they may consider the divine' (Pals 2009: 187, emphasis added). James warned against confounding 'the phenomena of mere tribal or corporate psychology', which he deemed 'religion's wicked intellectual partner', or 'dogmatic dominion' with 'manifestations of the purely interior life which are the exclusive object of our study' (Pals 2009: 187). Thus James differentiated 'first-hand religion' – that is, experiential, internal religious experience – from 'secondhand religion', or external religious doctrines, creeds and institutions. (*The Varieties of Religious Experience*, cited by Pals 2009: 172–5).

This distinction between religious experience at the individual as opposed to the corporate level is useful in explaining many paradoxes in the sociology of religion, such as why women (or slaves) might be more religious than men (or slave owners) – even though the doctrines to which they adhere discriminate against them. From a Jamesian viewpoint, the power of actual 'firsthand' religious experience, such as a woman's (or slave's) 'intimate communion with the divine', far outweighs any exploitative doctrinal and/or institutional 'secondhand' concerns.

James's distinction between an 'interior' spiritual life and 'corporate' religion also coincides well with the perspective of a growing contingent of people who consider themselves 'spiritual but not religious'. Like James, these people make a sharp distinction between institutionalized religion (of which they are sceptical) and the existence of a metaphysical, spiritual realm (which they not only accept, but often fervently embrace).

From a postmodern perspective, the increase in the number of people who call themselves 'spiritual but not religious' is unsurprising. In our hyper-mediated, sensation-driven, postmodern world, individual experience can be separated from institutions in ways that James could only have imagined. As the US religious historian Leigh Eric Schmidt states:

> In a mix and match world, why not create your own religion? Eclectic devotions, creedal crossings, consumer sampling, and individualistic expression are widely seen as the religious order of the day.
>
> (Schmidt 2005: 1)

Feminist spiritual writer Carol Lee Flinders adroitly encapsulates the 'pastiche spirituality' of the postmodern religious seeker when she states:

> I cannot describe my spiritual practice as Buddhist, or . . . as Hindu or Catholic or Sufi, though I feel that in a sense it is all of these . . . I meditate as best I can on Native American prayers and Taoist verses, on passages drawn from the Bible or the Upanishads, on passionate love songs composed for the One Beloved by a Spanish monk or an Indian princess-turned minstrel.
>
> (Flinders 1998: 24–5, cited by Schmidt 2005: 1)

Yet, from a cultural sociological perspective, the dividing line between the 'interior' and 'exterior' may be not quite as clear as James lets on. As Flinders's comment above reflects, so-called 'spiritual but not religious' beliefs and ideas are often simply religious ideas in a more narcissistic and disembodied form. Put in another way, our world may be more 'bric-a-brac' and hyper-mediated than ever before, but the human experience *is* always a complex blend of 'firsthand' (individual and experiential) and 'secondhand' (corporate) realms. For instance, US Protestants in particular have long been not only Bible readers, but 'practitioners of rigorous self-examination and introspective journaling' (Schmidt 2005: 1). '"My own mind is my own church," the revolutionary pamphleteer Thomas Paine insisted, with plenty of bravado, but little overstatement' (Schmidt 2005: 5). The

Protestant right of private judgement goes back at least to the Protestant Reformation (Schmidt 2005: 3).

That said, the 'internal' spiritual world is an increasingly popular object of study among neuroscientists, such as Michael Persinger. Using an apparatus they call the 'God Helmet', Persinger and his colleagues actually altered electromagnetic brain fields and induced 'spiritual' experiences (such as 'seeing God' or feeling an altered sense of self and a sense of oneness with the universe), thereby unlocking the complex neurological processes behind the types of religious experiences that so fascinated James. Persinger (1987) finds that there are significant differences in temporal lobe sensitivity in people, which helps explain the variability in individual religious and spiritual experience. At the extreme end of sensitivity are limbic epileptics, individuals who are more creative and also have extreme suggestibility – and researchers speculate that renowned religious prophets and saints, such as Muhammad, St Thérèse of Lisieux and St Ignatius of Loyola, may well have been limbic epileptics (a charge that infuriates many conservative religious adherents). At the other end of the spectrum are people, like Dawkins, who deny the very possibility of an actual spiritual realm.

Acclaimed sociologist of religion Robert Wuthnow (1998: 3–9) also distinguishes between two distinct types of religious experience. But Wuthnow's continuum is between 'dwelling' and 'seeking'. Whereas a spirituality of *dwelling* emphasizes 'habitation' and 'requires sharp symbolic boundaries to protect sacred space from its surrounding', a spirituality of seeking emphasizes 'negotiation' and 'draws fewer distinctions of such magnitude'. Dwelling-oriented spirituality emphasizes order, formal liturgy and tightly bound and formalized sets of rules – 'individuals are expected to conform to these rules, indeed to internalize them' – while seeker-oriented spirituality emphasizes the individual search for sacrality, which may well be found in everyday experience rather than formal institutional settings.

While Wuthnow (1998: 6) points out that 'the wisdom of Saint Benedict is that dwelling and seeking are both part of what it means to be human', he argues that some people are 'dwellers' (for example, religious fundamentalists) while others are 'seekers' (for example, spiritual progressives such as Flinders), and that historical eras too tend to be 'dweller' or 'seeker' based (for example, the United States in the 1950s and 1960s, as opposed to the 1960s and 1970s). Were he alive, Durkheim might emphasize that both scientists who are atheists and religious fundamentalists can be considered 'dwellers', sharing as they do a firm emphasis on a fixed set of standards (whether 'positivistic' or 'religious'). Just as the scientist must adhere to the scientific method in order to be a (practising) scientist, so too the Orthodox Jew must adhere to the Mishnah (the compiled rabbinical interpretations of scriptural ordinances) in order to be a (practising) Jew at all.

Religion and social change

Wuthnow's juxtaposition of 'dwellers' and 'seekers' recalls a pivotal symbolic dichotomy in the sociology of religion coined by Weber: 'this-worldly' and 'other-worldly'. For Weber was not simply interested in documenting the substantive differences between various religions, but also in assessing the psychological and social *consequences* of these distinct worldviews. Towards that end, he developed an ideal typical symbolic dichotomy between 'this-worldly' and 'other-worldly' religious orientations. According to Weber, 'other-worldly' orientations encourage the individual to transcend or escape 'this-world', steering them away from it. For instance, in Buddhist practices of meditation, change occurs internally rather than externally. The idea is not to rebel against the external causes of suffering, but to accept that life is suffering. Enlightenment is achieved not by 'meeting' desires, but by abandoning them. By contrast, 'this-worldly' orientations steer the individual towards enacting spiritual and religious teachings here on earth, thereby changing this world, making it a better place. Evangelical Protestants, for instance, might be compelled to proselytize to and convert unbelievers in order that they might be saved, or to engage in social action such as sheltering the homeless, feeding the poor, visiting the sick and comforting the dying. Weber maintained that Christians began to dominate the globe because of their 'this-worldly' approach. Theirs was an activist religion, and the social consequences of this orientation were both weighty and manifold.

Most interestingly, today we seem to be witnessing a resurgence of both 'this-worldly' and 'other-worldly' religion – or both 'dwelling' and 'seeking', in Wuthnow's terms. On one hand, as indicated previously, one of the fastest growing religions today is Islam, which is renowned for its orthodoxy and activism. The world's Muslim population is expected to increase by about 35 per cent over the next 20 years, rising from 1.6 billion in 2010 to 2.2 billion by 2030, a growth rate about twice the rate of the non-Muslim population. Some analysts contend that Islam will overtake Christianity as the most popular world religion some time in the mid-twenty-first century (Pew Research Center 2011). Yet it is not only traditional Islam that is thriving today. In Latin America and sub-Saharan Africa, especially, Pentecostalism and other revivalist forms of Christianity are flourishing, and since the collapse of the Soviet Union, we have seen a resurgence in Christianity in the former communist states as well. Pentecostals believe that God, acting through the Holy Spirit, continues to play a direct, active role in everyday life, as evident in spiritually renewing 'gifts of the Spirit' such as speaking in tongues and divine healing (Pew Forum on Pentecostalism 2006).

On the other hand, over the last few decades we have also been witnessing the 'Easternization of the West' (Campbell 2007). Not only are large numbers of Westerners increasingly fascinated by the wisdom of the East and turning enthusiastically to Eastern religions and spiritual techniques (what Campbell calls the 'yogaization of the West'); Westerners are increasingly becoming disillusioned with the wisdom of the West – that is, with 'rationalistic' approaches to the world. Specifically, in stark contrast to the Western notion of the divine as both personal and transcendent (that is, 'a perfect person'), as well as the secular version that there *is* no divine being, we are seeing Eastern conceptualizations of the divine as an *immanent* divine presence that pervades all things. Now the divine is being conceived of not in personal terms, but as a form of energy. In addition, we are seeing an increasing fascination with nature, animal rights and vegetarianism – all of which reflect a shift away from the dualistic assumption that humans and animals are entirely different forms of being – in favour of the notion that all life is in some measure divine. Instead of the (Western) notion that there is a single overriding principle guiding human history, a more cyclical notion of time or a belief in reincarnation and cosmic or spiritual evolution is now taking hold. In fact, one of the fastest growing religions today is said to be the Earth-based neo-pagan religion Wicca, which is reportedly doubling in size every 30 months (World Christian Encyclopedia 2001). And while the numbers of people claiming 'no religious denomination' are, as we have seen, rapidly rising (especially among American youth – see Putnam and Campbell 2010), it is important to remember that this category includes not only agnostics and atheists, but neo-pagans and other 'easternized' religionists as well.

This brings us to another important contemporary trend: the infiltration of religion into popular culture. Today religion is not only an explicit topic of choice in films such as Mel Gibson's infamous *The Passion of the Christ*, but issues of religion and spirituality proliferate in books and films such as J.K. Rowling's *Harry Potter* series, the *Matrix* trilogy and the vampire craze of recent years. 'Apocalyptic' themes have long been rampant on the silver screen (for example, *Dr Strangelove, Soylent Green, Logan's Run, Terminator 2, Mad Max, Waterworld*), providing a compelling way to address technological, environmental and nuclear fears and concerns (see Stone 2011). Moreover, an entire sociology of religion course can be found in *The Simpsons*, which not only lampoons but edifies the audience in religion and spiritual matters in relatively sophisticated ways. Because regular characters include a Hindu convenience store manager, a Jewish entertainer and an Evangelical neighbour, there is often somewhat detailed dialogue and discussion about these religions, and entire episodes have been devoted to Islam, Buddhism, Scientology and well-known biblical stories (Dalton, Mazur and Siems 2011). Of course, another site (pun intended) where popular culture and religion merge today is online. Virtual churches such as *Second Life* are thriving, further eroding 'the distinction between sacred and profane space' (Wagner 2011: 271).

Conclusion

In this chapter, we have examined pivotal theses by Durkheim, Weber, Marx, Freud, Wuthnow, Berger and James concerning the relationship between culture, society and religion. We have seen that all of these thinkers make significant contributions towards our understanding of the complex relationship between religion, culture and the individual. We have also seen that, despite a classic contention that religious worldviews and structures would erode and be replaced by impersonal technological rationality in modern and postmodern society, we are witnessing *both* secularization and the continued vitality of religion and spirituality today.

Review questions

10.1 Explain the extent to which religion and spirituality are apparent or important in your life (or not). How does your example intersect with the 'secularization thesis'?

10.2 Explain what Durkheim means by the 'sacred' and 'profane'. How are the sacred and profane apparent in your everyday life? What do you hold 'sacred'? How do you know?

10.3 Explain how religion and spirituality are viewed by Marx and Freud. What are the common elements in their views? What are the differences?

Note

1 Obama was a huge hit among spiritual progressives and progressive Christians when he spoke at a Call to Renewal conference on 28 June 2006. In this speech, Obama (finally) responded to the insidious assertion made by Senator Alan Keyes in the course of the 2004 senatorial elections that 'Christ would not vote for Barack Obama'. Rather than give the 'typically liberal response' that Obama did at the time – namely, that 'we live in a pluralistic society [and] that I can't impose my religious views on another . . . [and that] I was running to be the US Senator of Illinois and not the Minister of Illinois', in this speech Obama explicitly delineated his progressive Christian point of view and his own 'faith story'. Keyes's 'implicit accusation that I was not a true Christian nagged at me, and I was also aware that my answer didn't adequately address the role my faith has in guiding my own values and beliefs'. See Mansfield (2008); Obama (2006).

Further reading

Armstrong, K. (2000) *The Battle for God*, Knopf, New York.

Berger, P. (1967) *The Sacred Canopy*, Anchor, New York.

Campbell, C. (2007) *The Easternization of the West*, Paradigm, Boulder, CO.

Davidman, L. (1997) *Tradition in a Rootless World*, University of California Press, Berkeley, CA.

Durkheim, E. (1965 [1912]) *The Elementary Forms of Religious Life*, Free Press, New York.

James, W. (1936 [1902]) *The Varieties of Religious Experience*, Modern Library, New York.

Mansfield, S. (2008) *The Faith of Barack Obama*, Thomas Nelson, Nashville, TN.

Putnam, R. and Campbell, D. (2010) *American Grace*, Simon and Schuster, New York.

Weber, M. (1958 [1919]) *The Protestant Ethic and the Spirit of Capitalism*, Scribner, New York.

Part IV

Leisure and Lifestyle

11

Popular Music: Place, Identity, Community

Learning objectives

- To examine how cultural sociology can be used to understand the cultural significance of popular music as it informs notions of place, identity and community.
- To understand the importance of local and global flows of information in musically constructed meanings of space and place.
- To assess the extent and impact of the interaction between music, structure and agency in the fashioning and articulation of identity.
- To discern the impact of popular music on contemporary notions of community and belonging.

Introduction

The study of popular music is now an established sub-disciplinary field of contemporary sociological research. Although a topic of study from the early 1950s onwards (for example, see Howard Becker's (1951) highly valuable work on the world of the jazz musician), the sociology of popular music began to gather critical momentum in the early 1980s following the publication of Simon Frith's (1978) *The Sociology of Rock* (later republished as *Sound Affects*, see Frith 1983). Until relatively recently, sociological research on popular music was strongly focused on issues of production, mediation and performance. This was in many respects unsurprising, given the pivotal place of popular music within the media and cultural industries. As such, a significant body of work in the sociology of popular music has been centrally concerned with the tensions and contradictions between popular music as art and industrial product, and between

Cultural Sociology: An Introduction, First Edition. Les Back et al. © 2012 Les Back, Andy Bennett, Laura Desfor Edles, Margaret Gibson, David Inglis, Ronald Jacobs and Ian Woodward. Published 2012 by Blackwell Publishing Ltd.

issues of authenticity and commodification (see, for example, Frith and Horne 1987; Negus 1992; Peterson 1997). Although such work has made critical contributions to our understanding of popular music as a cultural form in late modern society, its theoretical and empirical emphases served to elide any sustained consideration of music audiences and issues of consumption. Clearly, however, such issues are of equal importance in facilitating an understanding of music's sociological significance.

As with other areas of sociological research and scholarship, the cultural turn has had a significant impact on the way in which music has been approached and interpreted by sociologists (Bennett 2008a). In particular, the shift among music sociologists to questions of culture has brought with it an increasing focus on the appropriation of musical texts and the inscription of meaning. Indeed, such issues are by no means limited to the consideration of popular music, with research focusing on a broader range of genres, including jazz and classical music (see, for example, DeNora 2000; Hennion 2003; Martin 1995). Arguably, though, it is in the cultural sociology of popular music where issues of music's everyday use have most effectively been mapped against other factors considered integral to the everyday production of cultural life, notably articulations of place, identity and community.

If notions of place, identity and community are now understood to be both highly complex and keenly contested, of equal interest to sociologists has been the way in which cultural forms such as popular music feed into and inform everyday cultural discourses surrounding these and other aspects of everyday contemporary culture and cultural practice. As scholarship published since the early 1990s illustrates, cultural sociological research on the relationship between popular music, place, identity and community has engaged with a wide-ranging field of issues spanning production, performance and consumption – and within these has considered aspects of youth, ageing, ethnicity, gender and sexuality. At the same time, this literature has also taken issue with previously accepted sociological frameworks for the study of music and place-related concepts of identity; this is exemplified by the emergence of post-subcultural theory (Muggleton 2000), a body of work that challenges structuralist interpretations of popular music's socio-cultural significance in the light of the postmodern, mediatization, consumerism and cultural fragmentation (Chaney 2004).

This chapter offers an overview of the main concepts and theories employed in the cultural sociology of popular music in both local and global contexts. In doing so, it introduces the reader to key studies that have emerged over the last 20 years. The chapter is divided into three main sections that focus respectively on popular music and place, popular music and identity, and popular music and community. The chapter concludes by offering some thoughts and observations relating to possible future trajectories for the cultural sociology of popular music as an increasingly central sub-discipline of the broader sociological field.

Popular music and place

Popular music has long been held to function as a critical marker of place. As Bennett (2008b: 72) observes, 'part of the process of associating music with place involves a desire to make the music "real", to give it roots and an everyday, "lived" context in which to explore its meaning and significance, lyrically, musically and culturally'. Since the emergence of blues and roots music in the early twentieth century, writers have sought to highlight connections between the sonic and lyrical components of particular popular music styles and their places of origin (see Palmer 1977; Guralnick 1978). Indeed, early studies focusing on music and place often claimed an organic or 'natural' connection between geography and sound. To a great extent, the ease with which such connections could be established related to the ready distinctions that could be made between, for example, urban industrial metropoles and rural, agrarian regions, or Western centres of culture and production compared with remote, non-Western communities on the global periphery. Significantly, however, the association between music and place has remained even in the wake of mediatization and the increasing influence of globalization. Thus, despite the emergence of the popular music 'star' as a mediated and packaged object of consumption, emphasis continues to be placed on the importance of place, together with class, ethnic and gender background, as a means of understanding the aesthetic qualities of music (Shumway 1992). For example, during the 1950s and early 1960s, great significance was attributed to the working-class origin of artists such as Elvis Presley and The Beatles, and the alleged connection between this origin and the grittiness and immediacy of these artists' music. In the case of Liverpool, home of The Beatles, this translated into a broader discourse about place and sound that crystallized in the label 'Merseybeat' – a reference both to the River Mersey and the wider Merseyside area, of which Liverpool is the principal city (see Cohen 1991). Such associations have continued in more recent times. For example, throughout the 1980s, US artist Bruce Springsteen was frequently discussed in relation to his working-class New Jersey roots, a factor that afforded him an increased aura of authenticity with his fanbase (Cavicchi 1998). Similarly, the grunge style made popular by groups such as Nirvana and Pearl Jam was considered by music journalists to be inextricable from its point of origin in the post-industrial city of Seattle in America's north-west (Bennett 2008b). Such spatializations of music and culture serve as potent metaphors through which individuals come to understand the meaning of popular music as a central aspect of late modern popular culture. It is, however, important to note that such representations of music embody their own powerful narratives, generated through the authoritative lens of print and visual media. To put this in a slightly different way:

> due to the way in which place, music and audience are positioned through and by global media flows, new representations of place emerge that superimpose their own fictive gloss to produce what Kahn-Harris refers to as a 'hybrid and flexible concatenation of the discursive and the real' (2006: 133). Through the power of media representation, place ceases to be a mere geographical space and assumes instead a powerful metaphorical significance that links accepted physical properties of a place with a series of inscribed qualities that are deemed to have given rise to particular sound and associated performative conventions.
>
> (Bennett 2008b: 71–2)

Yet it is not purely in the realm of mediatized representations that such narrative fictions of music and place materialize. On the contrary, cultural sociological research has also provided important insights concerning the interaction of such representations with everyday, localized sensibilities of space and place. For example, in his instructive work on the Chicago blues scene, Grazian (2004) demonstrates how Chicago's global reputation as the home of the blues style has become a powerful means of promoting potent myths about blues authenticity. Such myths play out both in the promotion of particular bars and venues as spaces for the performance of blues music and in the way that blues 'tourists' visiting Chicago map out and plan their visit to the city.

The Internet has also proven to be an important medium through which fans and consumers of music are able to map connections between music and place. During the late 1960s, the English cathedral city of Canterbury momentarily became a focus for music journalists due to the emergence from the city of a number of rock and jazz rock bands, including Caravan, Soft Machine and Gong. Some 30 years later, the 'Canterbury Sound' was suddenly revived as a result of the launching of 'Calyx', an Internet fansite dedicated to the bands mentioned above and others which had been associated with Canterbury. Among the many features of the web site, fans were given an opportunity to discuss definitions of the Canterbury Sound and its connection to the city:

> the online discussions of fans being informed by a shared image of Canterbury as an urban space that provided the necessary stimulus for the birth of the Canterbury Sound and which remains central to its 'spirit'. Thus, the fans inscribe Canterbury's streets, pubs, venues and other urban spaces with their own fictive interpretations (Chaney 1993), the latter becoming a crucial touchstone for the fans' collective belief in the inherent link between the 'Canterbury Sound' and the city of Canterbury.
>
> (Bennett 2004: 209)

As these brief examples illustrate, popular music serves as a highly potent resource in the narrativization of space and place. However, to fully comprehend the importance of music in such place-making processes, one must go beyond the notion of music and place as tied to local clusters of music production, or the mediated notion of a local sound or 'scene'. Indeed, as Bennett observes:

> For much of the time, popular music's relationship to the local has rather less to do with its being a local 'product' than with the way in which commercially available musical products are appropriated and reworked within the context of a given locality.
>
> (Bennett 2000: 60)

To pursue this point further, it follows that even within global flows of industrially produced music, new expressions of space and place can be cemented through the inscription of localized meanings by musicians and audiences. To a large extent, this relates to the malleability of popular music genres and texts. Although the latter are not entirely free-floating signifiers, at the same time they allow considerable scope for personal interpretation in terms of meaning and significance. Also important in this respect is the notion of 'ownership'. Thus, according to Frith (1987), individuals' ready association with and symbolic ownership of musical texts allows for the powerful inscription of meaning. As a critical means through which late modern individuals make sense of and relate to their everyday surroundings (DeNora 2000), the inscription of meaning in musical texts often assumes a place-related dimension. An effective illustration of this is provided through research into hip hop. Although, as Rose (1994) observes, most hip hop fans and practitioners recognize themselves as working out of a musical and stylistic basis with origins in New York during the early 1970s, at the same time the global spread of hip hop has resulted in highly nuanced localized versions of the style. In particular, rap – the musical dimension of hip hop and its most commercially exploited component – has assumed localized significance through experimentation with its musical and linguistic elements (Bennett 1999a, 1999b). Indeed, even within the same urban or regional setting, rap can give rise to very different localized variations of composition, performance and aesthetic meaning (see, for example, Harrison 2009). As this observation suggests, if popular music has become a significant resource in the narrativization of place, then it also offers the potential for multiple, and sometimes conflicting, narratives of place. Thus, as Bennett observes:

> in referring to the 'local', we are in effect speaking about a space which is crossed by a variety of different collective sensibilities each of which imposes a different set of expectations and cultural needs upon that space. In doing so, such sensibilities also construct the local in particular ways, a process which ensures that terms such as *locality* and *local identity* are always, in part at least, subjective elements which begin by utilising the same basic knowledges about the local, its social and spatial organisation, but supplement such knowledges with their own collectively held values to create particular narratives of locality.
>
> (Bennett 2000: 66)

Music, then, can be seen as both a source of commonality and a source of conflict in the creation of narratives of space and place. We will return to this point in the final section of the chapter, which considers the contribution of cultural sociology to our understanding of popular music's role in the construction and articulation of notions of community and belonging.

Popular music and identity

The impact of cultural sociological approaches on our understanding of popular music's role in the representation and everyday articulation of identity has also been highly significant. Initially, sociological research on music attempted to read the relationship between music and identity in terms of **structural determinism** – that is, structural factors such as class, gender and ethnicity were considered to have an over-arching effect on everyday cultural responses to music, and the acquisition and articulation of musical taste. A key example of this approach is seen in Willis's (1978) *Profane Culture*, a study of bikers and hippies in England during the early 1970s. Willis draws attention to the contrasting musical tastes of these two youth cultural groups, the bikers preferring short, musically straightforward rock'n'roll songs, while the hippies displayed an interest in progressive rock, a more musically complex, album-orientated variation of the rock genre (see also Moore 1993). Willis argues that the musical tastes of the bikers and hippies were a direct reflection of their differing class backgrounds:

> The [working class] motorbike boys preferred music . . . that clearly resonated and developed the particular interests and qualities of the boys' life-style. [Rock'n'roll] had an integrity of form and atmosphere as well as an immediate, informal confidence.
>
> (Willis 1978: 71)

In contrast, argues Willis, the more highly educated, middle-class hippies demanded music that *challenged* the listener. Not content with the 4/4 rhythms and gritty vocal and guitar sounds associated with rock'n'roll, the hippies sought music that offered a more diverse listening experience – something they found in the progressive rock music of groups such as Genesis, Yes and Pink Floyd. Moreover, in combination with psychedelic drugs, the complex rhythms and exotic soundscapes characteristic of progressive rock music became a way of achieving altered states of perception and awareness, subverting conventional notions of time: 'Electronic techniques . . . such as echo, feedback, stereo [and] loudness itself . . . [gave] the impression of space and lateral extension'. This experience was enhanced significantly through the use of marijuana and hallucinogenic drugs such as LSD (Willis 1978: 167).

Applying a conceptual approach closely related to Bourdieu's notion of cultural capital and its influence on patterns of taste as exhibited by different social groups, Willis's linking of musical taste with the class-based identity of the listener is cemented through the concept of **homology**. According to Willis, homology represents 'the continuous play between the group and a particular item which produces specific styles, meanings, contents and forms of consciousness' (1978: 191). Over the course of the next two decades, the concept of homology was to become an important term of reference in the sociological analysis of popular music. For example, in her ground-breaking study of heavy metal music, Weinstein (2000) maps the significance of heavy metal for a North American blue-collar audience in ways not at all dissimilar to Willis's approach. For Weinstein, the grittiness of heavy metal and the male-centric nature of its lyrics are both a product of the blue-collar class experience (the majority of heavy metal artists having working-class backgrounds) and resonate strongly with the everyday experience of the male-dominated, largely blue-collar audience.

As cultural sociologists have argued, however, a key problem with homological approaches to understanding the cultural meaning of popular music is the lack of **reflexivity** assigned to the social actor. In effect, homology is used 'as a means of uncovering the social processes that are perceived to underpin the acquisition of musical taste – the former then being used to explain away the latter' (Bennett 2008a: 422). Thus, according to homological explanations of musical taste and affect:

> what appear on the surface to be spontaneous responses on the part of social actors to music are, in fact, pre-determined by the structural experience of class. Far from being reflexive and creative agents in the creation of musical meaning and affect [social actors respond to music in subconscious ways] in accordance with structurally embedded antecedents which basically 'tell' them 'how' to react to particular aural and visual stimuli.
>
> (Bennett 2008a: 422)

As the above account illustrates, much of the problem concerning homology centres upon its positioning of class as a means of explaining away the cultural meaning and significance of music as a product of predetermined, largely subconscious factors. Thus, while class – together with other structural factors such as gender and race – clearly plays some part in shaping a person's life experience, we need to question how far we can assume that an individual's response to a musical text is a product of class, and for that matter the extent to which class can be considered a uniform barometer of the ways in which music is appropriated and used in everyday life. Homological interpretations of musical responses as largely subconscious and predetermined modes of reception are also highly problematic in that they afford the social actor little or no power in ascribing their own notions of significance and value in relation to music. Indeed, as Chaney (1994: 48) observes, a key problem with homologically informed approaches to the study of contemporary culture 'is that they try to close off the processes of the production of meaning'.

Thus it could be argued that homology presents a somewhat skewed picture of music's role in the production and representation of identity. Indeed, as a number of cultural sociological studies have endeavoured to illustrate, a more productive way of assessing and understanding the relationship between music and identity is to consider it a resource that offers the potential for multiple enunciations of identity, including those that strive to negotiate and/or transcend the parameters of class background and the expectations that this places on expressions of, for example, gender, ethnicity, sexuality and age.

Important in this respect is the work of Lewis (1992), which applies the concept of taste cultures as a means of engaging with the relationship between music and identity in a way that moves beyond homology. According to Lewis, taste cultures – a term originally developed by Gans (1967) – define a process whereby collective social identities are not merely reflections of social class and other manifestations of structural inequality, but are also informed by popular music and other forms of technologically mediated popular culture. Thus, argues Lewis, the connection between social class and taste is:

> not the clean and neat one that some, perhaps naively, have assumed it to be – especially in our modern, mass-mediated technological society. In such a society, under conditions of relatively high social mobility, greater discretionary income, easy credit, efficient distribution of goods, high diffusion rate of cultural products, conspicuous consumption, and a greater amount of leisure time, the link between social and cultural structures becomes a question, not a given. Rather than assume it to be simply correlative, it is perhaps better to view it as contingent, problematic, variable, and – to a higher degree than we might imagine – subjectively determined.
>
> (Lewis 1992: 141)

Lewis goes on to argue that three main dimensions can be identified in the formation of taste cultures – *demographics*, *aesthetics* and *politics*. *Demographics* cover factors such as age, gender, race and locality. Lewis argues that each of these dimensions can dramatically cut across class by providing a basis for attachment to a particular style of music. *Aesthetics* describes the process whereby personal preference for a particular music style and/or related cultural forms can feed into and inform a lifestyle politics that plays a significant part in the way individuals position themselves in the world and forge associations with others. Finally, *politics* connotes a perception on the part of the individual as to the relationship between a given music genre and the dominant power structure. Thus, as Lewis explains, whereas a genre such as country may be perceived as broadly supportive of the dominant power structure, punk and rap can be seen as assuming an oppositional stance. Thus, in adopting a preference for a particular kind of music, individuals both articulate their own political values and assert themselves in opposition to other musical taste groups.

Lewis's study is important in that, breaking with the tradition of looking for underlying structures that inform collective taste in music, it regards individuals as reflexive agents in the acquisition of musical taste and in the positioning of such taste in relation to their identity and lifestyle. Moreover, given that certain predetermined and external factors may play a part in this process, the latter do not, in Lewis's view, press down like dead weights on the individual. Rather, they serve as points of reference, acting on individuals at different levels and in different ways – producing a plurality of responses to musical genres rather than the type of monolithic response proffered in studies utilizing a homological perspective. Lewis's study, then, serves as a highly useful mapping schema for our understanding of the relationship between music, taste and identity in late modernity. Absent from Lewis's approach, however, is a more detailed consideration of specific examples through which individuals reflexively engage with music and associated cultural objects, images and texts.

In this respect, a number of later studies importantly attend to some of the empirical gaps evident in Lewis's work. For example, in his highly important work on the relationship between youth, identity and music, Back (1996) argues that musical styles such as reggae and, more recently, rap and bhangra have given rise to new expressions of collective identity among youth, whereby musical taste has acted as a primary frame of reference for expressions of association and affinity between youth from various ethnic backgrounds. Thus, according to Back, a mutual attraction to, for example, the reggae sound system or hip hop jam provides a basis upon which young people forge bonds and affinities with others. Although notions of neighbourhood, locality and community play a role here, that role is critically augmented by shared understandings of musical meaning that operate across such boundaries in ways that connote modes of inclusion and participation that rely as much upon common aesthetic values inscribed in musical texts as upon discourses of space and place.

The notion of popular music as a resource for the construction and articulation of identities grounded in shared understandings of aesthetics and textual meaning has also been deployed effectively in studies of music and gender. Schilt's (2004) study of the Riot Grrrl movement in the United States also marks an important point of departure in this respect through its mapping of the post-punk, indie guitar scene's transgression beyond male-centric representations of performance, production and consumption to offer more space for female involvement and articulations of female identity. Again, a shared taste in music – in this case, a guitar-centred style and accompanying DIY production and performance ethic – provides a basis through which individuals identify with and bond to create collective cultural understandings of themselves. As Schilt notes, the extent to which participation in the creation of the musical and extra-musical text of Riot Grrrl generated new, reflexive understandings of identity is demonstrated through musicians' and audience members' refusal to be labelled by the media as promoters of culturally ingrained discourses of feminism. Rather, argues Schilt (2004: 127), followers of Riot Grrrl 'were finding new ways to express their feminism' located within the realm of DIY cultural production.

Popular music's role in the construction of identities that cut across categories of class, gender and – increasingly – age has also been a significant point of consideration in more recent studies of music and sexuality. An effective case in point here is Taylor's (2010) study of the queer music scene in Brisbane, Australia. In particular, Taylor considers how the musical eclecticism of the queer scene mirrors a sensibility of inclusion and tolerance among scene members; the musical soundscape of the scene is, at one important level, a means through which individuals of varying ages and from different class and ethnic backgrounds can find a sense of connection with the scene, irrespective of their individual sexuality. At the same time, observes Taylor, such musical eclecticism also performs as a cultural code through which the queer scene can collectively express a critical distance from other, more openly commodified expressions of musicalized sexuality – notably that seen in urban gay clubs, where the musical repertoire is tightly focused around disco and contemporary dance music.

The function of popular music as a means through which discourses of belonging and distance can simultaneously be expressed within and across specific neighbourhoods and adjacent city spaces has also been considered in relation to the contemporary articulation of established regional identities. For example, in considering the appropriation of hip hop by white youth in Newcastle in the United Kingdom, Bennett illustrates how, through absorbing the discourses of hip hop, local followers sought to distance themselves from what they classed as 'townie' youth and their perceived parochial and racist attitudes. In doing so, local white hip hoppers sought to construct a new expression of local 'Geordie' identity that embraced a more open, cosmopolitan stance to issues of ethnic and cultural difference. For many local hip hoppers, their alternative outlook was a direct reflection of their investment in hip hop and their understanding of it as a global, multi-ethnic youth cultural form.

As the above examples illustrate, popular music functions as a critically important resource through which individuals forge identities that cut across lines of class, gender, sexuality and locality. One final point worth considering in this section of the chapter is how popular music underpins patterns of **trans-local** mobility that can in turn foster new, temporal expressions of identity. An illustrative example of this is seen in Dowd, Liddle and Nelson's (2004) work on music festivals. Dowd and colleagues argue that one of the key – and perhaps unintended – functions of the contemporary music festival is to facilitate experimentation with identity in a setting removed from the regular spaces and routines of everyday life. Thus, they observe:

> Drawn together from geographically dispersed locations and away from the expectations of everyday life, fans and performers can immerse themselves in a particular culture and experiment with different identities.
>
> (Dowd, Liddle and Nelson 2004: 149)

Dowd and colleagues' observations are significant here in that they offer an additional dimension through which to understand the relationship between music and identity in which issues of temporal experience in liminal spaces such as festivals impact on the way that individuals are able to construct and articulate identities. Although the relationship between music and identity may take a different, and in some cases less intense, form in the context of the festival where other activities and experiences may also inform the individuals' participation in the event, it is the music that underpins the essence of the collective festival experience, and that provides the cue for experimentation with identity.

Popular music and community

Among academic scholars, one of the most contested aspects of popular music is its function as a basis for expressions of community. In considering the claims of the late 1960s counter-cultural movement to have established the basis for a new, alternative community based around political rock music – as part of its rejection of the dominant, capitalist culture – Frith (1981) argues that this was in effect an ideological rather than physical community. Indeed, this notion of popular music as a catalyst for ideological spaces of resistance and opposition to mainstream society has been integral to sociological and cultural studies research for a number of years. During the 1970s, researchers based at the Centre for Contemporary Cultural Studies (CCCS) adopted and adapted the Chicago School concept of 'subculture' to explain working-class music and style-based youth cultures, from mods and skinheads to rockers and punks, as youth groupings whose ideological sensibilities made them distinct from the dominant culture of their parents, the school, work, and so on. In their now-famous study *Resistance Through Rituals*, Hall and Jefferson (1976) positioned the so-called youth subcultures as expressions of an ongoing British class struggle that had assumed a new spectacular dimension through the appropriation of consumer objects, such as music, fashion, jewellery and technology, and their symbolic repositioning as objects of resistance (see also Hebdige 1979).

As with the concept of homology (see previous section) criticisms of subcultural theory have suggested that it presents a too narrow and monolithic interpretation of music's impact on the listener. Moreover, it is argued, as the range of music-related consumer products has grown and given rise to articulations of music- and style-based identity that now often transcend youth (see Bennett 2006), it is increasingly hard to maintain a subculture–dominant culture binary (Chaney 2004). In response to this, a range of other models has been developed for examining music's role in the construction and articulation of community.

Modelling a term first introduced by Redhead (1990), Muggleton (2000) proposes the concept of post-subculture as a means of describing a new mode of musical and stylistic consumption in which notions of belonging and community are expressed through a multiplicity of aesthetic sensibilities grounded in reflexive individualized patterns of consumption. Such forms of 'post-subcultural' affiliation, Muggleton argues, gave rise to new articulations of collective association that were not grounded in uniform adoption of musical and stylistic resources but rather in common aesthetic sensibilities relating to a mixing and matching of styles and influences.

A further refinement of this approach is evident in Bennett (1999c) and Malbon's (1999) work on contemporary dance music utilizing Maffesoli's (1996) concept of the neo-tribe. Drawing on Maffesoli's contention that neo-tribal associations are under-pinned by the qualities of temporality evident in contemporary social groupings such as sports spectators and crowds in a shopping mall, Bennett and Malbon's respective studies conceptualize the dance music event as a temporal form of collectivity in which crowds connected by affective bonds of shared musical taste and perception of the cultural properties of the dance event gather together in short-lived bursts of sociality.

The concept of the scene is a further attempt to consider and understand the community-generating qualities of popular music. The idea of the scene was first applied in an academic context by Straw (1991) as a means of engaging with music's capacity to transcend the confines of locale, neighbourhood and other traditional perceptions of community in bringing together people to participate collectively in music events. According to Straw (1991: 379), scenes transcend particular localities, 'reflect[ing] and actualiz[ing] a particular state of relations between various populations and social groups, as these coalesce around particular coalitions of musical style'. Utilizing this approach, Kahn-Harris (2006) examines how such bonds articulated through common musical taste can operate across national borders, resulting in what he refers to as trans-local scenes. These are given further substance through a continual flow of recorded music, DVDs and literature, as well as touring groups, DJs, and so on. In this sense, music-informed notions of community become less about specific perceptions of space and place, and are enacted through specific forms of artistic and economically motivated cultural practice. Finally, and building still further on this concept of the music scene as ideologically managed and perpetuated, Peterson and Bennett (2004) coin the term 'virtual scene', suggesting that virtual scenes utilize Internet communication technology, thus allowing geographically dispersed fans to interact online. As they observe:

> Whereas a conventional local scene is kept in motion by a series of gigs, club nights, fairs, and similar events, where fans converge, communicate and reinforce their sense of belonging to a particular scene, the virtual scene involves direct net-mediated person-to-person communication between fans . . . This may involve, for example, the creation of chat-rooms or list-serves dedicated to the scene and may involve the trading of music and images on-line.
>
> (Peterson and Bennett 2004: 11)

The notion of the 'virtual' scene thus opens up a new means of conceptualizing scene membership, not necessarily as a face-to-face activity but as one that is conducted primarily, if not exclusively, in the virtual spaces of the Internet. In this way the Internet becomes an important new medium for forms of musicalized association, with the physical, face-to-face forms of interaction that characterize the local scene being replaced by new forms of interaction that centre primarily on articulations of knowledge, taste and authority that go along with a prolonged commitment to a particular genre or genres of music.

Conclusion

This chapter has examined the contribution of cultural sociology to our understanding of the relationships among popular music, place, identity and community. Core to this has been a consideration of the ways in which cultural sociologists have taken issue with more traditional sociological approaches grounded in structurally informed concepts such as homology and subculture. The key purpose of the chapter has been to define and discuss these concepts before going on to consider some of the problems identified with them and the alternative conceptual models offered by sociological theorists in the wake of the cultural turn. In examining concepts of place, identity and community and their relationship to popular music, this chapter has shown how cultural sociologists have attempted to move beyond a concentration on social structure to consider how music serves as a cultural resource for the reflexive construction of place, identity and community as 'discursive' rather than 'given'; as modes of socio-cultural being and practice in which social actors have a stake in the production and representation of their everyday lives.

The key contribution of the cultural sociological approach to popular music is arguably in supplying a new *reflexive* understanding of popular music's significance in everyday life. A critical aspect of this has involved the redefinition of musical meaning 'as a dynamic interactive process in which the everyday reception, appropriation and aestheticization of popular music texts, artefacts and associated resources are integral to the production of musical meaning and significance' (Bennett 2008a: 430). As the cultural sociology of popular music moves forward, a critical challenge will be to manage the development of the field in a way that continues to provide distinctive insights through the application of a reflexive sociological approach. Increasingly, a number of those working in the cultural sociology of popular music have backgrounds as musicians, producers, promoters, songwriters, and so on. Such a strong connection between the theory and practice of music has clear potential for the establishment of an everyday approach to sociology, as envisaged by Chaney (1994) in *The Cultural Turn*. In order to realize this effectively, however, the project of reflexivity, in the cultural sociology of popular music as in other areas of the cultural sociology sub-field, must continue to work hard in order to develop and maintain parameters of critical distance and objectivity (Bennett 2002). If this can be achieved, then there is ample scope for significant broadening of the field to take into account more recent and emerging issues: in the area of technology, examples include P2P file-sharing and issues of intellectual property; in the area of production, they include 'mash-ups' and other instances of DIY music production; in the field of consumption, we could look at ageing audiences and the increasing instance of multi-generational followings for genres such as rap, punk, hardcore and dance.

Review questions

11.1 What are considered to be the key differences between cultural sociological and more traditional approaches to the study of popular music?

11.2 Why is a consideration of the respective concepts of place, identity and community particularly pertinent to the cultural sociology of music?

11.3 What do you consider to be cultural sociology's most important contribution(s) to our understanding of the everyday significance of popular music?

Further reading

Bennett, A. (2008a) Towards a cultural sociology of popular music. *Journal of Sociology*, 4 (4), 419–32.

Lewis, G.H. (1992) Who do you love? The dimensions of musical taste, in *Popular Music and Communication* (ed. J. Lull), 2nd edn, Sage, London, pp. 134–51.

12

Fashion Logics and the Cultural Economy: The Social Power of Tastes, Aesthetics and Style

Learning objectives

- To examine how and why a fashion dynamic – which is at its core a process of diffusion and adoption of aesthetic innovation – has become central to many aspects of contemporary life.
- To understand the drive to be 'in fashion' as a manifestation of increased circulation of objects, images, ideas and identities in the contemporary social world.
- To understand arguments about the claimed collapse of taste and fashion hierarchies.
- To understand the influence of retro and street cultures on fashion.
- To understand the extent to which status in contemporary society has to a large degree become materialized and visualized.

Introduction

Whether we consider ourselves to be fashionable or not, the logic of fashion permeates our everyday lives in often-unacknowledged ways, and is also a central dynamic within the global culture system. Fashion – which we can define initially as the social systemic production, consumption and institutionalization of novelty – is a cultural phenomenon that integrates culture, the individual and the economy. Fashion is both an idea and an ideal. Yet it finds expression materially and visually in forms coded by colour, shape, texture and branding, and must be produced and circulated within cultural fields integrating local and global systems. Though clothing is the most visible and widespread example of fashion at work, fashion is not just a social process pertaining to clothing and

Cultural Sociology: An Introduction, First Edition. Les Back et al. © 2012 Les Back, Andy Bennett, Laura Desfor Edles, Margaret Gibson, David Inglis, Ronald Jacobs and Ian Woodward. Published 2012 by Blackwell Publishing Ltd.

dress. It is more of an expressive sensibility favouring novelty and individuality, which energizes facets of both economic production and personal consumption.

There are a number of important reasons why any analysis of contemporary culture must come to grips with the logic of fashion and its centrality to our everyday experiences. In general, fashion is fundamental to culture because it offers **aesthetic** forms in fields such as dress and clothing, philosophy and religion, music, habits and customs, through which individuals attach to, or demonstrate their difference from, various communities. As a cultural process, fashion is responsible for locating individuals within a constantly changing forest of objects, people, events, styles and practices to which they relate, about which they form opinions and which symbolically help to locate them within various social strata and communities. In this way, being 'in fashion', indifferent to it or actively claiming to reject fashion becomes an important technique for individuals to establish their social difference and individuality.

Fashion is elemental to our economies because it plays a significant part in energizing innovations, mobilizing design and aesthetic industries, and providing an ongoing impetus for creative economic production. Furthermore, fashion objects – whether they be clothes, shoes or items of furniture – allow us direct contact with the politics and economics of global economic systems, and provide a potential material site for people to consider questions of excess consumption, labour exploitation, the form of beauty or good more broadly, and potentially oppressive or alienating representations of embodiment and identity. Finally, whether it is expressed in the form of clothing or ideas, fashion represents an important set of resources or technologies for individuals to transform or change themselves; curiously, fashion both oppresses and liberates them, making them at once individuals and also a part of the social collective.

To help us think about what fashion is, we first need to dispel from our minds the idea that fashion is just about clothing, and especially *haute couture*, or the clothing of fashion show runways. Though clothing is a very visible and prominent example of the fashion dynamic at work, the logic of fashion infuses all aspects of our culture, from the shape, colour and style of motor cars to what we drink, eat and wear, our religious and philosophical beliefs, our use of technology and gadgets, what we read and listen to, the names children are given and even what types of pets we keep. The sociologist Georg Simmel (1997a), writing in a famous essay published over a century ago, noted this broader dimension of fashion as type of cultural logic, pointing out that fashion was not just about clothing styles, but was in fact a basic process that propelled modern life, and in turn its structuring of the psycho-social development of the modern person. In a more abstract sense, fashion, tastes and personal style represent much more than merely clothes, home decoration or jewellery: they are fundamental processes that form the individual, allowing them to belong to a group, but also to feel and communicate their uniqueness. Processes of conflict, compromise, elevation and adaption, imitation, acceptance and rejection are all part of the fashion dynamic, serving a basic sociological dialectic: uniformity versus individuality; generality and belonging to a group versus differentiation and uniqueness.

Defining fashion and its conceptual relatives

In this section, we will consider some elementary understandings of fashion, its relationships to clothes and dress, and also a range of other terms to which it is related. In what is the most famous – and still very relevant – sociological statement on the nature of fashion, Georg Simmel (1997a) situates fashion away from any one realm of social life and argues that fashion refers to a general phenomenon of all modern societies. In essence, fashion is a type of social horizon point where individual interests come up against the collective, and where the stability and conservatism of social customs are challenged by new and innovative aesthetic and behavioural forms. In Simmel's sense, fashion can thus be represented by any object – whether it be clothes, ideas or habits – but in essence it refers to any field of social action where the dynamic, sometimes antagonistic process of individual formation and collective integration is evident. To quote Simmel:

> fashion represents nothing more than one of the many forms of life by the aid of which we seek to combine . . . the tendency toward social equalization with the desire for individual differentiation and change.
>
> (Simmel 1997a: 543)

Other theorists define fashion more centrally within the realm of clothing – specifically the way clothing presents, shapes and narrates the human body. Entwistle (2000) defines fashion generally as a system of dress found in **modernity** – that is, a social system for encoding the presentation of bodies. From her perspective, fashion is a form of dress that essentially concerns the body – how it is presented and dressed, how it performs, and what messages it contains and represents. Entwistle comments:

> Fashion is about bodies: it is produced, promoted and worn by bodies. It is the body that fashion speaks to and it is the body that is presented in almost all social encounters . . . Fashionable dress is dress that embodies the latest aesthetic; it is dress defined at a given moment as desirable, beautiful, popular. In articulating the latest aesthetic, and in making available certain kinds of clothes, fashion provides the 'raw material' of daily dress.
>
> (Entwistle 2000: 1)

Likewise, Diana Crane's (2000) study principally locates fashion within the domain of clothing, which she highlights as providing rich insights into both norms of appropriateness and convention, and their possible breach through the abundant variety of clothing alternatives that are on offer. She thus takes clothing to be a particularly salient indicator of social categories like gender, class and social status, but also a particularly malleable and effective form for negotiating or even subverting the **symbolic boundaries** that define these categories. Being at the crucible of social change, playing with taboos around identities, the display of flesh and presentation of the body, fashionable clothing is an especially powerful and compelling form of communication. As an example, think of any musician of the last few decades who has caused shock in part through the messages their dress communicates about their body, sexuality and political values – David Bowie, Madonna, Marilyn Manson and Lady Gaga come to mind as key examples.

The anthropologist and linguist Edward Sapir (1931) agrees that clothing, being the field of expression most closely linked to the body and identity, may perhaps be the natural field for considering fashion, though he concedes that it can also exist in a range of other everyday fields such as furniture and leisure forms. Reflecting upon the phenomenon of fashion, Sapir (1931: 143) takes an interesting approach by linking fashion with the psyche, noting that 'fashion concerns itself closely with the ego'. Making the point that utility has a lesser priority in systems of fashion, he states: 'Functional irrelevance as contrasted with symbolic significance for the expressiveness of the ego is implicit in all fashion' (Sapir 1931: 144). Sapir's point suggests that an interesting route for us to use to think about fashion is through psychology and psychoanalytic frames, related to the drive to establish and communicate identity through embodied performance. For Sapir, fashion is properly located in the domain of the ego. We will consider this idea, and a range of other cultural explanations on offer, later in the chapter.

The social and cultural powers of fashion

We can think of fashion as a type of cultural resource, which is used by social actors to accomplish various aspects of identity, to differentiate and integrate themselves within communities, and to symbolize various ideals and values. These key dimensions of fashion are considered in the following section of the chapter.

Individual differentiation and collective

Perhaps the most powerful trick of fashion – and it is literally a kind of ideological trick – is to allow individuals to feel singular, unique and different, as though they are 'in fashion', somehow being a leader, specially charged or at the cutting edge. Yet to be 'in fashion', one must submit oneself to social processes, meaning that one must first belong to the group in order to differentiate oneself from it.

Fashion as a dynamic process

Another dimension of fashion is that it is a constantly moving process. Thus, while 'skinny jeans' or technological gadgets such as the iPod and iPad might seem so indispensable that they will remain an utterly essential accoutrement into the distant future, of course they are inevitably superseded relatively quickly by other forms that are functionally or aesthetically differentiated in ways which make them more desirable fashion objects. Some of the classical theories of fashion suggest that this movement follows a 'trickle-down' pattern, whereby the upper classes are the fashion leaders and fashions slowly trickle down to the middle classes. However, while fashions do move about society, they do not have to move in this way, as we shall discuss later in the chapter. Things can be said to have their own biography, as the anthropologist Kopytoff (1986) points out – akin to a type of life-course trajectory. Thus we could map the life course of fashion objects, from their birth, rise to fashionable status, inevitable decline to death and then their possible rebirth via later moments of the fashion cycle some years down the line.

Fashion as volatile container and communicator of cultural ideals

A further key power of fashion lies in fusing various aspects of social and cultural life into an object, style or idea. Fashion is a very powerful container, which allows its possessor to feel as if they are somehow at the very heart of a powerful cultural movement or force (Holt 2004; Wernick 1991). Whether a fresh colour, a visible brand motif, a discreet label only seen by the wearer, an inventive shape, cut or style, or something also worn or endorsed by a celebrity or esteemed fashion exemplar, the fashion object can be transformative – or indeed take on talismanic qualities – for individuals (Lightfoot 1997). At its heart, this container performs the powerful cultural trick of convincing its possessor that they are somehow unique, or belong to a small and privileged group of those who know or own such an object.

Fashion objects as mobile objects

Fashion is characterized by various spatio-temporal mobilities. In a spatial sense, fashion circulates local objects, aesthetics and practices globally. For example, the clothing fashions of Tokyo, Milan or New York circulate way beyond their place of origin. The inherently visual aspects of much fashion and many fashionable places, people and events allow them to be transmitted very quickly as image through the Internet, via blogs or photo-sharing sites, or magazines. As well, the global fashion system is also structured at a micro or local level. It happens on streets, in clubs and in shops, and relies on networks of interconnected users – designers, buyers, shoppers, blogs, magazines, music and television – for its dissemination. Fashion is also temporally structured, given its cyclical nature. Such cycles are not time-specific – some are shorter or longer than others.

The cultural mechanisms and functions of fashion

We consider three major theoretical models for understanding fashion. The first, best represented by classical modern theories of fashion in the work of Georg Simmel (1997a) and Thorstein Veblen (1899), articulates an elite–mass model of taste that relies heavily on notions of emulation, class distinction, imitation and conspicuousness. The second major model, marked by Herbert Blumer's (1969) article on collective tastes, emphasizes the communal and interactional negotiation of style and taste, apart from the need for distinction and emulation. The final model, most powerfully captured in the work of Pierre Bourdieu (1984), emphasizes the role of fashion objects as forms of cultural capital and social distinction, which are unevenly distributed through society and act to reproduce social inequalities.

Display, imitation and the elite–mass dynamic: Simmel and Veblen

As is the case with much of his oeuvre, Simmel's analysis of fashion and style is essentially an attempt to understand processes that propelled modernity, and in turn their impact on the psycho-social development of the modern person. Fashion and style, therefore, came to represent much more than merely clothes, home decoration or the adornment of jewellery; they were fundamental processes in individual formation, with fundamental social contours. Processes of conflict, compromise, elevation and adaption all serve the basic Simmelian dialectic: generality/uniformity versus individuality/differentiation. Simmel (1997a: 194) saw fashion as a kind of public playing out of taste mechanisms – it was a domain where levels of public taste were constantly established, then superseded. Imitation was a fundamental component of this process, because it was the central practice or technique for individuals to orient themselves to the social through imitating the styles and fashions of others. Because it sometimes involved reflection and mindless copying, Simmel (1997a: 188) characterized this central component of fashion as at once 'a child of thought and thoughtlessness'. For the modern person, imitation was not only a negative thing, for it did free the individual from the responsibility of maintaining self and the work of generating an authentic individual style. However, in the process of copying, the modern imitator forfeited creativity and genuine self-purpose. The modern fashion imitator was merely a 'vessel of social contexts', meaning a vessel of other people's choices (Simmel 1997a: 188).

Given that imitation was such a fundamental process in fashion, and hence a charac-teristic force of modernity as well, there must be a social group whose fashions served as models available to be imitated. It is because of this important demarcation between those who set the fashion agenda and those who follow that Simmel's analysis of fashion is largely a class-based model of emulation, where the lower classes constantly seek to imitate upper-class fashions. What Simmel goes on to argue is that fashion, in its purest form (that is, its latest version), is the domain of the upper classes. Technically, the lower class can possess few genuine fashions of their own, and thus perpetually occupy the role of imitator most easily. Because fashion is the relentless striving for a social balance between differentiation and integration, fashions constantly change as the lower classes effectively begin to imitate the fashions of the upper classes. The ruthless striving for difference is frantic, though it is a one-way process only – in Simmel's classical model, the lower classes routinely look to the upper classes for the direction of fashion. Fashion is thus a supremely modern tool for differentiation that has a unique power to set in place a class-based dialectic of destruction and creative vitality ultimately based upon zero-sum principles:

> The very character of fashion demands that it should be exercised at one time only by a portion of the given group, the great majority being merely on the road to adopting it. As soon as an example has been universally adopted, that is, as soon as anything that was originally done by only a few has really come to be practiced by all – as is the case in certain portions of our apparel and in various forms of social conduct – we no longer speak of fashion. As fashion spreads, it gradually goes to its doom.
>
> (Simmel, 1997a: 547)

In Thorstein Veblen's *The Theory of the Leisure Class* (1899) there is a more vulgar, witty and venomous expression of the same elite–mass emulation model developed by Simmel. However, while Simmel impresses with craftsmanship, subtlety and sociological force in the proposition of a class-based model of emulation, Veblen 'grinds away'

(Davis 1994: 111) relentlessly on the central idea of pecuniary honour – that is, the link between money and our evaluation of beauty. Veblen's work is a frequently entertaining and caustic dissection of pecuniary tastes in a variety of popular domains – flowers, lawns and pastures, animals and clothing are his main targets. Shots at contemporary fashion are rife. Both Veblen and Simmel, however, tend to share a vision of public taste that is fundamentally charged by distinctions of class and the psychological attraction of aesthetic difference that sheer volumes of money can cultivate.

Communities of fashion followers: negotiating the cool and beautiful

By way of contrast, Blumer's (1969) theory of fashion offers a more nuanced treatment of fashion and taste mechanisms than the work of earlier theorists. While class differentiation was seen to drive fashion in conventional accounts, using an **interactionist** approach, Blumer sought to elaborate a collective, almost market-driven dimension as the key element in the fashion and taste dynamic. In the first place, Blumer's analysis is an invitation to sociologists to take fashion seriously, and to grant it a significant place in any theorization of modernity. While Simmel (1997a: 203) was also cognizant of the way fashion increasingly was manifested in diverse social forms associated with the modern economy, Blumer's analysis – over half a century later – showed a more keen sense of how aesthetic work was becoming crucial to economic progress, and in some ways is a prefiguring of contemporary notions of **aestheticization** (see Featherstone 1990a; Lash and Urry 1994). The core of Blumer's (1969) case is his critique of Simmel's famous essay on fashion, and the proposition of a different model of fashion, which essentially posited a unique conception of the interactional mechanisms that shape fashions. The essence of Blumer's theory is that fashion and taste are formed collectively through a series of interactional chains, rather than set by privileged elites as Simmel had earlier suggested.

On the basis of **ethnographic** observation of the women's fashion industry in Paris, Blumer (1969: 278) identified a key feature of fashion to be 'an intensive process of selection'. Buyers in the industry developed a sharpened sense of discrimination, 'which guided and sensitized their perceptions, and which channelled their judgements and choices' (Blumer 1969: 279). What Blumer identified in the buyers was evidence of a common sense of the direction of public taste – a reading of codes, symbols and values inherent in new fashions, which involved both an orientation to, and extension of, accepted fashions and tastes. In Simmel's earlier version of the mechanism of taste and fashion, the elite are centrally important as they determine the direction of public tastes. In contrast, Blumer characterized the elite as incorporated into the emergence of new forms as much as the lower classes. They have a desire to be acceptable to emergent forms of public taste – *to be in fashion* is the key motivation. The following quotation from Blumer puts his argument directly:

> The fashion mechanism appears not in response to a need of class differentiation and class emulation but in response to a wish to be in fashion, to be abreast of what has good standing, to express new tastes which are emerging in a changing world. These are the changes that seem to be called for in Simmel's formulation. They are fundamental changes. They shift

fashion from the fields of class differentiation to the area of collective selection and center its mechanism in the process of such selection. This process of collective selection represents an effort to choose from among competing styles or models those which match developing tastes, those which 'click', or those which – to revert to my friends, the buyers – 'are stunning'.

(Blumer 1969: 282)

The taste for fashion: the materialization of social class

Prominent French sociologist Pierre Bourdieu (1984) offers not a theory of fashion, but complex theories of social tastes and a set of cultural concepts and theories for thinking about fashion. The first point to note about Bourdieu's understanding of taste is that it is manifested in everything people do and possess. He observes that taste is 'the basis of all that one has – people and things – and all that one is for others' (Bourdieu 1984: 56). That is, taste is not something reserved just for discussion of 'legitimate' painting, music or literature that is produced and consumed principally by what might be called the 'dominant' aesthetic classes. Rather, taste decisions are exercised in all social and personal domains across all social classes. This includes practical arts like fashion, hairstyles, home decoration and food preparation, along with leisure activities like reading, sport and cinema. In aggregate, the sum of these practices represents people's 'tastes'. As well as this, the bottom line of taste practice for Bourdieu (1984: 190) is manifested in the way people present their bodies: 'the body is the most indisputable materialization of class taste'. The body is a fundamental site for the expression of taste through clothing and hairstyles, objects of adornment, speech and manner. Additionally, the dimensions and shapes of the body as presented to others reveal the **embodied** nature of taste – for example, dimensions like body volume and weight, shape and posture are clues to the social conditions that manifest them and the attitudes people hold towards their own body. For Bourdieu, then, taste is a universal practice because it applies to all classes of people across social groups, and it is also an inevitable practice because participation in the social world requires expressions and commitments of taste, whether social actors are aware of such commitments or not.

Two important principles follow as a result of Bourdieu's assertion that taste plays a role in determining all our interactions in the social and material world. The first is that the practice of taste takes on an appearance of being a 'natural' judgement. Judgements of taste are so routinely pervasive in everyday life, and are determined to such an extent by people's conditions of existence, that separating social relations from aesthetic judgements becomes difficult. In this way, taste judgements in Bourdieu's model come to serve as an aesthetic playing out of social relations. Since tastes are so thoroughly incorporated into people's ways of being, acting and seeing in consumer society, they take on a 'natural' appearance and feel.

The second consequence of the chronic nature of taste judgements in consumer society is that there is a larger 'economy' of preference decisions available to be understood by the researcher. The economy of cultural goods is manifested in two ways for the researcher. First, it is identifiable in the particular combinations of cultural objects that classes of people consume. Second, in Bourdieu's analysis, other social classes relate to cultural objects in socially unique ways. For example, the bourgeois classes' mode of consumption attempts to emphasize authenticity and naturalness in their relation to culture, as though it were made especially for them. Alternately, the working-class aesthetic is dominated by a rejection of aestheticization and the cultivation of an art of living that is founded in modesty, pragmatism and simplicity.

The cultural economy of contemporary fashion: making and circulating fashion objects

The thrust of the classical approach to understanding fashion was about the social and cultural uses and effects of fashion, as opposed to studies of the properties of fashion itself, and its embeddedness and constitution in various social and personal spheres. As we saw in the previous sections of this chapter, sociology typically has theorized fashion as an aesthetic category for social differentiation and distinction. In the theories of Simmel, Veblen and Bourdieu, the role of fashion is basically representational in nature. It is a form of social communication that is socially available and visible, though unevenly distributed across social strata according to patterns of wealth, education, learning and the possession of cultural skills. More recently, a number of new approaches to fashion have developed. While sociologists have not abandoned this earlier conceptualization of fashion, these new approaches have emerged in response to rapid social changes related to what has been called the aestheticization and culturalization of the economy (Du Gay and Pryke 2002).

The increasing production of aesthetic goods

The predominance of commodification processes, the increasing importance assigned to displaying viable social identities and the cultural dominance of consumption are intrinsic counterparts to these processes, emphasizing what has been labelled the 'culturalizing' of the economy. Fredric Jameson (1998, 1991) was one of the first to highlight the widespread incorporation of aesthetic elements into commodity production, a trend that signifies postmodern tendencies regarding the breakdown of distinctions between high culture and mass culture as commodities become more like art and vice versa, and the increasing importance of aesthetic and narrative codes for successful commodity production. Thus objects that circulate in consumer society – including the examples used by Jameson (1998: 124) of clothes, furniture and buildings – are aestheticized as new waves of consumption are framed through design, style and art. The quantitative change in this sphere has been an 'immense dilation in the sphere of commodities, and a quantum leap in the aestheticization of reality' (Jameson 1998: 124). The iPod is perhaps the most outstanding recent example of this process of the aestheticization of the commodity: a minimalist, smooth, sleek white square that is accompanied by a rich seam of narrative and mythic gloss which, for many people, has become an essential personal and lifestyle accoutrement. The same can be said for many commodities with which we engage, whether they are motor vehicles, bicycles, shoes, tennis rackets or various types of food and drink objects. The most successful and memorable of these objects combine striking and powerful aesthetics with equally effective narrative and mythical traits.

The obvious currency here is the brand, a relatively new composite type of communicative object that, through the power of storylines, has the potential to make objects appear powerful – even magical (Holt 2004).

Brand objects

In studies of fashion, this link between cultural, aesthetic and economic activity is most clear in the branded object. The brand is probably the most important aspect of fashion, having a capacity to communicate a universe of meaning for consumers through simple visual and aesthetic forms such as a word or a colour (Holt 2004). Think of any popular shoe brand, for example – Nike, Adidas, Converse, Asics, Puma, among many others. Each is not just a simple shoe, but carries a much longer and richer history of storylines and narrative established by previous brand work, such as advertising, brand ambassadors or event sponsorship, giving it meaning and currency for consumers. From the perspective of consumers, what distinguishes one from another is rarely the technical features of the shoe, but price along with facets of the appeal of branding combined with aesthetic features. The broader point to be drawn here is that objects of fashion, or any successful or hip consumer object, are not just made in factories or workshops by industrialists who do nothing apart from produce or make such objects. On the contrary, production within many fields of economic activity must be thoroughly 'culturalized'. Any successful producer must master not just the production process efficiencies as they are understood rather narrowly in economics textbooks, but they must also understand the cultural work of communication necessary to establish their object as viable, desirable or necessary in the imaginations of consumers.

Networked objects

The realization of a fashion object – be it any item of clothing or footwear, a piece of technology or otherwise – from the stages of planning and conceptualization, through production, distribution, sale and consumption, is a thoroughly cultural activity. What makes it so? A large network of actors plays a part in bringing fashion objects into being: financiers and backers, producers, designers, people who source fabrics and new styles, workers in factories or workshops, advertisers, models, retail workers and, finally, consumers. In a famous study of what he called 'artworlds', Becker (1984) came to a similar conclusion, which can help us to understand the production of fashion objects. Becker points out that it is the collective physical, mental, cultural and economic effort of a range of people that brings aesthetic objects into being. This is sometimes very much physical, in transforming raw or processed materials into value-added objects, but also interpretive, collective and aesthetic due to its organization of the efforts of designers, artists and, in some cases, even 'cool hunters' who might be hired to ethnographically uncover the rules of certain consumer communities. At all stages, economic production processes must fuse the material design of an object with the rules of cultural myth and narrative if that object is to achieve success in the market (Belk, Wallendorf and Sherry

1989). Furthermore, there is no longer just one mass market, but markets stratified by as many cultural markers as one might imagine, from the obvious ones like age, income and gender through to more complex factors related to perceptions of authenticity, branding, celebrity endorsement or celebrity design. As Schulz (2008: 386) puts it in her review of the new cultural economies of fashion, 'this makes culture and economics amalgams: the realm of one is always influenced by the other'.

Drawing inspiration from street and youth culture

A further key development that needs to be taken into account in the circulation of fashion is the importance of street culture and Internet cultures. In fact, these are a reason for sociologists to rethink the classical theories of Simmel and Veblen discussed earlier in this chapter, which positioned fashion as driven by a class dynamic, underpinned by the desire of the upper class to materially communicate their difference and the desire of the middle class to use aesthetic goods as proof of their rising economic fortunes. These days, fashion is more likely to spring from youth cultures, working-class culture or socially marginalized groups which have acquired cultural capital that is ripe for mining by fashion producers. Fashion from the origins of the punk era in the 1970s is an excellent example, particularly the case of the designer Vivienne Westwood. Now a major fashion brand on high streets and upmarket malls around the world, Westwood started out producing her clothes inspired by punk themes of bondage, shock and sex, using everyday objects such as razor blades and safety pins. A participant in the punk subcultural scene, Westwood introduced the fashion motifs of the disenfranchised world of British youth to an increasingly middle-class clientele. Hers was an aesthetic of shock, which worked in part because it took everyday objects out of their usual contexts and also because it used materials, colours and styles that were unusual and often considered extreme. These were the central characteristics of punk fashion (Hebdige 1979). Over the last few decades, Westwood has continued to draw from and develop these fashion themes. Ironically, having started out giving material expression to the feelings of disenfranchisement and alienation driving punk culture, Westwood's designs remain challenging but are now very sought after, exclusive and expensive. Tellingly – and from this fact we can begin to think about the links between fashion, media and celebrity culture – one of Westwood's dresses features in a wedding scene in the movie *Sex and the City*.

In a similar way, we can see fashion designers and marketers drawing extensively from youth, street, sporting and working-class culture to generate contemporary fashion objects. For example, the ubiquitous denim jeans started as tough and durable outfitting for miners, and were first patented in America by German immigrant Levi Strauss in 1873. Worn by agricultural and industrial workers through the first half of the twentieth century as an item of long-lasting workwear, denim jeans were then appropriated by young people in the 1950s, who wore denim more expressively and with communicative intent. In symbolic contrast to earlier generations, for whom denim was tough and long-lasting, for young people denim jeans register their modern ideals of leisure, freedom and autonomy (see Miller and Woodward 2007; Sullivan 2006). The fashion industry has also directly been inspired by sport and music cultures. The sneaker is perhaps the most striking example in this regard. In sneaker stores of today, we see a huge range of styles and models, many having been revived by shoemakers who recycle models from the 1970s and 1980s. Reproducing such models recalls the original context of the shoe, often in sports such as basketball or wrestling, but inserts it into a contemporary fashion logic where the wearer may have only minimal knowledge of the shoe's sporting past, but places value on its general sense of wearing part of cultural history. Linked to famous sponsored sports stars – Michael Jordan or Kobe Bryant, for example, who have both had Nike models designed in their name – the sporting shoe has been incorporated into logics of collectorship, scarcity and prestige, a highly visible communicator of cultural affiliation when worn on the street or perhaps stored in pristine condition in its original box as a collector's item.

Mapping the consumer: producing and projecting desire

Let us put this dimension of fashion into a broader context related to aspects of its production. During the latter half of the twentieth century, a key element behind the construction of notions of consumer desirability, fashionability and style came from the burgeoning marketing and advertising industries of the era. This was not necessarily a simple case of advertisers exploiting the aimless and easily malleable desires of mindless consumers, but a project combining efforts in scientific disciplines of psychology, economics and the emergent sciences of management, which sought to know and understand the consumer in increasingly deep ways (Miller and Rose 1997). The goal of these new disciplines of consumer research was to map the subjectivities, habits and souls of consumers in order to better understand their relationship to particular commodities, and to broader ideals of lifestyle. The techniques for coming to know the desires of consumers were those of scientific study: social surveys, focus groups, psychological testing and emotion and brain activation testing allowed producers to know how, when and perhaps why their products had gained consumer attention.

This era was the birthplace of the consumer science disciplines, which are now widely integrated into academic disciplines such as marketing within universities. As Miller and Rose (1997) put it, what happened over time was the development of a 'passional economy', where sciences of knowing the consumer developed in line with brands that could effectively communicate to particular groups of consumers new products and new objects of desire. In the past, psychologically oriented research that was individualistic in style and also frequently quantitative and abstract in nature played a major role, but now much consumer research is almost a type of applied cultural sociology, utilizing ethnographic, visual and embodied techniques for knowing consumers. The larger result of all this is that consumers have entered a world where enchantment, seduction and entering meaningful relationships with various commodities are just as common as the cycle's downside – dissatisfaction, the loss of efficacy and disposal of the commodity, which go hand in hand with the search for things new and fresh. The passional economy constructs such cycles of pleasure as commonplace, and it is the perpetual restlessness of consumer desires that forms an important psycho-social basis of commodity capitalism (Illouz 2009). In recent years the iPod is perhaps the best example of this.

Contemporary social spaces for representing fashion: the street and the online blog

A very important contemporary dimension of fashion is the prevalence of so-called street fashion cultures, or 'street style'. Street style refers to the way specific fashion codes and fashions become associated with particular parts of our cities (Woodward 2009). Often based on music subcultures and the idea that certain 'types' of people inhabit particular geographic zones within our cities, street style becomes an important narrative informing our collective engagement with the city. The idea we have that certain parts of the city demand particular sartorial and cultural knowledges leads us to dress in ways that 'fit in', allowing us to participate smoothly within a social scene. A simple example of this tendency is that black-coloured clothing and denim are predominantly worn by audiences at rock gigs. A more complex example involves particular street scenes in parts of cities, such as Camden in London, Harajuku in Tokyo or Venice Beach in Los Angeles. Each is famous for a particular style of dress and cultural scene, known widely by locals and visitors alike. In fact, in the case of a place like Harajuku in Tokyo, street scenes become known very widely as an epicentre of youth subcultural activity. The street in Harajuku called Takeshita-Dori, for example, and the entrance to Yoyogi Park by Harajuku railway station, are widely known for being places where young people congregate to hang out, often dressed in very elaborate, decorative fashion ensembles (Kawamura 2006). As cautioned by Woodward (2009), such vibrant street scenes are not the norm, and for the most part people are led to make very modest and small-scale fashion innovations and differentiations. Furthermore, they do so using an ensemble of clothes that reflects things such as their budget and access to shops. Recycling and reusing clothing, combining high-street stock style with small creative flair, is much more common than purchasing something exclusive or new.

In conjunction with burgeoning and popular global street scenes, the last decade has seen fashion influenced heavily by the rise of the street blogger. Perhaps most notable here is 'The Sartorialist', a most influential and popular blog run by a fashion photographer and entrepreneur who photographs stylish, fashionable individuals in his travels around the world's fashion centres – principally Milan, Paris and New York. Another blog called 'The Selby' reproduces photographs of home interiors and the fashionable, creative individuals who have made them.

Conclusion

This chapter has shown how fashion is a unique and powerful force in social life. Fashion is a type of meeting point where, often through aesthetic and decorative forms, the individual confronts collective social forces, and where custom and taken-for-granted tradition meet the new, challenging and even shocking. Far from being mundane facets of individual choice, matters such as how low and baggy one's jeans are worn, whether one chooses to cover one's face in public, how short one wears a skirt, or the colour one dyes one's hair, really do have capacity to provoke, challenge and mobilize political, ethical and social action. In reviewing theories of fashion, this chapter has shown that sociologists typically emphasize the representational dimensions of fashion, especially the capacity of decorative novelty and innovation to symbolize social and cultural distance between groups in society. Thus, fashion has often been seen as the domain in which the upper class are able to demonstrate their dominance over other social classes, who constantly strive to imitate and catch up to those at the forefront of fashion. While this competitive dimension of fashion still exists to some degree, this chapter has also shown how sociologists have had to revise their theories of fashion, given the rapid social and cultural changes of the last 30 years. Things such as the Internet, the growing visibility of youth culture and the rise of the youth consumer, which have been complemented and driven by growth in the media and music industries, the increased emphasis on the aesthetic component of economic production, the growth of energetic and expressive street and working-class cultures and refinements in the way culture is made and marketed – for example, through celebrity icons – have meant that theories of fashion have had to engage with a much broader theoretical palette in order to remain relevant. In the contemporary mode of global capitalism, which is to a significant degree culturalized and aestheticized, such theoretical innovations are surely crucial to any complete theory of society.

Review questions

12.1 Discuss the shift from class and status to the street and celebrity culture as the principal generator of fashion in contemporary society.

12.2 What is the difference between fashion, style, taste and custom? In what ways might these concepts be related?

12.3 How is fashion linked to space and place? Use an example from your own town or city to illustrate this aspect of fashion.

12.4 Use current examples to discuss how fashion has a moral dimension.

12.5 How might fashion become a social resource for achieving symbolic domination or, alternatively, resistance?

Further reading

Bourdieu, P. (1984) *Distinction: A Social Critique of the Judgement of Taste*, Routledge, London.

Crane, D. (2000) *Fashion and Its Social Agendas: Class, Gender and Identity in Clothing*, University of Chicago Press, Chicago.

Entwistle, J. (2000) *The Fashioned Body: Fashion, Dress and Modern Social Theory*, Polity Press, Cambridge.

Holt, D.B. (2004) *How Brands Become Icons: The Principles of Cultural Branding*, Harvard Business School Press, Boston.

Jameson, F. (1998) Postmodernism and the consumer society, in *The Cultural Turn: Selected Writings on the Postmodern, 1983–1998* (F. Jameson), Verso, London, pp. 1–20.

Miller, P. and Rose, N. (1997) Mobilizing the consumer: assembling the subject of consumption. *Theory, Culture and Society*, 14 (1), 1–36.

Veblen, T. (1899[1934]) *The Theory of the Leisure Class: An Economic Study of Institutions*, Unwin, London.

13

Food, Eating and Culture

Learning objectives

- To examine how cultural sociology can understand food and eating today, especially as these are informed by processes of globalization.
- To understand the cultural dimensions of food crises and risks that increasingly plague global food systems.
- To assess the degree to which global food homogenization is promoted by 'McDonaldizing' socio-economic forces.
- To discern how globalization may promote the complexification of food identities and practices.

Introduction

Tell me what you eat, and I will tell you who you are.

(Alexis Soyer)

The words of the world's first celebrity chef, the nineteenth-century Frenchman Alexis Soyer, continue to ring true today. What a person eats tells us a very great deal about them – not just their tastes and their pleasures, their aspirations and their everyday routines, but also their sense of themselves, their gender, ethnicity, social class and many other things besides. Food is a real goldmine for the cultural sociologist, as it can reveal many aspects of a person, a social group and a society. How they eat, what they eat, how their food is made and distributed, their culinary passions and their dietary aversions – consideration of these sorts of matters can demonstrate many of the most fundamental aspects of both people and societies.

Cultural Sociology: An Introduction, First Edition. Les Back et al. © 2012 Les Back, Andy Bennett, Laura Desfor Edles, Margaret Gibson, David Inglis, Ronald Jacobs and Ian Woodward. Published 2012 by Blackwell Publishing Ltd.

This is because food is never just a physical and material object. It is also invested with profound symbolic significance. How a group or society defines a particular foodstuff may be radically different from how another group or society defines it. Contemporary Americans, Britons and Australasians would baulk at eating horse, but horsemeat is a familiar ingredient in certain parts of Italy, France and Belgium, national societies that are otherwise not too culturally distant from the English-speaking world. Like most foodstuffs that are, or have been, eaten in different parts of the world, there is nothing intrinsically dangerous to humans about horsemeat. Whether it is loved or loathed is a matter of cultural definition.

Each human group has its own distinctive, culturally shaped food likes and dislikes. Whether a particular food is avoided or adored owes little to biology and much to culture. Where, when and by whom a particular food is eaten, and how it is prepared for consumption, is very much marked by cultural forces (Douglas 1966). The Jewish and Islamic prohibitions on certain kinds of food consumption, such as eating pork, are well known. But every human group has its own ways of encouraging the consumption of some foods, and restricting – even banning outright – the eating of others (Leach 1964). Studying the specific nature of cultural rules and definitions to do with food – about what is edible and what is not, who can eat certain things and who cannot, when some items are to be eaten and when not – reveals much about the ideas, values, assumptions, practices and institutions of the social groups who have invented and live by those rules (Simmel 1997b).

The symbolically highly loaded nature of food makes it an ideal subject for cultural sociology, which is concerned primarily with the meanings and values that groups of people project on to the world around them, and how in turn those meanings and values (generally understood by the people involved as just 'natural' and not human creations at all) come to affect profoundly how those people think and act. People create cultures that invest foods with meaning, but the meanings of food then come to have wide-ranging effects on what those people think and do. Because its nature is always culturally informed, food can only be understood fully by the kinds of analyses that put culture and meaning at the forefront of their concerns, like cultural sociology.

Foodstuffs can still be studied usefully in ways that do not stress their cultural dimensions. Many social scientists concern themselves with considerations of the more 'material' aspects of food production and consumption – for example, analysing the dynamics of national, regional and world markets in food production (McMichael 1994). Cultural sociologists, as well as others such as anthropologists, tend to focus much more on micro-level contexts of food preparation and eating, endeavouring to unpack the symbolic and meaningful dimensions of food-related activities, such as how meals are organized according to specific cultural conventions (Inglis, Gimlin and Thorpe 2007). However, cultural sociology can also be used to examine how macro-level, 'material' factors in food production impact upon more micro-level 'symbolic' processes and, crucially, how the latter can impact upon the former in important ways.

In this chapter, we will see how cultural sociology can understand food and eating today, especially as these are informed by processes of globalization (see Chapter 9). The main issues to be examined are the cultural dimensions of food crises and risks that increasingly plague global food systems; alleged global food homogenization caused by so-called 'McDonaldizing' socio-economic forces; and apparent food heterogenization and changing food identities and practices. We will see how the cultural sociology of food gives us sophisticated understandings of many of the most crucial aspects of present-day food consumption, and the increasingly complex global cultural conditions within which eating takes place today.

Food crises and cultural definitions

People's food conditions vary radically across the world, from the African and Asian peasant facing constant near-starvation to the affluent urban Westerner enjoying an apparent surfeit of food products from every part of the globe (Humphery 1998). Under conditions of advanced globalization (see Chapter 9), these diverse conditions are profoundly connected with each other: the food wealth of some parts of the world is made possible by, and exists side by side with, the food poverty of other parts (Chossudovsky 2008).

However, even for the relatively rich populations living in North America, Europe, Australasia and parts of Asia, contemporary food conditions are still problematic. Over the last 30 years, the increasingly globalized food production systems upon which people in these regions rely have become ever more subject to crises that can have long-term, often highly destabilizing, effects. From pandemics among animal populations such as swine flu and chicken flu, through BSE ('mad cow disease') and outbreaks of foot-and-mouth disease, to ethical and health concerns about factory-farmed animals, genetically modified crops and world agriculture's contribution to environmental crises like global warming, food production across the world today is in a state of rupture, uncertainty and ambivalence (Fischler 1999). These are all hallmarks of what the German sociologist Ulrich Beck (1992) calls 'world risk society', a planet-encompassing condition whereby human activities create problems that can spiral out of control, beyond the reach of any particular institution to deal with them effectively. A sense of constant crisis prevails, especially as attempts to solve certain problems can rebound, generating further crises.

These crises are part of a globalized, although unevenly integrated, food production system that stretches across the whole planet. This system has been developing since at least the late nineteenth century (Friedmann 1994). Rapid and massive urbanization in Europe and North America created a situation whereby constantly expanding urban populations needed to be fed. Agriculture was transformed to keep up with rising demand, involving such innovations as the development of mass agricultural and livestock production systems (that is, factory farms), the application of innovative scientific knowledge to both animals and crops in order to encourage ever greater yields, the **massification** and rationalization of animal-breeding techniques and slaughtering systems, and the development of international food transportation systems (for example, cattle-rearing in Brazil and Argentina) for Western consumption (Fernandez-Armesto 2001). All of these originally European and North American innovations have come to have increasingly world-level ramifications and consequences (Sobal 1999), such as the crises mentioned above, which are potentially planet-spanning in reach (*The Economist* 2008).

Even as recently as the 1970s, the globalized food production systems upon which developed world consumers rely were not widely perceived to be in constant crisis. However, these production systems are nowadays thought by many people, including food consumers, to be in severe conditions of crisis. What were once features of food production that generally remained uncommented on, such as factory farming and the keeping of food animals in very small spaces, are now very much the subjects of ethical and political contestation and controversy. While fast food – such as hamburgers – was consumed without many qualms until the 1980s, it is now the source of a series of fears about growing levels of obesity among the population in many countries, as well as being seen by many as being ethically problematic, such as in the hamburger industry's intensive cattle-farming techniques (Schlosser 2001).

Cultural sociology can help us to understand why senses of crisis and risk are now so central in the world of food production and consumption. Even apparently purely 'material' phenomena like diseases and pandemics have to be culturally processed in order for people to make sense of them. What people think phenomena like avian flu or mad cow disease 'are', and what their effects might be, are the result of cultural framing (Beck 2000). Problems faced by the globalized industrial food production system today, such as complaints and protests against factory farming, are not problems in and of themselves. They are only problems if they are defined by some people as such. The definition depends on a whole series of culturally based assumptions about what is good and bad, acceptable and unacceptable, and other ethical and moral judgements – for example, that factory farming practices are a fundamental breach of animal rights.

Cultural sociology can demonstrate that, in a relatively simple cultural context, the way in which a particular phenomenon is defined will likely be uncontroversial, as all individuals sharing a common cultural outlook will all view the issue in the same way. But in a more culturally complex situation – as applies in most cases in the world today – where there are multiple and rival ways of defining a phenomenon or issue, different groups will struggle to define the object in ways that suit their own specific interests (Bourdieu 1984). They may well seek to define it in ways that they think are 'natural' – for them, the object in question 'really is like that', and other people need to be persuaded of that fact. Thus members of the defining group may be consciously aware that they are seeking to redefine the object – for example, to show others that factory farming is morally dubious – but they may also believe that their definition is not just one way of looking at the object, but is in fact the *only* true way of looking at it (Becker 1963).

The more possible ways of defining a particular phenomenon there are in a given social context, the more uncertainty there may be for relatively uncommitted groups and individuals as to what a phenomenon really is like. A supermarket consumer today may be torn between different definitions of the food he or she buys: is the chicken on the shelf as healthy and nutritious as the food industry wants the consumer to believe, or is it to be shunned as part of the ethically abhorrent and environmentally unsustainable factory farming system, as critics of the industry would have it (Tulloch and Lupton 2002)? The more potential, and contradictory, ways there are of defining a particular food or food-related issue, the more uncertainty – and thus sense of risk and crisis – there is likely to be (Gergen 1991). In particular, the more ways that exist of categorizing certain phenomena as problems, the more problems come to 'exist' that then have to be dealt with.

These general considerations allow us to grasp one very important reason why industrial food production systems have come to be seen as increasingly in crisis over recent years. Over the last 30 years, food successfully has been redefined by different activist groups as a highly political and controversial area of human life (Fischler 1999). Due to the often very effective campaigns of animal rights and environmentalist groups in the developed world (Lien and Nerlich 2004), globalized systems of food production have been opened up to ever more public scrutiny and questioning (Nibert 2002). Concerns about such issues as animal rights and the consequences of the genetic modification of plant and animal life have become increasingly visible, being debated in the media and becoming objects of social and political concern and controversy. Thus the activities of animal rights and environmental campaign groups have very much helped to shape the now-widespread view that food production is a realm in the grip of multiple problems and crises (Macnaghten 2004).

One aspect of these developments is the undermining of the power of scientists to define for everyone what is true and false, good and bad. Previously enjoying high prestige and status, scientists and their claims are nowadays compelled to compete within a marketplace of differing views and opinions (Beck 2000). Indeed, different groups of scientists today seem (at least to food consumers) constantly to be generating contradictory findings. Scarcely a week goes by without journalists reporting scientific findings that seem to go completely against previous sets of findings about food, drink and health. Consumers today wonder what is good for their health, given the apparently huge diversity of opinions as to what foods are healthy or not, and which kinds of diets are beneficial or dangerous. As scientists no longer enjoy a monopoly on what counts as the truth about food and diet, public opinion can be strongly shaped by other groups, such as political activists. Thus the advocates of genetically modified (GM) crops, such as spokespeople for the powerful Monsanto company (one of the world's largest and most influential agricultural biotechnology companies), might in the past have had a relatively easy time convincing public opinion as to the benefits of this technology (for example, helping to eradicate famines in the developing world). But their task in this regard is much more difficult today (Keen 1999). This is because increasing public scepticism towards scientific claims means that the views of anti-biotechnology campaigners may well be taken as seriously as, if not more so than, those of industry representatives or those scientists seen to be in the pay of corporate interests (Charles 2001). People who regard themselves as ethically informed 'global citizens' may well be more receptive to the cultural framings of food matters offered by campaign groups than those offered by scientists – especially if scientists are thought to be in the pockets of large corporations (Guptill and Wilkins 2002).

Campaigners today have – at least potentially – the power to change other people's understandings of what is good or bad to eat, for health reasons or for reasons of ethics and morality, such as respecting animal rights. The Norwegian anthropologist Marianne Elizabeth Lien (2004) has shown how campaign groups working across national borders have successfully created new food taboos, encouraging people in different countries to reject the attempted defining by the meat industry of certain animals, such as kanga-roos, as fit for human consumption. Just as food production systems have become ever more transnationalized, so too have certain food prohibitions and dispositions towards what is ethically unacceptable food consumption. Classic analyses of food prohibitions (for example, Douglas 1966; Leach 1964) examined how particular small-scale, relatively homogeneous societies created and used cultural definitions of which foods were disgust-ing, polluting and dangerous. But in today's highly globalized world, groups, societies and cultural forms have all become much more complex and heterogeneous. Particular food-related groups, such as vegans, now exist in diverse places across the planet, but their members share certain food prohibitions with others like them, no matter where they happen to live. These food prohibitions have often been promoted by campaign groups carrying new ideas about food and morality across national borders, often in explicit opposition to scientists and the large corporations that run the globalized food production system. This system is today very much a realm where differing cultural definitions of edible and inedible, healthy and unhealthy, ethical and unethical are in constant conflict with each other.

Global food homogenization?

One crucial aspect of food-related activities today involves the worldwide spread of the great American food brands: Coca-Cola, Pepsi, KFC, Burger King and so on. These are alleged by their critics to eliminate totally more 'local' food cultures in their all-conquering path. No brand has been subjected to more criticism than McDonald's. Growing from one single outlet in San Bernardino, California in 1940, by the late twentieth century McDonald's had spread to 117 countries worldwide, with a new branch opening somewhere in the world every eight hours in the mid-1990s. Although this boom had subsided by the first few years of the twenty-first century, the symbolic importance of McDonald's as the great champion of the globalization of American-style fast food across the globe remains undimmed (Watson and Caldwell 2005: 2). McDonald's is often seen today as the great symbol of American-led cultural globalization, going hand in hand with the other products of alleged American 'cultural imperialism', like Hollywood films and television (Tomlinson 1997).

Perhaps the most influential contribution to the defining of McDonald's as emblematic of present-day globalized conditions is the work of US sociologist George Ritzer. For Ritzer (2000), the four central features of the McDonald's approach to food production, preparation and serving are efficiency, calculation, predictability and control. Every aspect and detail of food consumption is strictly regulated according to fine-grained measurements. This applies from the weight and size of the burgers (wholly standardized) to the methods of assembling them in restaurants (according to the same principles as a factory production line), the regulation of staff (all trained in exactly the same manner) and the control of the customers. Measures to deal with the latter in as efficient a manner as possible include the deliberate selection of uncomfortable seating in the restaurants in order to prevent consumers from lingering, thus freeing up space for the next wave of customers. Ritzer's ideas imply that in the sector of food production and consumption, such principles will become ever more important in all parts of the globe. Even if it is not the McDonald's company itself that is the actual motor of such developments, it is nonetheless these principles that increasingly will control and structure the nature of food production and consumption worldwide.

Should McDonald's, and other food chains originating in the United States like KFC and Pizza Hut, be seen as symbols and leaders of American-led cultural control and domination over the rest of the world? This would certainly be the view of those associated with the 'anti-globalization' political movement. One of the heroes of this movement, possessed of a media profile stretching far beyond the borders of his homeland, is French farmer José Bové, who famously bulldozed a branch of McDonald's France in protest at what he saw as the degradation of French culture in general, and food culture in particular, by creeping processes of Americanization (Bové, Dufour and de Casparis 2002).

A lot of the academic discussion about alleged McDonaldization of food has centred on the nature of the spatial organization of fast-food restaurants. Such spaces can plausibly be understood in terms of what the French anthropologist Marc Augé (1995) calls 'non-places' – spaces that are totally culturally **deterritorialized**, such as international hotel lobbies, and the departure lounges and duty-free stores of large airports all across the world. A McDonald's restaurant in Manchester or Philadelphia has the same sort of layout as an equivalent outlet in Moscow or Singapore. From the viewpoint of critics sympathetic to the anti-globalization movement, such places are locales where local people – especially younger people – are inculcated into Western-style eating practices, and so increasingly enticed away from more indigenous and 'local' foods and ways of eating. The same claims could also be made about American-style coffee-shop chains, the foremost of which is Starbucks, which have spread over the last 15 years or so to many countries of the world. Such spaces have been particularly enthusiastically embraced by younger, more socially aspirant social groups. A case in point here is the increasing popularity of Starbucks among younger, socially mobile people in the People's Republic of China, where 'hanging out' in Starbucks is regarded as a very cool activity (Harrison *et al.* 2005). The cultural studies scholar Tim Simpson's (2008) study of the development of Starbucks and similar chains in the former Portuguese colony of Macau (control of which returned to the Chinese government in 1999) indicated that over time more traditional, collectivist modes of drinking and eating (for example, family-centred meal times) were significantly eroded as more and more middle-class people started to structure their daily routines around coffee shops. More individualistic eating practices were encouraged, and older, more family-centric forms of eating and drinking were diminished.

Such studies suggest that everyday routines can be restructured by globalized eating and drinking spaces, with potentially significant effects on people's identities and senses of self. However, we can also look at such spaces in a different light, regarding them and the goods sold within them as being without any intrinsic meaning in themselves – as relatively blank backdrops against which the activities of everyday life are played out (Ritzer 2004). It is possible going to McDonald's or Starbucks may have few profound effects on people's cultural activities. It is in fact possible that these spaces and products may themselves come to be colonized by 'local' cultural ideas and activities. A great number of ethnographic studies of everyday food routines around the world seem to support these possibilities. Much of this research was carried out in the 1990s, against the background of the spread of McDonald's and other such chains to the former Soviet bloc and a China that was rapidly becoming ever more capitalist in its economic relations (Watson 1997; D. Miller 1998; Caldwell 2004; Lozado 2005). One of the key aims driving such research was to criticize what these researchers took to be often overly simple assertions about worldwide food **homogenization** and Americanization put forward by anti-globalization critics (D. Miller 1998). Ethnographic studies of customer activities within McDonald's and similar outlets in places like Moscow and Beijing stressed that fast-food restaurants and related innovations did not actually fundamentally restructure everyday activities and ways of thinking, and so had not radically altered culture as lived in mundane ways and contexts. Instead, once such places had lost their initial novelty and the glamour attendant upon it, they rapidly became part of, and were appropriated by, already-existing forms of everyday life.

For a writer like the globalization analyst John Tomlinson (1997), fast-food restaurants, coffee shops and similar locales may at first glance look as if they are all the same around the world. But in fact they are arenas for all sorts of different activities, sometimes more universal in nature (for example, quickly eating a hamburger meal), but often also expressing more established local and regional ways of eating, thinking and acting. However, we have to note that the ethnographic studies above are not beyond criticism. They sometimes assume that 'local' and 'national' food-related habits and ways of thinking, as enacted in everyday contexts and locations, are relatively static and unchanging, and are sufficiently robust to withstand any alleged colonization by Western-style fast-food influences. These analyses sometimes operate with overly romantic assumptions about the continuing vibrancy of what are taken to be distinctively local and national ways of eating. The cultural sociology of food has to be sensitively attuned both to the possibly culturally erosive and transformative nature of food globalization processes and to the potential continuing vitality of food-related activities that express more specific, localized cultural orientations and identities.

Fearing homogenization, creating heterogenization

One of the great strengths of cultural sociology is its ability to examine how particular social circumstances are shaped and structured by particular sets of ideas, mental dispositions and symbolic forms. It is within cultural forms that we can find expressed many of the most profound hopes and fears of people living in particular places at particular times. Cultural dispositions towards food are particularly fruitful sources to analyse in this regard, because thoughts about food that were prevalent during a given period often contain both worries and aspirations about the world at that time.

The sorts of fears about food in the present day that we looked at above are not historically unprecedented. Consideration of historical sources reveals that worries about the destruction of national and local cuisines by external influences have been around for at least a century or more in various European countries. In France just after World War I:

> Frenchmen began to feel that the unprecedented influx of foreign tourists hurrying through the country in fast cars, Riviera or Biarritz bound, not caring what they ate or drank so long as they were not delayed on their way, was threatening the character of their cookery far more than had the shortages and privations of war. Soon, they felt, the old inns and country restaurants would disappear and there would be only modern hotels serving mass produced, impersonal food which could be put before the customers at a moment's notice, devoured, paid for, and instantly forgotten.
>
> (David 1970: 6)

So worries as to the advent of 'mass produced, impersonal food' served in homogenous non-places are not just a feature of contemporary France, but have been a feature of French culture for eight decades or more (Fantasia 1995). French cultural fears as to what is seen today as the disastrous overturning of national culinary culture by the forces of American-led globalization follow a cultural script that was written at least 80 years ago (Ross 1996).

Such culturally patterned worries are not peculiar to France. Other national cultures (or, more precisely, intellectual groups within them) have fretted about perceived threats to national culinary purity over the last hundred years or so. For example, it was in the mid-1920s that the first pan-Greek cookery books were written, texts that codified for the first time what were to be taken as quintessentially 'Greek' ingredients, flavours and means of preparation. At exactly the same time, it was also the case that Greek authors started to depict food and eating as key areas of Greek culture that were 'in danger of being swept away by the onslaught of a cosmopolitan modernity' (Peckham 1998: 173). These two processes are fundamentally interconnected. Perceived threats to what are taken as authentically 'national' food habits – in this case, the threats posed by the first appearance in Greece of American- and British-style canned foods – compel authors to compile what they then present as the national culinary heritage. But once that heritage has been identified, the apparent threats to it loom ever larger in the cultural imaginary, provoking further, ever more fraught attempts to freeze in time what is taken as the 'pure essence' of the national food culture.

The French and Greek cases point to the **dialectical** nature of cultural symbolizations of food. When particular phenomena are perceived by certain groups of people as homogenizing and destructive of what they take to be the purity of a particular culture or cultural form, those people may very likely engage in projects – sometimes more, sometimes less self-conscious in nature – that stress the value of what they imagine to be cultural 'purity'. As the social theorist Manuel Castells (1997: 2) argues, when people in particular parts of the world feel threatened by the apparently homogenizing forces of (what they think of as) 'globalization', they may well turn towards 'expressions of collective identity that challenge globalization . . . on behalf of cultural singularity and people's control over their lives and environment[s]'. So, far from destroying more local and specific senses of cultural belonging, identity and affiliation, globalization processes may help not only to reinvigorate these, but in fact to create them.

Over the last decade, a notable feature of public discourses about food has been the rise and subsequent ubiquity of critiques of fast-food outlets and supermarkets, both in book form (for example, Schlosser 2001; Blythman 2005) and in cinema documentaries (for example, Spurlock 2004). Critiques of the food homogenization processes allegedly carried out by supermarkets and global food brands, and their apparently very negative social, cultural and medical effects, have become an important element of the contemporary world food system. The large companies that are under attack have had to deal with the barrage of criticisms in various ways, such as public relations campaigns and rebranding exercises, and changing the nature of the actual goods being offered for consumption. Up until the early 1980s, bad publicity and adverse media coverage were quite uncommon in the world of food production. However, over the last two decades or so, food corporations have had to make ever greater, and more fraught, efforts to deal with negative media coverage – often with many unpredictable consequences (Humphery 1998). With critiques of the food industry now a standard part of contemporary media culture, a much wider spread of people than was the case in the past is being influenced by ways of thinking that stress the threats of supposed food homogenization and degradation. This in turn increases the likelihood of a proliferation of projects to promote either culinary **heterogenization** or alleged cultural purity in food (Boyle 2004).

Ironically, it is the large supermarket chains themselves that to a large extent have been responsible for certain types of culinary heterogenization in the countries of the developed world. As noted by British anthropologist Allison James (1996), one key feature of food globalization in developed world countries over the last several decades has been the mass production of 'foreign' food. In the 1950s, food writer Elizabeth David encountered great resistance to her attempts to introduce 'Mediterranean' textures and flavours into the repertoire of British cookery (McLean 2004). Yet now what are taken to be 'typically' southern Italian, southern French, Spanish, Greek, Indian, Mexican, Chinese and Thai ingredients and recipes are available in practically every Western European, North American and Australasian supermarket, with these cuisines now integrated into everyday domestic and leisure activities (Warde, Martens and Olsen 1999). As the large supermarket chains from the 1960s onwards both reflected and themselves cultivated changing public attitudes towards food, more and more items that had previously been regarded as highly exotic, such as Chinese ingredients, became indigenized and familiar. Supermarkets have been keen to promote apparent heterogenization of tastes, even if the underlying material substructure of production and distribution that they have developed is best understood as primarily homogenizing in nature (Inglis and Gimlin 2010).

Another ironic development concerns what Allison James (1996) calls the 'connoisseurship' of national cuisines. Against the perceived threats of culinary homogenization posed by fast food companies and supermarkets are cultural counter-trends that involve defining and defending the parameters of particular 'national' and 'regional' cuisines. In these cases, certain people – such as authors and activists – claim to have found the supposed cultural 'essence' of a particular cuisine, be it associated with a nation, a region or a particular ethnic group. A sector of the publishing industry has sprung up to cater for this market, selling cookbooks that claim to present, for example, the 'real Tuscany' or the 'true taste of Morocco' (Boyle 2004). There is a concerted effort not only to capture the 'essence' of each particular cuisine, but also to adjudicate as to what are truly 'real' or unacceptably 'inauthentic' versions of particular dishes. Today a whole series of culinary entrepreneurs – cookbook authors, food journalists, television food programme hosts, certain kinds of activists, and so on – are all concerned with dictating what is 'authentic' in a cuisine (Lu and Fine 1995).

A good example of these trends is the Slow Food movement, which sprang up in northern Italy in the 1980s as a social movement of the intellectual middle class, dedicated to what it saw as 'saving' local cuisine and eating habits from the apparent destructive effects of food globalization (Leitch 2003). Ironically, given the success of the movement among a primarily middle-class audience in Italy and beyond, the movement is now itself transnational, having active branches across the developed world, including in the supposed stronghold of food homogenization itself, the United States. Here is the paradoxical case of a social movement dedicated to the preservation of the so-called 'national' and 'local' in food – and in culture more generally – that is itself global in reach and organization. This mirrors the transnationalization of groups dedicated to other related causes such as organic food production and Fair Trade distribution (Wright and Madrid 2007). The apparently 'local' struggles against the negatively conceived 'global' in food terms have themselves become significantly globalized (Leitch 2003). So we see again how globalization creates not just threats to national and local cultures, but in fact the revitalization and even wholesale (re)invention of these.

Within the cultural symbolism of the Slow Food movement and similar groups, 'hybrid' culinary forms are often disparaged, with what are viewed as trendy fusion cuisines particularly held up to ridicule (Petrini 2003). But what this sort of culinary policing has to forget is something about which cultural sociology can remind people. Many of the cuisines that apparently have been untouched for many centuries are themselves hybrids, created as the result of very long-term processes of migration and trade. The trans-Atlantic food transactions that resulted from the European colonization of the Americas from the early 1500s onwards in fact marked the beginning of modern food globalization. The 'Columbian' movement of foodstuffs, animals, plants and people between the old world and the new world was as wide-ranging and as disruptive of previous patterns of food cultivation, distribution and consumption as the effects of the globalized food regimes of today (Mintz 2008).

Many of the ingredients and tastes that have characterized European food cultures over the last five centuries originated in the Americas and were wholly unknown to Europeans before the conquerors brought them back to their mother countries. Without the expansion of the Spanish empire throughout the sixteenth century, we would not today be familiar with the tastes of either chocolate or peanuts – crops that are now grown in other parts of the world but which were once available only in the Americas (Rebora 2001). Even more peculiar is the thought that the potato would probably not play such an important role in north European food cultures if it had not been brought back from South America by the means of European conquest (Fernandez-Armesto 2001). In subsequent European history, allegedly 'national' food cultures were made possible by a collective cultural forgetting of the originally non-indigenous, often far-off origins of certain foodstuffs.

As a result of fears about global food homogenization, there exist today growing tendencies to draw demarcation lines around supposedly 'true' expressions of a food culture, and to condemn what are seen as mere imitations of these. The reclaiming of the 'local' or 'regional' in food often involves actually reinventing these. For example, you may think that artisan-produced (that is, not mass-produced) pasta is a key part of ancient southern Italian food culture. But pasta only became widespread in the region in the eighteenth century, hardly a period long enough away from our own to count as 'ancient' (Serventi and Sabban 2003). Likewise, nothing seems more essentially 'southern Italian' than the tomato, but it first came from the Americas, along with 'north Italian' staples like gnocchi (made from potatoes) and polenta (made from maize, another South American crop). Similarly, one today associates chillis with the cooking of India and Far Eastern countries, yet they too are indigenous to South America. A converse process of trans-Atlantic movement in foodstuffs has also occurred over the last several centuries: from Europe and Africa to the Americas and the Caribbean came crops such as rice and bananas, and animals such as beef cattle. Nothing sounds more authentically 'Mexican' than chilli con carne, but as it involves both beef and rice, it uses ingredients that came to the Americas as a result of global economic and political forces.

In a world-condition characterized for many people by perceived flux, movement and uncertainty, cultures that seem authentic can be a great source of comfort, of much-needed **ontological security**, in a world of apparently constant upheaval (Giddens 1990). The taste of a 'traditional dish', served in a comfortingly 'local' setting, accompanied by symbols of culinary heritage, can provide powerful forms of reassurance in a highly globalized world that seems to be characterized by a constant sense of risk and crisis. In a world seeming to involve uncertain futures and never-ending change, food can meet desires for security, homeliness, belonging, community and cultural stability. But the great irony here is that food that is presented as truly 'local' and 'authentic' is often itself a product of long-term globalization processes, and the desire for culinary authenticity is itself an expression of a world that has been globalizing for at least 500 years.

Conclusion

Food is a ripe source of inquiry for the cultural sociologist because of its heavily symbolic character. Such symbolism is always highly charged, both emotionally and politically. Indeed, it is precisely the intertwined emotionality and politicized nature of food that cultural sociology is so well placed to discern, in addition to showing how social conditions both create and are in turn structured by food's symbolic capacities. Globalization is in large part about different sorts of people imagining in their own distinctive ways what the world around them is like, and how it affects their lives (Appadurai 1996). Given its focus on the symbolic, meaningful and affective dimensions of human existence, cultural sociology is particularly well placed to investigate such matters with a sensitive but critical eye. In this chapter, we have seen what cultural sociology can say about the many different locations and roles of food in the present day, from the apparently wholly authentic 'local' restaurant to the apparently homogenizing, globally ubiquitous fast-food outlet. In all such cases, food and eating are constituted by, and communicated through, cultural symbolism that expresses the hopes and aspirations, and the fears and anxieties, of different sorts of people living across the globe today.

Review questions

13.1 Do globalization processes inevitably destroy local food cultures?
13.2 In what ways are food traditions actually recent social inventions?
13.3 What are the main problems and risks in food production and consumption today? How do they impact on your everyday life? How do you try to control them?

Further reading

Inglis, D. and Gimlin, D. (eds) (2010) *The Globalization of Food*, Berg, Oxford.
Nützenadel, A. and Trentmann, F. (eds) (2008) *Food and Globalization*, Berg, Oxford.

14

Media, Culture and Public Life

Learning objectives

- To find out about the culture of democracy, and how it shapes our understanding of rationality and entertainment.
- To learn what constitutes the public sphere.
- To discover the difference between an official public and an informal public, and the role of the media in each.
- To explore the meanings people attribute to the media, and examine how these meanings relate to the ways people think about public life and democracy.
- To learn how the entertainment media contribute to public debate, in both official and informal publics.
- To find out why some people treat entertainment media as unimportant, and as unworthy of serious public attention.

Introduction

Media play a significant role in all aspects of social life. This is particularly true for politics and public communication, which are unimaginable without the presence of media institutions. But what meanings do people attribute to media, and how do these meanings relate to the way in which people think about public life and democracy? Are certain types of media culturally privileged over others? How do the non-privileged media contribute to public life?

In order to answer these questions, it helps to recognize how media are organized into two opposed cultural categories: *news* and *entertainment*. News is the privileged

Cultural Sociology: An Introduction, First Edition. Les Back et al. © 2012 Les Back, Andy Bennett, Laura Desfor Edles,
Margaret Gibson, David Inglis, Ronald Jacobs and Ian Woodward. Published 2012 by Blackwell Publishing Ltd.

category. It is considered more important to democracy, and more worthy of everyday discussion. Entertainment, on the other hand, is viewed with more suspicion. At best, it is a mindless diversion. At worst, it is a dangerous distraction from more important matters. This distinction is related to the larger culture of democracy, which treats rationality as the preferred form of argument, and seriousness as the preferred attitude.

This chapter explores the cultural organization and social consequences of different media formats, and the social consequences that these media formats have for the organization of democratic public life. The first part of the chapter examines the culture of rationality, and the role this culture plays in the formation of an idealized picture of the public sphere. The second part of the chapter distinguishes between official publics and informal publics, outlining the role of media in each. The third part of the chapter explores how these publics are organized around a cultural hierarchy that privileges news and politics over entertainment. The final part of the chapter considers the different ways in which entertainment media contribute to debate in the public sphere.

Culture and rationality in modern public life

One of cultural sociology's central contributions is its development of a more meaning-centred theory of civil society and democracy. Most political scientists and political theorists who have written about these issues have concerned themselves with evaluating how well societies match up against idealized visions of democracy, and suggesting ways to encourage such cherished principles as critical rationality (Habermas 1989, 1996), autonomy (Fraser 1992; Bourdieu 2005), inclusion (Barber 1984; Young 2000), deliberation (Benhabib 2002; Gutmann and Thompson 1996) and generalized trust (Putnam 2001). All of these are important principles, and they inform the idealized images that most democratic societies paint for themselves; however, this approach provides an incomplete and distorted picture of how 'real democracies' actually operate in practice.

Rather than evaluating how well real societies match up to idealized principles, cultural sociology has chosen to study the cultural organization of democracy and public life itself. In studies of war (Smith 2005), race (Eyerman 2001; Jacobs 2000; Alexander 2006), religion (Alexander 2006; Lichterman 2005), sexuality (Seidman 2002; Meeks 2001) and democratization (Ku 1999; Baiocchi 2006), cultural sociologists have demonstrated that democratic virtues are only made meaningful through the symbolic identification of democratic vices. Furthermore, because ideals are always part of a larger cultural system, they can be used to promote exclusion as well as inclusion. For example, people can strive to be more rational, or they can use the principle of rationality as a symbolic weapon to exclude from the public sphere those who are claimed to lack sufficiently rational qualities. Trust can be used to create solidarity and mutual understanding, or it can be used to symbolically pollute and exclude those who are seen as cynical, self-interested and distrustful.

Once we have distinguished between idealized hopes and actual practices of democracy, it becomes easier to understand the relationship between rationality and the public sphere. The **public sphere** refers to those common spaces where individuals gather to discuss matters of common concern. The creation of a public sphere was crucial for the development of democracy, because the discussions taking place in the public sphere encouraged individuals to believe that 'the public' was the ultimate source of authority – even more important than kings or monarchs or other political leaders. Believing that those in power ultimately were responsible to the public, individuals came to demand that representatives of government justify themselves and their positions in the public sphere, and to give good reasons for the policies they wanted to implement.

Historically, the power of the public sphere has been based on a belief in **rationality**, implying that (i) people would give good reasons to justify their positions on an issue, (ii) they would engage in spirited debate with others who were committed to different positions, and (iii) they were willing to be persuaded by the force of the better argument. If people in the public sphere committed themselves to these three principles, it was believed, then society would make better collective decisions. For this to work as effectively as possible, participants needed to be reasoned instead of emotional, serious instead of playful, and open-minded instead of strategic. They would also have to be inclusive, providing an opportunity for everyone who was potentially affected by an issue to participate in the public sphere debate.

Because cultural sociologists are interested in the difference between idealized beliefs and actual practices, they have identified two problems with this commitment to rationality in the public sphere. First, it is impossible to eliminate emotion, playfulness and rhetoric from the public sphere. People do not simply state their position and then wait to see whether their arguments are the most rational or the most convincing. If they have any skills at all, they will develop their arguments by telling stories, making emotional appeals and relying on other rhetorical techniques to express and authorize their arguments. The second problem, as we have already suggested, is that exclusion is inevitable. If people believe that rationality is important, they will seek to exclude from the public sphere all those they deem to be too emotional or irrational. As Zygmunt Bauman (1990) argues, people often spend more time trying to disqualify their adversaries as legitimate participants in the public sphere than they spend debating with people who hold different views. Worse still, history is full of examples where women, racial minorities and members of the working class were disqualified from full public participation because they were thought to lack the necessary qualities of rationality. In other words, the ideal of rationality has too often been used as a symbolic weapon designed to exclude.

Media and the public sphere: the relationship between formal and informal publics

To explore the issue of exclusion further, we also need to consider the technological limits that prevent complete inclusion in the public sphere. In the large, complex societies in which we live today, it is impossible for all people to gather together in a common public space and debate the merits of different social or policy positions. In fact, the only 'common public space' is the media. But media do not really create a single public sphere in which everybody participates. Instead, media connect people together through multiple and overlapping publics of various size and influence.

In order to understand how media connect different types of publics, most cultural sociologists and political theorists distinguish between formal and informal publics.

Informal publics refer to small-group discussions that take place among regular individuals. These discussions can be face to face, or they can be organized through communication technologies such as Internet forums, blogs and social media such as Facebook. Informal publics are important because anyone can participate in them. While it is very difficult to gain an appearance on television or in the largest newspapers, it is easy to have a discussion with friends, make a post on a blog or participate on a social media site such as Facebook. Because informal publics are so inclusive, they are often the place where new problems are first identified, where new approaches to existing problems are developed, and where new collective identities are formed.

The 2011 revolution in Egypt provides a good example of the power of informal publics. Many of the early protests that started this revolution were organized on Facebook. Wael Ghonim, a marketing manager for Google, had volunteered to run the Facebook page for Mohamed ElBaradei, a leader of the Egyptian opposition and a winner of the 2005 Nobel Peace Prize. ElBaradei's Facebook page became very popular, and Ghonim began using it to reach out to Egyptian youth, encouraging them to collaborate and share content about Egyptian government repression and the need for democratic reform. The January 2011 protests were organized largely through Facebook and Twitter. These protests were so large and successful that they attracted the attention of major media organizations throughout the world, encouraging many of the world's political leaders to pressure Egyptian president Hosni Mubarak to resign.

By attracting the attention of the major media organizations and encouraging commentary from leading politicians worldwide, the protests in Egypt managed to become a central part of the official public sphere. These **official publics** refer to public discussions that take place between government officials, politicians, experts, journalists and other representatives of the public interest. Compared with informal publics, the discussions that take place in official publics occur under conditions of maximum publicity within open and transparent forums, so that third parties can watch and hold speakers accountable for their arguments. Official publics are almost always organized within the largest media organizations: in major newspapers and on television channels and web sites.

In the idealized image of the official public sphere, journalists are the guardians and representatives of the public interest. In this idealized picture, journalists are supposed to monitor the social political environment, looking for emergent issues of potential concern and identifying informal publics that can bring an original new position to the public debate. They are supposed to provide a platform for dialogue between those who represent the official public sphere (that is, representatives of the state, as well as major stakeholders from the largest bureaucracies) and those who represent civil society (that is, representatives from social movements, non-profit organizations, and other associations and interest groups). They should seek to uncover and unmask all forms of strategic communication – what today is commonly called 'spin'. Finally, they should speak to their readers as citizens who are interested in and capable of making sense of these issues.

As with all other parts of the culture of democracy, however, there is a difference between the idealized picture and the actual practice of journalism in the official public sphere. In practice, the official public sphere is organized around a set of meanings about what counts as a serious issue, and which types of media formats deserve serious attention. For example, discussions about the economic implications of tax policy are deemed important, while discussions about the latest episode of *American Idol* are dismissed as trivial and unimportant. In other words, the relationship between official publics and informal publics is shaped by the distinction between two different kinds of media: news and entertainment.

The cultural preference for news over entertainment

In the official public sphere, the understanding of media is shaped by the central cultural distinction between news and entertainment. News is understood and evaluated in terms of its ability to provide objective facts about important issues. This helps to explain why news and editorial are kept separate in most newspapers. It also helps to explain why the most serious punishments in politics and journalism are directed at people who make things up and try to pass them off as facts. Finally, it helps to explain why there is so much public concern about the growing influence of entertainment values within the news divisions of television stations and newspapers. After all, as Barbie Zelizer (1992, 1998) has shown, journalists get their status from being eyewitnesses and chroniclers of history, not from telling good stories.

While it appears natural to us today, the distinction between factual news and fictional entertainment was actually a historical achievement. In the sixteenth century, the main defining characteristic of news was that it was *new*, a feature it shared with literary novels as a way of asserting a distinction against ancient stories and myths; the idea that news should be *factual* did not develop until the seventeenth and eighteenth centuries, as journalists attempted to distinguish themselves from novelists (Davis 1983).

By the nineteenth century, journalists – together with historians (see White 1978) – had successfully managed to identify truth with fact. As the opposite of truth, fiction and entertainment came to be criticized as trivial diversions that got in the way of a more sober, serious understanding of the world. In fact, most theories of democracy and the public sphere view entertainment as a dangerous intrusion preventing a more rational civil society (for example, Habermas 1989; Putnam 2001; Adorno and Horkheimer 2001; Bourdieu 1998). This fear – that people are 'amusing themselves to death' (Postman 1985) – is widely shared by politicians and public figures. Newton Minow, who was chairman of the Federal Communications Commission, provided one of the most influential and significant criticisms of entertainment media in the United States in a 1961 speech he gave to the National Association of Broadcasters:

> When television is good, nothing – not the theatre, not the magazines or newspapers – nothing is better. But when television is bad, nothing is worse. I invite each of you to sit down in front of your television set when your station goes on the air and stay there for a day without a book, without a magazine, without a newspaper, without a profit and loss sheet or a rating book to distract you. Keep your eyes glued to that set until the station signs off. I can assure you that what you will observe is a vast wasteland.
>
> (Minow 1961)

Minow's speech was widely credited with building the necessary support that led to the 1967 Public Broadcasting Act. This in turn resulted in the formation of the first public television network in the United States, which was established with a mandate to create more serious and enlightened television that was more than just entertainment.

What are the consequences of this deeply held cultural distinction, which privileges serious talk about politics and policy, and which calls into question the importance of entertainment and other supposedly trivial diversions? People who have deep commitments to entertainment media know that the possibility always exists that they will be called upon to justify the seriousness of their pursuits and the importance of their discussions. This leads to a certain defensiveness, which makes it less likely that they will participate in the official public sphere.

We can see this symbolic hierarchy at work in the public persona of Jon Stewart, and the public commentary that swirls around his award-winning political-media satire, *The Daily Show*. When Stewart and his programme are the object of discussion in mainstream newspapers and other parts of the official public sphere, he receives overwhelmingly positive attention. Yet Stewart himself is always quick to dismiss the show's relevance, emphasizing that it is about 'fake news', and that its only motivation is to be funny. Critics of Stewart rely on the same argument, dismissing him for being a 'mere comedian' who does not understand the complexity of the public issues that he is using as fodder for his routines. These criticisms place the entertainer on the polluted side of the serious/non-serious binary, a positioning that demands justification, and which explains the wariness many entertainers have about venturing into the official public sphere. The same cultural formula is used repeatedly to criticize entertainment celebrities who attempt to participate in the official public sphere – people such as Bono, Sean Penn, George Clooney or Elton John.

This suggestion that their pursuits are insufficiently serious also follows the audience for entertainment. To the extent that the audience accepts such a positioning, there is a lower likelihood that they will recognize the programmes they are watching as serious commentary about important public issues. Instead, they will tend to consume the texts of popular culture in a more passive and distracted way, failing to develop an elaborated discourse about their cultural consumption and its place in their social worldview. In this sense, it is possible to see the passive and distracted consumer of popular culture as being not so much a product of the cultural industry, but rather the product of the culture of media and democracy, which privileges seriousness over entertainment, and establishes these as binary and mutually exclusive categories. This, of course, was the point that Raymond Williams (1983: 289) was trying to make when he argued that there were no masses, only discourses about masses.

It is because of this symbolic pollution of entertainment, and the way it is deeply institutionalized within the discourse of civil society, that cultural critics are so important. When Jack Gould wrote his television columns in the *New York Times* during the 1950s and 1960s, he was signalling to his readers that talk about television was indeed a serious matter of common concern. In more recent times, when critics have written about the deep sociological insight of critically acclaimed television programmes such as *The Wire* or *Mad Men*, they remind the reader that there are important things to be learned from the texts of popular culture, particularly if the reader is careful to sample from the quality genres.

Even when entertainment programmes are included as part of the conversation about an important public issue within the official public sphere, there is always a risk of ridicule for the individual who introduces the entertainment programme into the debate. We can see this clearly with the case of US vice-president Dan Quayle, who famously used a quarrel with the fictional television character Murphy Brown in order to successfully get the conservative 'family values' issue on to the national agenda. But Quayle accomplished this at great personal cost, as he saw his approval ratings plummet, and as he (once again) became the object of public critique. As *New York Times* columnist A.M. Rosenthal commented:

> [Quayle's] aides were well aware that they were straying into dangerous political territory, but no one expected the firestorm Quayle set off. Once again, the barbs were brutal: 'Quayle also says there should be more honesty on television,' Johnny Carson said. 'He said there's no way a coyote could live after swallowing all that dynamite.'
>
> (*New York Times*, 5 July 1992, F11).

The point is that it is risky to take entertainment programming as a serious object of commentary in the official public sphere unless the motivation is to criticize the programming as an obstacle to more serious pursuits. This is unfortunate, because of the many different ways that entertainment media manage to provide penetrating social and cultural commentary about matters of common concern. It is equally unfortunate in the way that the seriousness/entertaining binary works to position the committed fan of entertainment as being somehow outside of civil society.

Entertainment media and the public sphere

Despite the social risks associated with treating entertainment media as an important part of the public sphere, it remains the case that fictional media and entertainment do have an impact on public life. We can identify three different ways in which this works. First, entertainment media have an impact on **social imagination**, by providing cultural scripts that individuals use in order to make sense of themselves and the world around them. Second, entertainment media are part of an **aesthetic public sphere**, because they frequently get linked to discussions about important matters of common concern. Third, because many people do in fact care a lot about entertainment media, they are often the focus of debates about **cultural policy**.

Social imagination

Supporters of 'the arts' have long claimed that fictional media offer a penetrating look into the 'true nature of things', which is based on how things might be rather than how they are at the moment (Williams 1983). Rather than trying to reflect actual worlds that are constrained by 'mere facts', those in the arts offer characters and stories that consumers can use to re-describe the world around them (Alexander 2006). For example, the novels of Charles Dickens provided a penetrating look into the lives of the industrial working class, while Jane Austen's novels encouraged readers to think more critically about gender, marriage and social status. In fact, as political theorist Jürgen Habermas

(1989, 1996) has argued, the novels that bourgeois families were reading in the 1700s and 1800s helped to encourage the values of empathy and understanding that were so important for democratic communication in the public sphere.

Today, while novels and other arts are still powerful sources of social imagination, they are less influential than the cultural industries of film and television. The cultural industries make a lot more money than the arts, but they have less prestige. This makes it more difficult to treat entertainment media as a serious source of social imagination and public worth. In the arts, critics have tended to argue that the rare outstanding products have a greater influence than the more common and mediocre ones, because they attract the most critical attention and most powerfully engage the imaginative moral faculties of their audience (Williams 1983). In contrast, where the cultural industries are concerned, most critics have tended to adopt a somewhat different perspective, arguing that the mediocrity that defines most products overwhelms the ability of any of the quality products to attract attention or inspire imagination (for example, see Postman 1985; Adorno 1990). Yet outstanding products from the cultural industries do exist, they do attract critical attention and they do encourage moral reflection.

We can see how the quality texts from entertainment media provide imaginative moral discourses for their audiences by examining the television industry. In the initial years of the US television networks, there was a significant amount of quality live theatre. Programmes such as *Philco Television Playhouse*, *Goodyear Television Playhouse* and *Kraft Television Theater* were big attractions to writers from the New York theatre, including such luminaries as Rod Serling, Reginald Rose, Tad Mosel and Paddy Chayefsky (Barnouw 1990: 154–65). Ultimately, this 'golden age of television' was done in by a number of factors, including the switch from live video to film (Gould 2002: 41–3), the rising popularity of formula series (such as comedies, Westerns) and the growing influence of blacklist pressures (Barnouw 1990: 166–7). In its early years, though, television was seen as an excellent medium for screening quality drama.

What were the aesthetic, moral and subjunctive qualities of these early programmes? One of the most promising possibilities of the early medium was its intimacy and immediacy, as well as its ability to provide a 'disciplined appreciation of reality in everyday life' (Gould 2002: 44). In other words, television dramas provided compelling portraits of social life, as individuals struggled to find meaning and dignity in the modern world. Paddy Chayefsky's 1953 production of *Marty*, for example, offered a poignant portrayal of a shy and plain-looking working-class man, and his struggles with loneliness (Gould 2002: 43–4; Barnouw 1990: 157–9). Reginald Rose's *Thunder on Sycamore Street* provided a portrait of neighbourhood intolerance, in a teleplay inspired by a racial incident that had taken place in suburban Illinois. Rod Serling's *Requiem for a Heavyweight* told the story of an ageing boxer and his unscrupulous manager, while J.P. Miller's *Days of Wine and Roses* offered a tragic portrait of alcoholism (Gould 2002: 49–51).

What these programmes had in common was the desire to dramatize a social issue, through an intimate portrait of individuals in pain, all trying to salvage some degree of moral dignity in a cold and heartless world. These dramas did not simply entertain through easy formulae or ideological messages about happiness through consumption. Instead, they challenged their viewers to empathize with the damaged, the weak and the compromised. At the same time, these dramas expanded the collective understanding of what counted as a matter of common concern. Breaking down the barrier between public and private, these psychological portraits were deeply sociological in the way they suggested a link between biographical problems and sociohistorical structures.

While these golden age dramas gave way during the 1960s to formula series, television scholars such as Thompson (1997) have argued that the 1970s and 1980s ushered in a 'second golden age' of American television, which was defined by aesthetic quality, public relevance and self-reflexivity. The idea that entertainment programmes could deal successfully and popularly with 'serious' issues of the day had been demonstrated with the runaway success of *All in the Family*, which was the most popular show on television from 1971 to 1976. The real turning point, Thompson argues, was the appearance of two new shows that appeared in the 1980s: *Hill Street Blues*, a police drama that ran from 1981 to 1987; and *St Elsewhere*, a medical drama that ran from 1982 to 1988. These shows received extensive critical praise, and established new formulae for a host of other quality dramas that emerged during the 1980s and 1990s.

The quality programmes of the 1980s all relied upon a number of devices that allowed them to produce a particular kind of moral discourse. First, they had large ensemble casts, which allowed them to develop multiple storylines – some of them resolved in a single episode and others developed over a longer period of time. Second, most of the programmes included an examination of the conflict between work life and private life, showing how the two were connected in complex and often contradictory ways. Third, and perhaps most importantly, these programs dealt to a greater extent than ever before with 'real-life' issues of the time, such as urban decay, hospital administration, anti-abortion violence, racial conflict and baby boomer angst. And they did all this while maintaining the sense of intimacy and empathy that has always characterized quality television.

The engagement with current social issues allowed the quality programmes of this 'second golden age' to create something like an alternative public sphere, in which fictional individuals gathered together to discuss matters of politics and common concern. Rather than limiting their presentation to the standard techniques of mainstream journalism, political speeches or press conferences, these alternative public discussions increased their power by maintaining a connection to the ongoing character development and overlapping storylines that had characterized the programmes. Indeed, because the writers of these programmes could assume that their viewers had an ongoing relationship with (and attachment to) the programmes, they were able to present their fictional public discussions in a way that was consistently thematic, in contrast to the disconnected and episodic nature of so much news coverage of public problems. (On the episodic framing that tends to dominate most news coverage, particularly on television, see Iyengar 1994.)

The aesthetic public sphere

As the engagement with current issues became a staple of many programmes, the alternative publics of quality television increasingly have found themselves penetrating the discussions taking place in 'real' public spheres. For example, medical dramas such as *ER* and *Chicago Hope* have portrayed health maintenance organizations (HMOs) as the villain in their dramatic plots, crystallizing a growing dissatisfaction that put HMOs on the defensive and forced them to justify their actions (*New York Times*, 8 November 1998, B30). As mentioned previously, in 1992 the political debate about family values and single mothers was carried out in large part as a debate between Vice-President Dan Quayle and the fictional television character Murphy Brown. More recently, episodes of the critically acclaimed *Mad Men* have provoked a good deal of public reflection about changing gender roles in the workplace, while various episodes of *The Wire* have produced public discussion about urban crime, politics and the media (*New York Times*, 8 November 1998, B30). These programmes clearly engage the moral sensibilities and critical capacities of their viewers, and they do so in informal as well as official publics.

As we have suggested above, fictional entertainment media do not only enter the social imaginary through internal dialogues within the self (though these are certainly important); they also help to organize and motivate collective public dialogues about matters of common concern. In other words, entertainment media are part of an *aesthetic public sphere*. By combining cultural criticism with social commentary, aesthetic publics infuse popular media with a sense of public relevance, engaging the civic identities of their audiences at the same time as they provide the communicative infrastructure for constituting a critical public sphere. Today, entertainment media have all the infrastructure that is necessary to form a critical public sphere: texts that challenge public authority; a space of criticism (in the academic and journalistic fields) that serves to define the criteria for making evaluative judgements; and a set of overlapping communicative spaces where individuals participate in collective television criticism.

The spaces of expert criticism are of particular importance, because they allow television's civic influence to extend beyond the discussions taking place in informal publics that are largely invisible from the official public sphere. Indeed, the fact that television criticism is a regular part of the newspaper means it is connected to the 'official' or 'dominant' public sphere – which, after all, is organized primarily by mainstream news media. In other words, we can think about the 'Arts' section of the newspaper as an important part of the public sphere whose significance tends to be overlooked by researchers as well as by privileged political actors.

Cultural policy

The massive participation in entertainment media and the corresponding discussions that swirl around them have done more than simply draw people into the public sphere in a way that leaves it unchanged. Entertainment media have also helped to redefine how people think about citizenship. While most theories of citizenship emphasize a subject who is engaged in debates about political and social policies, Toby Miller (1998) suggests that the subject of cultural citizenship is more likely to think about the public good in terms of *cultural* policy. It is common for these discussions to centre around the kinds of culture that ought to be available in order to make a 'better' society; this usually involves advocating for the protection of children, local cultures, minority cultures, heritage cultures, elite 'high culture' or something else. Regardless of which kind of debate is taking place, the point is that cultural citizens have a significant *moral* investment in entertainment media. For many individuals, their participation in entertainment media, along with their arguments about it, constitutes their most significant civic practice.

In the United States, these debates tend to assume the model of American commercial media, and thus tend to be organized through a market discourse that emphasizes the freedom to consume whatever culture one likes, with the market determining what will be available. From this cultural framework, it comes as no surprise that the most active debates about television policy tend to be connected to social movements, which usually focus on specific programmes that are viewed as unfair, uncivil or dangerous to children. Furthermore, because these social movements also assume a market model for mass media, their critique usually takes the form of pressuring advertisers and viewers to boycott a specific programme.

Outside of the United States, the situation is more complex. In many nations, there is a long tradition of debate about television policy, and specifically about how to counter the threat of American hegemony. These debates actually began in the 1920s, as the US film industry achieved a position of global dominance; shifting to the issue of television policy in the 1950s, the debates have intensified since the 1980s, with the decline of the public service broadcasting model and the strengthening position of US television products (Gorman and McLean 2003). As a result of these debates, many countries have specific legislation in place to limit foreign (that is, US) media content. In France, current laws require that 40 per cent of all television content be produced in France, with 60 per cent being of European origin. Laws in Australia and Canada are similar, mandating that between 50 and 60 per cent of media content must be produced domestically. The Sri Lankan government has tried a different approach, recently introducing a tax on all imported film and television content. Despite the specific policy differences between countries, what is common among all of them is the regular debate about the need to protect national popular culture against US media. These debates came together in the 2005 UNESCO Convention on the Protection and Promotion of Diversity of Cultural Expressions, where participating nations overwhelmingly approved a document affirming the rights of nations to enact legislation protecting cultural expression from foreign competition.

Debates about cultural policy proceed through two types of argument. The first contrasts the American free-market view of culture with an alternative (French) model, which views culture as a central component of national heritage. In this argument, restrictions on foreign content are necessary to preserve national identity. In the second argument, (US) popular culture is defined by sexuality and violence, and cultural policies limiting American content are seen as necessary to protect children from a morally degraded culture. In these arguments, debates about media violence are also debates about Americanization, in which the violence of American television is linked to the violence of American society more generally. In such a situation, the comparative context helps to legitimate the cultural policy debates, because most of the violent content comes from foreign programming, which reflects an outside culture that can be held up as a threat to the national good.

Conclusion

As we have argued, the culture of democracy is based on a set of distinctions that privilege news over entertainment, seriousness over playfulness and rationality over rhetoric. These distinctions influence the kinds of issues, individuals and cultural styles that are most likely to attract the attention of the official public sphere. This makes the official public sphere less inclusive than it might be, and it places people who enjoy (and like to discuss) entertainment on the defensive. Fearing that their interests can so easily be marginalized and dismissed, fans of entertainment media become less visible and less active in their public participation. In other words, they become the victims of symbolic exclusion.

This marginalization of entertainment media from the official public sphere is not surprising. As we have suggested throughout this chapter, cultural sociology encourages us to distinguish between the idealized images and the actual practices of democracy, recognizing that the idealized images often lead to cultural distinctions and social exclusions.

On the other hand, the symbolic exclusion of entertainment media is limited by several important factors. Because entertainment media are a much bigger source of revenue than news media, the audience for entertainment media is courted aggressively by advertisers and programmers, whose interest in profit is at least as strong as (if not stronger than) their concern for democracy. This has important consequences for informal as well as official publics. In informal publics, social media make it easy for fans to discuss their favourite entertainment programmes. In official publics, arts journalism and entertainment reporting take up a significant part of the news budget, and occupy a good deal of the news space. In combination, this guarantees that entertainment media will continue to be the object of public discussion, and will frequently become part of the debate about more 'serious' issues. As cultural sociology helps us to recognize, this means that media have a more complicated relationship with democracy and the public sphere than idealized images and hopes might suggest.

Review questions

14.1 Why are news media treated as more important than entertainment media?
14.2 How are official publics and informal publics connected to one another? What is the role of the mass media in each?
14.3 How do the entertainment media contribute to debate and discussion in the public sphere?

Further reading

Alexander, J.C. (2006) *The Civil Sphere*, Oxford University Press, London.
Habermas, J. (1989 [1962]) *The Structural Transformation of the Public Sphere* (trans. T. Burger), MIT Press, Cambridge, MA.
Habermas, J. (1996) *Between Facts and Norms: Contributions to a Discourse Theory of Law and Democracy*, MIT Press, Cambridge, MA.
Williams, R. (1983) *Culture and Society, 1780–1950*, Columbia University Press, New York.

References

Abercrombie, N., Hill, S. and Turner, B.S. (1994) *The Penguin Dictionary of Sociology*, Penguin, Ringwood.

Adorno, T. (1990) Culture industry reconsidered, in *Culture and Society: Contemporary Debates* (eds J.C. Alexander and S. Seidman), Cambridge University Press, New York, pp. 275–282.

Adorno, T. and Horkheimer, M. (1986) *Dialectic of Enlightenment*, Verso, London.

Adorno, T. and Horkheimer, M. (2001) The culture industry: Enlightenment as mass deception, in *Media and Cultural Studies: Key Works* (eds M. Durham and D. Kellner), Blackwell, Oxford, pp. 71–101.

Alberti, J. (2004) *Leaving Springfield: The Simpsons and the Possibility of Oppositional Culture*, Wayne State University Press, Detroit, MI.

Albrow, M. (1996) *The Global Age*, Polity Press, Cambridge.

Alexander, J.C. (1995) *Fin de Siècle Social Theory: Relativism, Reduction, and the Problem of Reason*, Verso, New York.

Alexander, J.C. (2003) *The Meanings of Social Life: A Cultural Sociology*, Oxford University Press, New York.

Alexander, J.C. (2004a) From the depths of despair: performance, counterperformance, and 'September 11'. *Sociological Theory*, 22 (1), 88–105.

Alexander, J.C. (2004b) Cultural pragmatics: social performance between ritual and strategy. *Sociological Theory*, 22 (4), 527–73.

Alexander, J.C. (2006) *The Civil Sphere*, Oxford University Press, New York.

Alexander, J.C. (2010) *The Performance of Politics. Obama's Victory and the Democratic Struggle for Power*, Oxford University Press, New York.

Alexander, J.C., Jacobs, R. and Smith, P. (2011) Introduction: cultural sociology today, in *Oxford Handbook of Cultural Sociology* (eds J.C. Alexander, R. Jacobs and P. Smith), Oxford University Press, New York.

Alexander, J.C. and Smith, P. (2003) The strong program in cultural sociology: elements of a structural hermeneutics, in *The Meanings of Social Life* (ed. J.C. Alexander), Oxford University Press, Oxford, pp. 11–26.

Cultural Sociology: An Introduction, First Edition. Les Back et al. © 2012 Les Back, Andy Bennett, Laura Desfor Edles, Margaret Gibson, David Inglis, Ronald Jacobs and Ian Woodward. Published 2012 by Blackwell Publishing Ltd.

Alexander, J.C. and Smith, P. (2010) The strong program: origins, achievements, and prospects, in *Handbook of Cultural Sociology* (eds J. Hall, L. Grindstaff and M. Lo), Routledge, London, pp. 13–24.

Amenta, E., Bonastia, C. and Caren, N. (2001) US social policy in comparative perspective: concepts, images, arguments, and research strategies. *Annual Review of Sociology*, 27, 213–34.

Anderson, E. (1990) *Streetwise. Race, Class and Change in an Urban Community*, University of Chicago Press, Chicago.

Anthias, F. and Yuval-Davies, N. (1993) *Racialised Boundaries: Race, Nation, Gender, Colour and Class and the Anti-Racist Struggle*, Routledge, London.

Appadurai, A. (1996) *Modernity at Large: Cultural Dimensions of Globalization*, University of Minnesota Press, Minneapolis.

Arimoto, T. (2010) Body culture and nationalism in modernising Japan from 1868 to 1920s. PhD thesis. Goldsmiths, University of London, London.

Armstrong, K. (2000) *The Battle for God*, Knopf, New York.

Augé, M. (1995) *Non-Places: Introduction to an Anthropology of Supermodernity*, Verso, London.

Back, L. (1996) *New Ethnicities and Urban Culture: Racisms and Multiculture in Young Lives*, UCL Press, London.

Back, L. and Solomos, J. (2009) *Theories of Race and Racism: A Reader*, Routledge, London.

Baiocchi, G. (2006) The civilizing force of social movements: corporate and liberal codes in Brazil's public sphere. *Sociological Theory*, 24 (4), 285–311.

Balsamo, A. (1996) On the cutting edge: cosmetic surgery and new imaging technologies, in *Technologies of the Gendered Body*, Duke University Press, Durham, NC, pp. 56–79.

Barber, B. (1984) *Strong Democracy*, University of California Press, Berkeley, CA.

Barber, B. (2003) *Fear's Empire: War, Terrorism, and Democracy in an Age of Interdependence*, W.W. Norton & Co., New York.

Barker, M. (1981) *The New Racism*, Junction Books, London.

Barnouw, E. (1990) *Tube of Plenty: The Evolution of American Television*, 2nd edn, Oxford University Press, New York.

Barrett, M., *et al.* (1979) *Ideology and Cultural Production*, Croom Helm, London.

Barthes, R. (1967) *The Fashion System*, University of California Press, Berkeley, CA.

Barthes, R. (1968) *Elements of Semiology*, Hill and Wang, New York.

Barthes, R. (1993 [1957]) *Mythologies* (trans. A. Lavers), Vintage, London.

Bauman, Z. (1987) *Legislators and Interpreters on Modernity: Post-modernity and Intellectuals*, Polity Press, Cambridge.

Bauman, Z. (1989) *Modernity and the Holocaust*, Polity Press, Cambridge.

Bauman, Z. (1990) *Thinking Sociologically: An Introduction for Everyone*, Blackwell, Oxford.

Bauman, Z. (1992) *Intimations of Postmodernity*, Routledge, London.

Beck, U. (1992) *Risk Society: Towards a New Modernity*, Sage, London.

Beck, U. (2000) *What Is Globalization?*, Polity Press, Cambridge.

Becker, H. (1951) The professional dance musician and his audience. *American Journal of Sociology*, 57, 136–44.

Becker, H. (1963) *Outsiders: Studies in the Sociology of Deviance*, The Free Press, New York.

Becker, H. (1984) *Art Worlds*, University of California Press, Berkeley, CA.

Belk, R.W., Wallendorf, M. and Sherry, J.F. Jr (1989) The sacred and profane in consumer behaviour: theodicy on the odyssey. *Journal of Consumer Research*, 16 (1), 1–38.

Benhabib, S. (2002) *The Claims of Culture*, Princeton University Press, Princeton, NJ.

Benjamin, W. (1999) *Illuminations*, Pimlico, London.

Benn Michaels, W. (2007) *The Trouble with Diversity: How We Learned to Love Identity and Ignore Inequality*, Metropolitan Books/Henry Holt & Company, New York.

Bennett, A. (1999a) Rappin' on the Tyne: white hip hop culture in northeast England – an ethnographic study. *Sociological Review*, 47 (1), 1–24.

Bennett, A. (1999b) Hip hop am main: the localisation of rap music and hip hop culture. *Media, Culture and Society*, 21 (1), 77–91.

Bennett, A. (1999c) Subcultures or neo-tribes?: Rethinking the relationship between youth, style and musical taste. *Sociology*, 33 (3), 599–617.

Bennett, A. (2000) *Popular Music and Youth Culture: Music, Identity and Place*, Macmillan, Basingstoke.

Bennett, A. (2002) Researching youth culture and popular music: a methodological critique. *British Journal of Sociology*, 53 (3), 451–66.

Bennett, A. (2004) New tales from Canterbury: the making of a virtual music scene, in *Music Scenes: Local, Trans-Local and Virtual* (eds A. Bennett and R.A. Peterson), Vanderbilt University Press, Nashville, TN, pp. 205–20.

Bennett, A. (2005) *Culture and Everyday Life*, Sage, London.

Bennett, A. (2006) Punks not dead: the significance of punk rock for an older generation of fans. *Sociology*, 40 (1), 219–35.

Bennett, A. (2008a) Towards a cultural sociology of popular music. *Journal of Sociology*, 4 (4), 419–32.

Bennett, A. (2008b) Popular music, media and the narrativisation of place, in *Sonic Synergies: Music, Identity. Technology and Community* (eds G. Bloustien, M. Peters and S. Luckman), Ashgate, Aldershot, pp. 69–78.

Bennett, T., Martin, G., Mercer, C. and Woollacott, J. (1981) *Culture, Ideology and Social Process*, Open University Press, London.

Bennett, T., Savage, M., Silva, E., Warde, A., Gayo-Cal, M. and Wright, D. (2009) *Culture, Class and Distinction*, Routledge, London.

Berger, P. (1967) *The Sacred Canopy*, Anchor, New York.

Berger, P. (2002) The cultural dynamics of globalization, in *Many Globalizations* (eds P. Berger and S. Huntington), Oxford University Press, Oxford, pp. 1–16.

Beyer, P. (1994) *Religion and Globalization*, Sage, London.

Bhabha, H. (1994) *The Place of Culture*, Routledge, London.

Bhatt, C. (2004) Contemporary geopolitics and alterity research, in *Researching Race and Racism: Social Research Today Series* (eds M. Bulmer and J. Solomos), Routledge, London, pp. 16–36.

Bhatt, C. (2006) The fetish of the margin: religious absolutism, anti-racism and postcolonial silence. *New Formations: Special Issue – Postcolonial Studies After Iraq*, 59, 98–115.

Biddiss, M. (ed.) (1970) *Gobineau: Selected Political Writings*, Cape, London.

Biddiss, M. (ed.) (1979) *Images of Race*, Leicester University Press, Leicester.

Biernacki, R. (2009) After quantitative cultural sociology: interpretive science as calling, in *Meaning and Method: The Cultural Approach to Sociology* (eds I. Reed and J.C. Alexander), Paradigm, Boulder, CO, pp. 119–208.

Bleier, R. (1991) Science and gender, in *A Reader in Feminist Knowledge* (ed. S. Gunew), Routledge, London, pp. 249–56.

Blumer, H. (1969) Fashion: from class differentiation to collective selection. *Sociological Quarterly*, 10, 275–91.

Blythman, J. (2005) *Shopped: The Shocking Power of British Supermarkets*, Harper Perennial, London.

Bordo, S. (1993) 'Material girl': the effacements of postmodern culture, in *Unbearable Weight* (S. Bardo), University of California Press, Berkeley, CA, pp. 245–76.

Bordo, S. (1999) *The Male Body*, Farrar, Straus and Giroux, New York.

Bourdieu, P. (1977) *Outline of a Theory of Practice*, Cambridge University Press, Cambridge.

Bourdieu, P. (1984) *Distinction: A Social Critique of the Judgement of Taste* (trans. R. Nice), Routledge & Kegan Paul, London.

Bourdieu, P. (1990) *The Logic of Practice*, Stanford University Press, Stanford, CA.

Bourdieu, P. (1998) *On Television*, New Press, New York.

Bourdieu, P. (2005) The political field, the social science field, and the journalistic field, in *Bourdieu and the Journalistic Field* (eds R. Benson and E. Neveu), Polity Press, Cambridge, pp. 29–47.

Bové, J. Dufour, F. and de Casparis, A. (2002) *The World is Not for Sale: Farmers Against Junk Food*, Verso, London.

Boyle, D. (2004) *Authenticity: Brands, Fakes and the Lust for Real Life*, Harper Perennial, London.

Briggs, A. (1970) *History of Broadcasting in the United Kingdom*, Oxford University Press, Oxford.

Butler, J. (1997 [1988]) Performative acts and gender constitution. An essay in phenomenology and feminist theory, in *Writing on the Body: Female Embodiment and Feminist Theory* (eds K. Conboy, N. Medina and S. Stanbury), Columbia University Press, New York, pp. 519–31.

Caldwell, M.L. (2004) Domesticating the French fry: McDonalds and consumerism in Moscow. *Journal of Consumer Culture*, 4, 5–26.

Campbell, C. (2007) *The Easternization of the West*, Paradigm, Boulder, CO.

Cantril, H., Gaudet, H. and Herzog, H. (1940) *The Invasion from Mars: A Study in the Psychology of Panic*, Princeton University Press, Princeton, NJ.

Castells, M. (1997) *The Power of Identity, The Information Age: Economy, Society and Culture*, Vol. 2, Blackwell, Oxford.

Castoriadis, C. (1992) Reflections on racism. *Thesis Eleven*, 32, 1–12.

Cavicchi, D. (1998) *Tramps Like Us: Music and Meaning Among Springsteen Fans*, Oxford University Press, New York.

Chaney, D. (1993) *Fictions of Collective Life: Public Drama in Late Modern Culture*, Routledge, London.

Chaney, D. (1994) *The Cultural Turn: Scene Setting Essays on Contemporary Cultural History*, Routledge, London.

Chaney, D. (1996) *Lifestyles*, Routledge, London.

Chaney, D. (2002) *Cultural Change and Everyday Life*, Palgrave, Basingstoke.

Chaney, D. (2004) Fragmented culture and subcultures, in *After Subculture: Critical Studies in Contemporary Youth Culture* (eds A. Bennett and K. Kahn-Harris), Palgrave, Basingstoke, pp. 36–48.

Charles, D. (2001) *Lords of the Harvest: Biotech, Big Money and the Future of Food*, Perseus, Cambridge, MA.

Chossudovsky, M. (2008) Global famine. *Global Research*, May, http://www.globalresearch.ca/index.php?content=va&aid=8877 (accessed 20 September 2011).

Chu, H. (2009) Spreading the atheist word; a supporter explains the surprisingly popular British bus ads. *Los Angeles Times*, 12 January.

Clark, T.J. (1999) *Farewell to an Idea: Episodes from a History of Modernism*, Yale University Press, London.

Clark, T.N. and Lipset, S.M. (1991) Are social classes dying? *International Sociology*, 6 (4), 397–410.

Cohen, P. & Bains, J. (1988) *Multi-racist Britain*, Macmillan, London.

Cohen, S. (1985) *Visions of Social Control: Crime, Punishment and Class*, Polity Press, Cambridge.

Cohen, S. (1991) *Rock Culture in Liverpool: Popular Music in the Making*, Clarendon Press, Oxford.

Collins, F.S. (2004) What we do and don't know about 'race', 'ethnicity', genetics and health at the dawn of the genome era. *Nature Genetic Supplement*, 36 (11), S13–15.

Condry, I. (1999) The social production of difference: imitation and authenticity in Japanese rap music, in *Transactions, Transgressions, Transformations: American Culture in Western Europe and Japan* (eds H. Fehrenbach and U. Poiger), Berghan Books, Providence, RI, pp. 166–84.

Cooper, R.S., Kaufman, J. and Ward, R. (2003) Race and genomics. *New England Journal of Medicine*, 348 (12), 1166–70.

Corner, J. (1991) *Popular Television in Britain: Studies in Cultural History*, British Film Institute, London.

Cox, O.C. (1970) *Caste, Class and Race: A Study in Social Dynamics*, Monthly Review Press, New York.

Crane, D. (2000) *Fashion and Its Social Agendas: Class, Gender and Identity in Clothing*, University of Chicago Press, Chicago.

Cregan, K. (2006) *The Sociology of the Body: Mapping the Abstraction of Embodiment*, Sage, London.

Curtin, P.D. (1964) *Images of Africa: British Ideas and Action*, University of Wisconsin, Madison, WI.

Cvetkovich, A. and Kellner, D. (1997) Thinking global and local, in *Articulating the Global and the Local* (eds A. Cvetkovich and D. Kellner), Westview, Boulder, CO, pp. 1–30.

Dalton, L., Mazur, E. and Siems, M. (2011) Homer the Heretic and Charlie Church: parody, piety, and pluralism on *The Simpsons*, in *God in the Details* (eds E. Mazur and K. McCarthy), 2nd edn, Routledge, New York, pp. 231–47.

Daly, M. (1973) *Beyond God the Father: Toward a Philosophy of Women's Liberation*, Beacon Press, Boston.

David, E. (1970 [1960]) *French Provincial Cooking*, Penguin, Harmondsworth.

Davidman, L. (1997) *Tradition in a Rootless World*, University of California Press, Berkeley, CA.

Davies, N. (2008) *Flat Earth News: An Award-winning Reporter Exposes Falsehood, Distortion and Propaganda in Global Media*, Chatto and Windus, London.

Davis, F. (1994) *Fashion, Culture and Identity*, University of Chicago Press, Chicago.

Davis, L. (1983) *Factual Fictions: The Origins of the English Novel*, Columbia University Press, New York.

Dayan, D. and Katz, E. (1992) *Media Events: The Live Broadcasting of History*, Harvard University Press, Cambridge, MA.

de Beauvoir, S. (1954) *The Second Sex* (ed. and trans. H.M. Parshley), Alden Press, London.

de Certeau, M. (1984) *The Practice of Everyday Life*, Vol. I, University of California Press, Berkeley, CA.

de Saussure, F. (1966 [1916]) *Course in General Linguistics*, Peter Owen, London.

Dennis, N., Henriques, F. and Slaughter, C. (1969) *Coal is Our Life: An Analysis of a Yorkshire Mining Community*, Tavistock, London.

DeNora, T. (2000) *Music in Everyday Life*, Cambridge University Press, Cambridge.

Douglas, M. (1966) *Purity and Danger: An Analysis of Concepts of Pollution and Taboo*, Routledge, London.

Douglas, M. (1970) *Natural Symbols: Explorations in Cosmology*, Penguin, Harmondsworth.

Dowd, T.J., Liddle, K. and Nelson, J. (2004) Music festivals as scenes: examples from serious music, womyn's music and skatepunk, in *Music Scenes: Local, Translocal and Virtual* (eds A. Bennett and R.A. Peterson), Vanderbilt University Press, Nashville, TN, pp. 149–67.

Du Bois, W.E.B (1989 [1903]) *The Souls of Black Folk*, Bantam, New York.

Du Gay, P. and Pryke, M. (eds) (2002) *Cultural Economy, Cultural Analysis and Commercial Life*, Sage, London.

Durkheim, É. (1965 [1912]) *The Elementary Forms of Religious Life*, Free Press, New York.

Durkheim, É. and Mauss, M. (1963) *Primitive Classification*, University of Chicago Press, Chicago.

Durkheim, É. (1995) *The Elementary Forms of Religious Life* (trans. K. E. Fields), Free Press, New York.

Eagleton, T. (ed.) (1989) *Raymond Williams: Critical Perspectives*, Polity Press, Cambridge.

Eagleton, T. (2008) Determinacy kills. *London Review of Books*, 30, 12.

Edles, L.D. (2002) *Cultural Sociology in Practice*, Blackwell, Oxford.

Edwards, A. (1989) The sex/gender distinction: has it outlived its usefulness? *Australian Feminist Studies*, 10, 1–12.

Elias, N. (2000) *The Civilizing Process: Sociogentic and Psychogentic Investigations* (trans. Edmund Jephcott), Blackwell, Oxford.

Eliot, T.S. (1948) *Notes Towards the Definition of Culture*, Faber, London.

Elsom, J. (1976) *Post-war British Theatre*, Routledge and Kegan Paul, London.

Emmison, M. and Smith, P. (2000) *Researching the Visual: Images, Objects, Contexts and Interactions in Social and Cultural Inquiry*, Sage, London.

Entwistle, J. (2000) *The Fashioned Body: Fashion, Dress and Modern Social Theory*, Polity Press, Cambridge.

Evans, P.B., Ruechemeyer, D. and Skocpol, T. (1985) On the road toward a more adequate understanding of the state, in *Bringing the State Back In* (eds P.B. Evans, D. Ruechemeyer and T. Skocpol), Cambridge University Press, New York, pp. 347–65.

Eyerman, R. (2001) *Cultural Trauma: Slavery and the Formation of African-American Identity*, Cambridge University Press, New York.

Fanon, F. (1980) Racism and culture, in *Towards an African Revolution* (F. Fanon), Writers and Readers Publishing Collective, London, pp. 31–44.

Fanon, F. (1986) *Black Skins, White Masks*, Pluto Press, London.

Fantasia, R. (1995) Fast food in France. *Theory and Society*, 24 (2), 201–43.

Featherstone, M. (1990a) Perspectives on consumer culture. *Sociology*, 24 (1), 5–22.

Featherstone, M. (ed.) (1990b) *Global Culture: Nationalism, Globalization and Modernity*, Sage, London.

Featherstone, M., Hepworth, M. and Turner, B. (1991) *The Body: Social Process and Cultural Theory*, Sage, London.

Fekete, L. (2009) *A Suitable Enemy: Racism, Migration and Islamophobia in Europe*, Pluto Press, London.

Fernandez-Armesto, F. (2001) *Food: A History*, Macmillan, Basingstoke.

Finke, R. and Iannaccone, L. (1993) Supply-side explanations for religious change. *Annals, AAPSS*, 527, 27–39.

Finney, N. and Simpson, L. (2009) *Sleepwalking to Segregation? Challenging Myths about Race and Migration*, Policy Press, Bristol.

Fischler, C. (1999) The 'mad-cow' crisis: a global perspective, in *Food in Global History* (ed. R. Grew), Westview Press, Boulder, CO, pp. 207–31.

Flinders, C.L. (1998) *At the Root of This Longing: Reconciling a Spiritual Hunger and a Feminist Thirst*, Harper, San Francisco.

Foucault, M. (1963) *The Birth of the Clinic: An Archaeology of Medical Perception*, Gallimard, Paris.

Foucault, M. (1964) *Madness and Civilisation: A History of Insanity in the Age of Reason*, Gallimard, Paris.

Foucault, M. (1975) *Discipline and Punish: The Birth of the Prison*, Gallimard, Paris.

Foucault, M. (1976–84) *The History of Sexuality* (3 vols), Gallimard, Paris.

Fraser, N. (1992) Rethinking the public sphere: a contribution to the critique of actually existing democracy, in *Habermas and the Public Sphere* (ed. C. Calhoun), MIT Press, Cambridge, MA, pp. 109–42.

Fredrickson, G.M. (2002) *Racism: A Short History*, Princeton University Press, Princeton, NJ.

Freud, S. (1961 [1927]) *Civilization and its Discontents*, W.W. Norton, New York.

Freud, S. (1986 [1923]) The ego and the id, in *The Essentials of Psychoanalysis: The Definitive Collection of Sigmund Freud's Writings* (trans. J. Strachey), Penguin, London, pp. 439–83.

Friedman, T. (1999) *The Lexus and the Olive Tree*, HarperCollins, London.

Friedmann, H. (1994) The international relations of food: the unfolding crisis of national regulation, in *Food: Multidisciplinary Perspectives* (eds B. Harriss-White and R. Hoffenberg), Blackwell, Oxford, pp. 174–204.

Frisby, D. and Featherstone, M. (1997) *Simmel on Culture: Selected Writings*, Sage, London.

Frith, S. (1978) *The Sociology of Rock*, Constable, London.

Frith, S. (1981) The magic that can set you free: the ideology of folk and the myth of rock. *Popular Music*, 1, 159–68.

Frith, S. (1983) *Sound Effects: Youth, Leisure and the Politics of Rock*, Constable, London.

Frith, S. (1987) Towards an aesthetic of popular music, in *Music and Society: The Politics of Composition, Performance and Reception* (eds R. Leppert and S. McClary), Cambridge University Press, Cambridge, pp. 113–49.

Frith, S. (1992) The cultural study of popular music, in *Performing Rites: On the Value of Popular Music* (eds L. Grossberg, C. Nelson and S. Frith), Oxford University Press, Oxford, pp. 174–86.

Frith, S. and Horne, H. (1987) *Art into Pop*, Methuen, London.

Froese, P. (2001) Hungary for religion: a supply-side interpretation of the Hungarian religious revival. *Journal for the Scientific Study of Religion*, 40 (2), 251–68.

Frow, J. (1987) Accounting for tastes: some problems in Bourdieu's sociology of culture. *Cultural Studies*, 1 (1), 59–73.

Furedi, F. (2004) *Therapy Culture: Cultivating Vulnerability in an Uncertain Age*, Routledge, London.

Gagne, P., Tewksbury, R. and McGaughey, D. (1997) Coming out and crossing over: identity formation and proclamation in a transgender community. *Gender and Society*, 11 (4), 478–501.

Gans, H.J. (1967) Popular culture in America, in *Social Problems: A Modern Approach* (ed. H.S. Becker), John Wiley & Sons, Inc., New York, pp. 549–620.

Gatens, M. (1983) A critique of the sex/gender distinction, in *Beyond Marxism? Interventions After Marx* (eds J. Allen and P. Patten), Sydney: Intervention, pp. 143–60.

Gatens, M. (1991) A critique of the sex/gender distinction, in *A Reader in Feminist Knowledge* (ed. S. Gunew), Routledge, London, pp. 139–57.

Geertz, C. (1973) *The Interpretation of Cultures*, Basic Books, New York.

Gergen, K. (1991) *The Saturated Self*, Basic Books, New York.

Ghosh, J. (2009) Will the crisis reverse global migration? Yaleglobal On-Line, Yale University, http://yaleglobal.yale.edu/content/crisis-reverse-global-migration (accessed 23 September 2011).

Gibson, M. (2001) Guiltless credit and the moral economy of salvation. *Journal of Social and Political Thought*, 1 (3), http://www.yorku.ca/jspot/3/mgibson.htm (accessed 23 September 2011).

Gibson, M. (2006) Bodies without histories: cosmetic surgery and the undoing of time. *Australian Feminist Studies*, 21 (49), 51–63.

Giddens, A. (1990) *The Consequences of Modernity*, Polity Press, Cambridge.

Giddens, A. (1991) *Modernity and Self-Identity: Self and Society in the Late Modern Age*, Polity Press, Cambridge.

Giddens, A. (1994) *The Transformation of Intimacy: Sexuality, Love and Eroticism in Modern Societies*, Polity Press, Cambridge.

Gilman, S.L. (1991) *The Jew's Body*, Routledge, New York.

Gilman, S.L. and Katz, S.T. (eds) (1991) *Anti-Semitism in Times of Crisis*, New York University Press, New York.

Gilroy, P. (1987) *There Ain't No Black in the Union Jack: The Cultural Politics of Race and Nation*, Unwin Hyman, London.

Gilroy, P. (1993) *The Black Atlantic: Modernity and Double Consciousness*, Verso, London.

Gilroy, P. (2000) *Between Camps: Nations, Culture, and the Allure of Race*, Allen Lane, London.

Gilroy, P. (2004) *After Empire: Melancholia of Convivial Culture*, Routledge, London.

Gilroy, P. (2010) *Darker Than Blue: On the Moral Economies of Black Atlantic Culture*, Belknap Press of Harvard University Press, Cambridge, MA.

Gitlin, T. (1993) *The Sixties: Years of Hope, Days of Rage*, Bantam, New York.

Goffman, E. (1959) *The Presentation of Self in Everyday Life*, Doubleday, New York.

Goffman, E. (1972) Embarrassment and social organization, in *Interactional Ritual: Essays on Face-to-Face Interaction* (E. Goffman), Penguin, Harmondsworth, pp. 97–112.

Goldberg, D. (2002) *The Racial State*, Blackwell, Oxford.

Gorman, L. and McLean, D. (2003) *Media and Society in the Twentieth Century*, Blackwell, Oxford.

Gould, L. (ed.) (2002) *Watching Television Come of Age: New York Times Reviews*, University of Texas Press, Austin, TX.

Gramsci, A. (1971) *Selections from the Prison Notebooks*, Lawrence and Wishart, London.

Grazian, D. (2004) The symbolic economy of authenticity in the Chicago blues scene, in *Music Scenes: Local, Trans-Local and Virtual* (eds A. Bennett and R.A. Peterson), Vanderbilt University Press, Nashville, TN, pp. 31–47.

Greeley, A. (1991) American exceptionalism, in *Is America Different?* (ed. B. Shafer), Clarendon Press, Oxford, pp. 116–37.

Greenberg, C. (1986 [1939]) Avant-garde and kitsch, in *Clement Greenberg: The Collected Essays and Criticism, Vol. I – Perceptions and Judgments 1939–1944* (ed. J. O'Brian), University of Chicago Press, Chicago, pp. 22–40.

Griswold, W. (2004) *Cultures and Societies in a Changing World*, Pine Forge Press, Thousand Oaks, CA.

Grosz, E. (1994) *Volatile Bodies: Toward a Corporeal Feminism*, Allen & Unwin, Sydney.

Guptill, A. and Wilkins, J.L. (2002) Buying into the food system: trends in food retailing in the US and implications for local foods. *Agriculture and Human Values*, 19, 39–51.

Guralnick, P. (1978) *Feel Like Going Home: Portraits in Blues and Rock 'n' Roll*, Omnibus, London.

Gutmann, A. and Thompson, D. (1996) *Democracy and Disagreement*, Harvard University Press, Cambridge, MA.

Habermas, J. (1989 [1962]) *The Structural Transformation of the Public Sphere* (trans. Thomas Burger), MIT Press, Cambridge, MA.

Habermas, J. (1996) *Between Facts and Norms: Contributions to a Discourse Theory of Law and Democracy*, MIT Press, Cambridge, MA.

Hage, G. (1998) *Against Paranoid Nationalism: Searching for Hope in a Shrinking Society*, Pluto Press, Sydney.

Hall, S. (1973) *Encoding and Decoding in the Television Discourse*, CCCS, Birmingham.

Hall, S. (1993) Culture, community, nation. *Cultural Studies*, 7 (3), 349–63.

Hall, S., Critcher, C., Jefferson, T., Clarke, J. and Roberts, B. (1978) *Policing the Crisis: Mugging, the State and Law and Order*, Palgrave Macmillan, London.

Hall, S. and Jefferson, T. (eds) (1976) *Resistance Through Rituals: Youth Subcultures in Post-War Britain*, Hutchinson, London.

Harding, S. (1993) *The 'Racial' Economy of Science: Toward a Democratic Future*, Indiana University Press, Bloomington, IN.

Harrison, A.K. (2009) *Hip Hop Underground: The Integrity and Ethics of Racial Identification*, Temple University Press, Philadelphia, PA.

Harrison, J.S., *et al.* (2005) Exporting a North American concept to Asia: Starbucks in China, *Cornell Hotel and Restaurant Administration Quarterly*, 46 (2), 275–83.

Hartley, J. (2003) *A Short History of Cultural Studies*, Sage, London.

Harvey, D. (1989) *The Condition of Postmodernity: An Enquiry into the Origins of Cultural Change*, Blackwell, Oxford.

Hebdige, D. (1979) *Subculture: The Meaning of Style*, Routledge and Kegan Paul, London.

Held, D. and McGrew, A. (2000) *The Global Transformations Reader: An Introduction to the Globalization Debate*, Polity Press, Cambridge.

Held, D., McGrew, A., Goldblatt, D. and Perraton, J. (eds) (1999) *Global Transformations: Politics, Economics and Culture*, Polity Press, Cambridge.

Hennessey, P. (2006) *Never Again: Britain 1945–51*, Penguin, London.

Hennion, A. (2003) Music and mediation: towards a new sociology of music, in *The Cultural Study of Music: A Critical Introduction* (eds M. Clayton, T. Herbert and R. Middleton), Routledge, London, pp. 80–91.

Hertz, R. (2007) The pre-eminence of the right hand, in *Beyond the Body Proper: Reading the Anthropology of Material Life* (eds M. Lack and J. Farquhar), Duke University Press, Durham, NC, pp. 30–40.

Hesmondhalgh, D. (2002) *The Culture Industries*, Sage, London.

Hickman, M., Walter, B., Morgan, S. and Bradley, J. (2005) The limitations of whiteness and the boundaries of Englishness: second-generation Irish identifications and positionings in multi-ethnic Britain. *Ethnicities*, 5 (2), 160–82.

Hill, J. (1986) *Sex, Class and Realism: British Cinema 1956–1963*, British Film Institute, London.

Hobsbawm, E. (1998) The nation and globalization. *Constellations*, 5 (1), 1–9.

Hoggart, R. (1957) *The Uses of Literacy: Aspects of Working Class Life*, Chatto and Windus, London.

Holt, D.B. (2004) *How Brands Become Icons: The Principles of Cultural Branding*, Harvard Business School Press, Boston, MA.

Hout, M. and Fischer, C. (2002) Why more Americans have no religious preference: politics and generations. *American Sociological Review*, 67 (2), 165–90.

Howes, D. (ed.) (1996) *Cross-Cultural Consumption: Global Markets, Local Realities*, Routledge, London.

Humphery, K. (1998) *Shelf Life: Supermarkets and the Changing Cultures of Consumption*, Cambridge University Press, Cambridge.

Huq, R. (1999) Living in France: the parallel universe of hexagonal pop, in *Living Through Pop* (ed. A. Blake), Routledge, London, pp. 131–45.

Illouz, E. (2009) Emotions, imagination and consumption: a new research agenda. *Journal of Consumer Culture*, 9 (3), 377–413.

Inglehart, R. (1990) *Culture Shift in Advanced Industrial Society*, Princeton University Press, Princeton, NJ.

Inglis, D. and Gimlin, D. (eds) (2010) *The Globalization of Food*, Berg, Oxford.

Inglis, D., Gimlin, D. and Thorpe, C. (2007) *Food and Society: Critical Concepts in the Social Sciences* (4 vols), Routledge, London.

Irigaray, L. (1985 [1974, in French]) *The Speculum of the Other Woman*, Cornell University Press, Ithaca, NY.

Irigaray, L. (1996) *I Love to You: Sketch of a Possible Felicity in History* (trans. A. Martin), Routledge, New York.

Iyengar, S. (1994) *Is Anyone Responsible? How Television Frames Political Issues*, University of Chicago Press, Chicago.

Jacobs, R.N. (2000) *Race, Media, and the Crisis of Civil Society: From Watts to Rodney King*, Cambridge University Press, Harvard, MA.

Jacobs, R.N. and Glass, D.J. (2002) Media publicity and the voluntary sector: the case of non-profit organizations in New York. *Voluntas: International Journal of Voluntary and Nonprofit Organizations*, 13 (3), 235–52.

Jacobs, R.N. and Sobieraj, S. (2007) Narrative and legitimacy: US Congressional debates about the nonprofit sector. *Sociological Theory*, 25 (1), 1–25.

Jacobs, R.N. and Townsley, E. (2011) *The Space of Opinion: Media Intellectuals and the Public Sphere*, Oxford University Press, New York.

James, A. (1996) Cooking the books: global or local identities in contemporary British food cultures?, in *Cross-Cultural Consumption: Global Markets, Local Realities* (ed. D. Howes), Routledge, London, pp. 77–93.

James, W. (1918 [1890]) *The Principles of Psychology*, H. Holt, London.

James, W. (1936 [1902]) *The Varieties of Religious Experience*, Modern Library, New York.

Jameson, F. (1991) *Postmodernism, or, The Cultural Logic of Late Capitalism*, Verso, London.

Jameson, F. (1998) Postmodernism and the consumer society, in *The Cultural Turn: Selected Writings on the Postmodern, 1983–1998* (F. Jameson), Verso, London, pp. 1–20.

Jessop, B., Bonnett, K., Bromley, S. and Ling, T. (1988) *Thatcherism: A Tale of Two Nations*, Polity Press, Cambridge.

Jones, G. (1980) *Social Darwinism and English Thought: The Interaction Between Biological and Social Theory*, Harvester, London.

Jordan, W.D. (1968) *White Over Black: American Attitudes Toward the Negro 1550–1812*, W.W. Norton, New York.

Kahn-Harris, K. (2006) 'Roots?': The relationship between the global and the local within the extreme metal scene, in *The Popular Music Studies Reader* (eds A. Bennett, B. Shank and J. Toynbee), Routledge, London, pp. 128–36.

Kaplan, G. and Rogers, L.J. (2003) *Gene Worship: Moving Beyond the Nature/Nurture Debate over Genes, Brain, and Gender*, Other Press, New York.

Katz, D. (1960) The functional approach to the study of attitudes. *Public Opinion Quarterly*, 24, 163–204.

Katz, E. and Lazarsfeld, P. (1955) *Personal Influence*, The Free Press, New York.

Katz, E. and Liebes, T. (1985) Mutual aid in the decoding of *Dallas*, in *Television in Transition* (eds P. Drummond and R. Paterson), British Film Institute, London, pp. 187–98.

Kawamura, Y. (2006) Japanese teens as producers of street fashion. *Current Sociology*, 54 (5), 784–801.

Keen, B. (1999) Restructuring food for corporate profit: the corporate genetics of Cargill and Monsanto. *Agriculture and Human Values*, 16, 161–7.

Kopytoff, I. (1986) The cultural biography of things: commoditization as process, in *The Social Life of Things: Commodities in Cultural Perspective* (ed. A. Appadurai), Cambridge University Press, Cambridge, pp. 64–94.

Kovel, J. (1970) *White Racism: A Psychohistory*, Columbia University Press, New York.

Ku, A. (1999) *Narratives, Politics, and the Public Sphere: Struggles Over Political Reform in the Final Transitional Years in Hong Kong*, Ashgate, Aldershot.

Lamont, M. (1992) *Money, Morals and Manners: The Culture of the French and the American Upper-Middle Class*, University of Chicago Press, Chicago.

Lash, S. (1990) *Sociology of Postmodernism*, Routledge, London.

Lash, S. and Urry, J. (1987) *The End of Organised Capitalism*, Polity Press, Cambridge.

Lash, S. and Urry, J. (1994) *Economies of Signs and Space*, Sage, London.

Lazarsfeld, P., Berelson, B. and Gaudet, H. (1944) *The People's Choice*, Columbia University Press, New York.

Leach, E. (1964) Anthropological aspects of language: animal categories and verbal abuse, in *New Directions in the Study of Language* (ed. E.H. Lenneberg), MIT Press, Cambridge, MA, pp. 23–63.

Leavis, F.R. (1977) *The Living Principle: 'English' as a Discipline of Thought*, Chatto and Windus, London.

Leavis, Q.D. (1932) *Fiction and the Reading Public*, Chatto and Windus, London.

Leitch, A. (2003) Slow food and the politics of pork fat: Italian food and European identity. *Ethnos*, 68 (4), 437–62.

Lemarchand, R. (1996) *Burundi: Ethnic Conflict and Genocide*, Cambridge University Press, Cambridge.

Lentin, A. (2008) *Racism: A Beginner's Guide*, Oneworld, Oxford.

Lévi-Strauss, C. (1962) *Totemism* (trans. R. Needham), Penguin, Harmondsworth.

Lévi-Strauss, C. (1966 [1962]) *The Savage Mind*, University of Chicago Press, Chicago.

Lévi-Strauss, C. (1973) *Tristes Tropiques*, Picador, London.

Lévi-Strauss, C. (1979) *Myth and Meaning: Cracking the Code of Culture*, Schocken, New York.

Lewis, G.H. (1992) Who do you love? The dimensions of musical taste, in *Popular Music and Communication*, 2nd edn (ed. J. Lull), Sage, London, pp. 134–51.

Lichterman, P. (2005) *Elusive Togetherness: Church Groups Trying to Bridge America's Divisions*, Princeton University Press, Princeton, NJ.

Lien, M.E. (2004) Dogs, whales and kangaroos: transnational activism and food taboos, in *The Politics of Food* (eds M.E. Lien and B. Nerlich), Berg, Oxford, pp. 179–97.

Lien, M.E. and Nerlich, B. (eds) (2004) *The Politics of Food*, Berg, Oxford.

Lightfoot, C. (1997) *The Culture of Adolescent Risk-Taking*, Guilford Press, New York.

Lorimer, D.A. (1978) *Colour, Class, and the Victorians: English Attitudes to the Negro in the Mid-nineteenth Century*, Leicester University Press, Leicester.

Lovejoy, A. (1964) *The Great Chain of Being: A Study of the History of an Idea*, Harvard University Press, Cambridge, MA.

Lozado, E.P. Jr (2005) Globalized childhood? Kentucky Fried Chicken in Beijing, in *The Cultural Politics of Food and Eating: A Reader* (eds J.L. Watson and M.L. Caldwell), Blackwell, Oxford, pp. 163–79.

Lu, S. and Fine, G.A. (1995) The presentation of ethnic authenticity: Chinese food as a social accomplishment. *Sociological Quarterly*, 36 (3), 535–53.

Macleod, A.E. (1991) *Accommodating Protest: Working Women, the New Veiling, and Change in Cairo*, Columbia University Press, New York.

Macnaghten, P. (2004) Animals in their nature: a case study on public attitudes to animals, genetic modification and 'nature'. *Sociology*, 38 (3), 533–51.

Maffesoli, M. (1996) *The Time of the Tribes: The Decline of Individualism in Mass Society* (trans. D. Smith), Sage, London.

Malbon, B. (1999) *Clubbing: Dancing, Ecstasy and Vitality*, Routledge, London.

Mansfield, S. (2008) *The Faith of Barack Obama*, Thomas Nelson, Nashville, TN.

Markula, P. (2008) Governing obese bodies in a control society. *Junctures: The Journal for Thematic Dialogue*, 11, 53–65.

Marshall, G. (1997) *Repositioning Class. Social Inequality in Industrial Societies*, Sage, London.

Martin, P.J. (1995) *Sounds and Society: Themes in the Sociology of Music*, Manchester University Press, Manchester.

Marx, K. (1978 [1844]) Contribution to the critique of Hegel's philosophy of right, in *The Economic and Philosophical Manuscripts* (K. Marx, trans. M. Milligan), Dover, New York, pp. 3–129.

Marx, K. and Engels, F. (1978) The German ideology, in *The Marx-Engels Reader* (ed. R. Tucker), W.W. Norton & Co., New York, pp. 146–201.

Mason, T. (1989) Football, in *Sport in Britain: A Social History* (ed. T. Mason), Cambridge University Press, Cambridge, pp. 146–86.

Mattelart, A. (2000) *Networking the World, 1794–2000*, University of Minnesota Press, Minneapolis.

Maxwell, I. (1994) *Phat Beats, Dope Rhymes: Hip Hop Down Under Comin' Upper*, Wesleyan University Press, Middletown, CT.

McDonnell, J. (ed.) (1991) *Public Service Broadcasting: A Reader*, Routledge, London.

McKibbin, R. (2008) What can Cameron do? *London Review of Books*, 30, 20.

McLean, A. (2004) Tasting language: the aesthetic pleasures of Elizabeth David. *Food, Culture and Society*, 7, 1.

McMichael, P. (1994) *Development and Social Change: A Global Perspective*, Pine Forge Press, Thousand Oaks, CA.

McRobbie, A. (1991) *Feminism and Youth Culture: From Jackie to Just Seventeen*, Macmillan, London.

McRobbie, A. (2009) *The Aftermath of Feminism: Gender, Culture and Social Change*, Sage, London.

Mead, G.H. (1932) *The Philosophy of the Present*, Prometheus, Amherst, NY.

Mead, G.H. (1934) *Mind, Self, and Society*, University of Chicago Press, Chicago.

Meeks, C. (2001) Civil society and the sexual politics of difference, *Sociological Theory*, 19, 325–43.

Melly, G. (1970) *Revolt into Style: The Pop Arts in Britain*, Allen Lane, London.

Michaels, W.B. (2009) What matters. *London Review of Books*, 31 (16), 11–13.

Miles, S. (2000) *Youth Lifestyles in a Changing World*, Open University Press, Buckingham.

Miller, D. (1992) The young and restless in Trinidad: a case of the local and global in mass consumption, in *Consuming Technology* (eds R. Silverstone and E. Hirsch), Routledge, London, pp. 163–82.

Miller, D. (1998) *Material Cultures: Why Some Things Matter*, University of Chicago Press, Chicago.

Miller, D. and Woodward, S. (2007) Manifesto for a study of denim. *Social Anthropology*, 15 (3), 335–51.

Miller, P. and Rose, N. (1997) Mobilizing the consumer: assembling the subject of consumption. *Theory, Culture and Society*, 14 (1), 1–36.

Miller, T. (1998) *Technologies of Truth: Cultural Citizenship and the Popular Media*, University of Minnesota Press, Minneapolis.

Mills, C.W. (1956) *The Power Elite*, Oxford University Press, New York.

Minow, N. (1961) Television and the public interest. Speech delivered to the National Association of Broadcasters, Washington, DC, 9 May.

Mintz, S.W. (2008) Food, culture and energy, in *Food and Globalization* (eds A. Nutzenadel and F. Trentmann), Berg, Oxford, pp. 207–19.

Mitchell, T. (1996) *Popular Music and Local Identity: Rock, Pop and Rap in Europe and Oceania*, Leicester University Press, London.

Mohr, J. (1998) Measuring meaning structures. *Annual Review of Sociology*, 24, 345–70.

Moore, A.F. (1993) *Rock: The Primary Text: Developing a Musicology of Rock*, Open University Press, Buckingham.

Morgan, D. (1993) You too can have a body like mine: reflection on the male body and masculinities, in *Body Matters: Essays on the Sociology of the Body* (eds S. Scott and D. Morgan), Falmer Press, London, pp. 69–88.

Morley, D. (1992) *Television, Audiences and Cultural Studies*, Routledge, London.

Mosse, G.L. (1964) *The Crisis of German Ideology: Intellectual Origins of the Third Reich*, Weidenfeld & Nicolson, London.

Mosse, G.L. (1985) *Toward the Final Solution: A History of European Racism*, University of Wisconsin Press, Madison, WI.

Muggleton, D. (2000) *Inside Subculture: The Postmodern Meaning of Style*, Berg, Oxford.

Myrdal, G. (1944) *An American Dilemma: The Negro Problem and Modern Democracy*, Harper & Bros, New York.

Nairn, T. (1993) Internationalism and the second coming. *Daedalus*, 122 (3), 155–70.

Nash, K. (2007) *Contemporary Political Sociology*, Wiley-Blackwell, Oxford.

Nathanson, P. and Young, K.K. (2001) *Spreading Misandry: The Teaching of Contempt for Men in Popular Culture*, McGill-Queen's University Press, Montreal, Quebec.

Nayak, A. (2006) After race: ethnography, race and post-race theory. *Ethnic and Racial Studies*, 29 (3), 411–30.

Nederveen Pieterse, J. (1995) Globalization and collective action, in *Globalization and Social Movements* (eds P. Hamel, H. Lustiger-Thaler, J. Nederveen Pieterse and S. Roseneil), Palgrave, Basingstoke, pp. 61–85.

Nederveen Pieterse, J. (2001) Hybridity, so what? The anti-hybridity backlash and the riddles of recognition. *Theory, Culture & Society*, 18 (2–3), 219–45.

Negus, K. (1992) *Producing Pop: Culture and Conflict in the Popular Music Industry*, Edward Arnold, London.

Nibert, D. (2002) *Animal Rights/Human Rights: Entanglements of Oppression and Liberation*, Rowman and Littlefield, Lanham, MD.

Nützenadel, A. and Trentmann, F. (eds) (2008) *Food and Globalization*, Berg, Oxford.

Obama, B. (2006) *The Audacity of Hope*, Crown Books, Lake Arbor, MD.

O'Sullivan, S. (1982) Passionate beginnings: ideological politics 1969–72. *Feminist Review*, 11, 70–86.

Owen, D. (1997) *Sociology After Postmodernism*, Sage, London.

Pakulski, J. (1993) The dying of class or of Marxist class theory. *International Sociology*, 8 (3), 279–92.

Pakulski, J. and Waters, M. (1996a) The reshaping and dissolution of social class in advanced society. *Theory and Society*, 25, 667–91.

Pakulski, J. and Waters, M. (1996b) *The Death of Class*, Sage, London.

Palmer, T. (1977) *All You Need is Love: The Story of Popular Music*, Futura, London.

Pals, D. (2009) *Introducing Religion*, Oxford University Press, Oxford.

Park, R. (1922) *The Immigrant Press and Its Control*, Harper, New York.

Park, R. (1938) Reflections on communication and culture. *American Journal of Sociology*, 44, 187–205.

Patterson, M. (2004) The rise of global fundamentalism. *National Catholic Reporter*, 5 July.

Patterson, O. (1982) *Slavery and Social Death: A Comparative Study*, Harvard University Press, London.

Peckham, S. (1998) Consuming nations, in *Consuming Passions* (eds S. Griffiths and J. Wallace), Times Higher Education Supplement, London, pp. 171–82.

Persinger, M. (1987) *Neuropsychological Bases of God Beliefs*, Praeger, New York.

Peterson, R.A. (1997) *Creating Country Music: Fabricating Authenticity*, Chicago University Press, Chicago.

Peterson, R.A. and Bennett, A. (eds) (2004) Introducing music scenes, in *Music Scenes: Local, Translocal and Virtual* (eds A. Bennett and R.A. Peterson), Vanderbilt University Press, Nashville, TN, pp. 1–16.

Petrini, C. (2003) *Slow Food: The Case for Taste*, Columbia University Press, New York.

Pew Forum on Pentecostalism (2006) Pentecostal resource page, http://pewforum.org/Christian/Evangelical-Protestant-Churches/Pentecostal-Resource-Page.aspx (accessed 23 September 2011).

Pew Research Center (2011) The future of the global Muslim population, 27 January, http://pewforum.org/The-Future-of-the-Global-Muslim-Population.aspx (accessed 23 September 2011).

Postman, N. (1985) *Amusing Ourselves to Death: Public Discourse in the Age of Show Business*, Penguin, New York.

Power, D. and Scott, A.J. (2004) *Culture Industries and the Production of Culture*, Routledge, London.

Prothero, S. (2008) *Religious Literacy*, HarperOne, New York.

Putnam, R. (2001) *Bowling Alone*, Simon and Schuster, New York.

Putnam, R. and Campbell, D. (2010) *American Grace*, Simon and Schuster, New York.

Reardon, J., Dunklee, B. and Wentworth, K. (2006) Race and crisis. SSRC Webforum – Is Race Real? http://raceandgenomics.ssrc.org/Reardon (accessed 23 September 2011).

Rebora, G. (2001) *Culture of the Fork: A Brief History of Food in Europe*, Columbia University Press, New York.

Redhead, S. (1990) *The End-of-the-Century Party: Youth and Pop Towards 2000*, Manchester University Press, Manchester.

Reed, I. and Alexander, J.C. (2009) *Meaning and Method: The Cultural Approach to Sociology*, Paradigm Press, Boulder, CO.

Reese, J. (2004) Heterosexual masculinity in the sitcom genre: the creation and circulation of the male idiot character type, MA thesis, Georgetown University, Washington, DC.

Ritzer, G. (2000) *The McDonaldization of Society*, Pine Forge Press, Thousand Oaks, CA.

Ritzer, G. (2004) *The Globalization of Nothing*, Sage, London.

Robertson, R. (1992) *Globalization: Social Theory and Global Culture*, Sage, London.

Rojek, C. and Urry, J. (eds) (1997) *Touring Cultures: Transformations of Travel and Theory*, Routledge, London.

Rose, T. (1994) *Black Noise: Rap Music and Black Culture in Contemporary America*, Wesleyan University Press, London.

Ross, K. (1996) *Fast Cars, Clean Bodies: Decolonization and the Reordering of French Culture*, MIT Press, Cambridge, MA.

Roszak, T. (1971) *The Making of a Counter-culture: Reflections on the Technocratic Society and Its Youthful Opposition*, Faber and Faber, London.

Rowbotham, S. (2001) *Promise of a Dream: Remembering the Sixties*, Penguin, Harmondsworth.

Rubin, G. (2006) The traffic in women: notes on the political economy of women, in *Feminist Anthropology: A Reader* (ed. E. Lewin), Blackwell, Oxford, pp. 87–106.

Sandbrook, D. (2006) *White Heat: A History of Britain in the Swinging Sixties*, Little Brown, London.

Sapir, E. (1931) Fashion, in *Encyclopaedia of the Social Sciences*, Vol. 6, Macmillan, New York, pp. 139–44.

Scannell, P. (1991) *A Social History of British Broadcasting, Vol. 1 – 1922–39: Serving the Nation*, Blackwell, Oxford.

Schaeffer, F. (2008) National Public Radio, *Fresh Air*, hosted by T. Gross, 9 December, transcription, http://www.npr.org/templates/story/story.php?storyId=97998654 (accessed 16 August 2011).

Schechner, R. (1993) *The Future of Ritual: Writings on Culture and Performance*, Routledge, London.

Schechner, R. (2002) *Performance Studies: An Introduction*, Routledge, New York.

Schilt, K. (2004) 'Riot Grrrl is . . .': contestation over meaning in a music scene, in *Music Scenes: Local, Trans-local and Virtual* (eds A. Bennett and R.A. Peterson), Vanderbilt University Press, Nashville, TN, pp. 115–30.

Schlosser, E. (2001) *Fast Food Nation: The Dark Side of the All-American Meal*, Houghton Mifflin, New York.

Schmidt, L.E. (2005) *Restless Souls: The Making of American Spirituality*, Harper, San Francisco.

Schudson, M. (1978) *Discovering the News*, Basic Books, New York.

Schuerkens, U. (2003) The sociological and anthropological study of globalization and localization. *Current Sociology*, 51, 209–22.

Schulz, S. (2008) Our lady hates viscose: the role of the customer image in high street fashion production. *Cultural Sociology*, 2, 385–405.

Seabrook, J. (2004) *Consuming Cultures: Globalization and Local Lives*, New Internationalist, London.

Seidman, S. (1994) *Contested Knowledge: Social Theory in the Postmodern Era*, Blackwell, Oxford.

Seidman, S. (2002) *Beyond the Closet: The Transformation of Gay and Lesbian Life*. Routledge, New York.

Serventi, S. and Sabban, F. (2003) *Pasta: The Story of a Universal Food*, Columbia University Press, New York.

Shiach, M. (1999) *Feminism and Cultural Studies*, Oxford University Press, Oxford.

Shumway, D. (1992) Rock and roll as a cultural practice, in *Present Tense: Rock and Roll and Culture* (ed. A. DeCurtis), Duke University Press, Durham, NC, pp 117–34.

Simmel, G. (1997a [1904]) The philosophy of fashion, in *Simmel on Culture* (eds D. Frisby and M. Featherstone), Sage, London, pp. 187–206.

Simmel, G. (1997b) The sociology of the meal, in *Simmel on Culture* (eds D. Frisby and M. Featherstone), Sage, London, pp. 130–5.

Simpson, T. (2008) The commercialization of Macau's cafés. *Ethnography*, 9 (2), 197–234.

Skeggs, B. (2004) *Class, Self, Culture*, Routledge, London.

Skocpol, T. (1979) *States and Social Revolutions: A Comparative Analysis of France, Russia, and China*, Cambridge University Press, Cambridge.

Skocpol, T. (1985) Bringing the state back in: strategies of analysis in current research, in *Bringing the State Back In* (eds P.B. Evans, D. Ruechemeyfer and T. Skocpol), Cambridge University Press, Cambridge, pp. 3–42.

Skocpol, T. (1996) *Boomerang: Clinton's Health Reform and the Turn Against Government*, Norton, New York.

Skocpol, T. and Amenta, E. (1986) States and social policies. *Annual Review of Sociology*, 12, 131–57.

Skrbis, Z. and Woodward, I. (2007) The ambivalence of ordinary cosmopolitanism: investigating the limits of cosmopolitan openness. *Sociological Review*, 55 (4), 730–47.

Smith, P. (2000) Culture and charisma: outline of a theory. *Acta Sociologica*, 43 (2), 101–11.

Smith, P. (2001) *Cultural Theory: An Introduction*, Blackwell, Oxford.

Smith, P. (2005) *Why War? The Cultural Logic of Iraq, the Gulf War, and Suez*, University of Chicago Press, Chicago.

Snowden, F. (1983) *Before Color Prejudice: The Ancient View of Blacks*, Harvard University Press, Cambridge, MA.

Sobal, J. (1999) Food system globalization, eating transformations and nutrition transitions, in *Food in Global History* (ed. R. Grew), Westview, Boulder, CO, pp. 171–93.

Sobieraj, S. (2011) *Soundbitten: The Perils of Media-Centered Political Activism*, New York University Press, New York.

Solomos, J. and Back, L. (1996) *Racism and Society*, Palgrave Macmillan, London.

Spillman, L. (2002) Introduction: culture and cultural sociology, in *Cultural Sociology* (ed. L. Spillman), Blackwell, Oxford, pp. 1–16.

Spurlock, M. (2004) *Super Size Me*, documentary, Showtime Networks.

Stark, R. and Finke, R. (2000) *Acts of Faith*, University of California Press, Berkeley, CA.

Stead, P. (1989) *Film and the Working Class: The Feature Film in British and American Society*, Routledge, London.

Stocking, G. (1968) *Race, Culture and Evolution: Essays in the History of Anthropology*, The Free Press, New York.

Stone, J. (2011) A fire in the sky: apocalyptic themes on the silver screen, in *God in the Details* (eds E. Mazur and K. McCarthy), 2nd edn, Routledge, New York, pp. 62–79.

Storey, J. (2003) *Inventing Popular Culture: From Folklore to Globalization*, Blackwell, Oxford.

Strassoldo, R. (1992) Globalism and localism: theoretical reflections and some evidence, in *Globalisation and Territorial Identities* (ed Z. Mlinar), Avebury, Aldershot, pp. 35–59.

Straw, W. (1991) Systems of articulation, logics of change: communities and scenes in popular music. *Cultural Studies*, 5 (3), 368–88.

Strinati, D. (1995) *An Introduction to Theories of Popular Culture*, Routledge, London.

Sullivan, J. (2006) *Jeans: A Cultural History of an American Icon*, Gotham Press, New York.

Swidler, A. (1986) Culture in action. *American Sociological Review*, 51 (2), 273–86.

Taylor, C. (1911) *Principles of Scientific Management*, Harper, New York.

Taylor, J. (2010) Queer temporalities and the significance of 'music scene' participation in the social identities of middle-aged queers. *Sociology*, 44 (5), 893–907.

The Economist (2008) The silent tsunami: the food crisis and how to solve it. 19–25 April.

Thompson, D. (1964) *Discrimination and Popular Culture*, Penguin, Harmondsworth.

Thompson, J. (2005) *The Media and Modernity*, Stanford University Press, Stanford, CA.

Thompson, R. (1997) *Television's Second Golden Age*, Syracuse University Press, Syracuse, NY.

Thornham, S. (2000) *Feminist Theory and Cultural Studies: Stories of Unsettled Relations*, Arnold, London.

Thornton, J. (1992) *Africa and Africans in the Making of the Atlantic World, 1400–1800*, Cambridge University Press, Cambridge.

Tilley, C., Keane, W., Kuechler, S., Rowlands, M. and Spyer, P. (2006) *Handbook of Material Culture*, Sage, London.

Tilly, C. (1984) *Big Structures, Large Processes, Huge Comparisons*, Russell Sage Foundation, New York.

Todorov, T. (1984) *The Conquest of America: The Question of the Other*, Harper & Row, New York.

Tomlinson, J. (1997) *Cultural Imperialism: A Critical Introduction*, Pinter, London.

Tucker, R.C. (1978) *The Marx-Engels Reader*, 2nd edn, W.W. Norton, New York.

Tudor, A. (1999) *Decoding Culture: Theory and Method in Cultural Studies*, Sage, London.

Tulloch, J. and Lupton, D. (2002) Consuming risk, consuming science: the case of GM foods. *Journal of Consumer Culture*, 2, 363–83.

Tunstall, J. (1977) *The Media are American*, Constable, London.

Turkle, S. (1995) *Life on the Screen: Identity in the Age of the Internet*, Simon and Schuster, New York.

Turkle, S. (2009) *Simulation and Its Discontents*, MIT Press, Cambridge, MA.

Turner, B. (1984) *The Body and Society*, Blackwell, Oxford.

Turner, V. (1982) *From Ritual to Theatre: The Human Seriousness of Play*, Performing Arts Journal Publications, New York.

Vargas-Silva, C. (2011) The global international migration stock: the UK and international comparison. *The Migration Observatory*, Oxford University, http://www.migrationobser vatory.ox.ac.uk/briefings/global-international-migrant-stock-uk-international-comparison (accessed 23 September 2011).

Veblen, T. (1899 [1934]) *The Theory of the Leisure Class: An Economic Study of Institutions*, Unwin, London.

Wagner, R. (2011) Our Lady of Persistent Liminality: virtual church, cyberspace and *Second Life*, in *God in the Details* (eds E. Mazur and K. McCarthy), 2nd edn, Routledge, London, pp. 271–90.

Walvin, J. (1992) *Black Ivory: A History of British Slavery*, Harper Collins, London.

Warde, A., Martens, L. and Olsen, W. (1999) Consumption and the problem of variety: cultural omnivorousness, social distinction and dining out. *Sociology*, 33, 105–27.

Waters, M. (1995) *Globalization*, Routledge, London.

Watson, J.L. (1997) Transnationalism, localization and fast foods in East Asia, in *Golden Arches East: McDonalds in East Asia* (ed. J.L. Watson), Stanford University Press, Stanford, CA, pp. 1–38.

Watson, J.L. and Caldwell, M.L. (2005) 'Introduction', in *The Cultural Politics of Food and Eating: A Reader* (eds J.L. Watson and M.L. Caldwell), Blackwell, Oxford, pp. 1–10.

Wearing, B. (1996) *Gender: The Pain and Pleasure of Difference*, Longman, Melbourne.

Weber, M. (1946) *From Max Weber: Essays in Sociology* (eds H. Gerth and C. Mills), Oxford University Press, New York.

Weber, M. (1958 [1919]) *The Protestant Ethic and the Spirit of Capitalism*, Scribner, New York.

Weber, M. (1978) *Economy and Society: An Outline of Interpretive Sociology*, University of California Press, Berkeley, CA.

Weinstein, D. (2000) *Heavy Metal: The Music and Its Culture*, 2nd edn, Da Capo Press, New York.

Welton, D. (ed.) (1998) *Body and Flesh: A Philosophical Reader*, Blackwell, Oxford.

Wernick, A. (1991) *Promotional Culture: Advertising, Ideology and Symbolic Expression*, Sage, London.

White, H. (1978) *Tropics of Discourse*, Johns Hopkins University Press, Baltimore, MD.

Willener, A. (1970) *The Action-Image of Society: On Cultural Politicization*, Tavistock, London.

Williams, E. (1964) *Capitalism and Slavery*, Andre Deutsch, London.

Williams, R. (1958) *Culture and Society 1780–1950*, Chatto & Windus, London.

Williams, R. (1961) *The Long Revolution*, Penguin, Harmondsworth.

Williams, R. (1980) *Problems in Materialism and Culture*, Verso, London.

Williams, R. (1983) *Culture and Society, 1780–1950*, Columbia University Press, New York.

Willis, P. (1978) *Profane Culture*, Routledge and Kegan Paul, London.

Wilson, S. (1982) *Ideology and Experience: Anti-Semitism in France at the Time of the Dreyfus Affair*, Fairleigh Dickinson University Press, Rutherford, NJ.

Wittig, M. (1992) *The Straight Mind and Other Essays*, Beacon Press, Boston.

Wolff, N. (2002) *No Logo*, Picador, London.

Woodward, I. (2007) *Understanding Material Culture*, Sage, London.

Woodward, S. (2009) The myth of street style. *Fashion Theory*, 13 (1), 83–102.

World Christian Encyclopedia (2001) *World Christian Encyclopedia: A Comparative Survey of Churches and Religions in the Modern World*, Oxford University Press, New York.

Wright, C. and Madrid G. (2007) Contesting ethical trade in Colombia's cut-flower industry: a case of cultural and economic injustice. *Cultural Sociology*, 1 (2), 255–75.

Wright, E.O. (1997) *Class Counts: Comparative Studies in Class Analysis*, Cambridge University Press, Cambridge.

Wright, E.O. (2005) Social class, in *Encyclopedia of Social Theory* (ed. G. Ritzer), Sage, London, pp. 719–22.

Wuthnow, R. (1998) *After Heaven: Spirituality in America since the 1950s*, University of California Press, Berkeley, CA.

Young, I.M. (2000) *Inclusion and Democracy*, Oxford University Press, Oxford.

Zelizer, B. (1992) *Covering the Body: The Kennedy Assassination, the Media, and the Shaping of Collective Memory*, University of Chicago Press, Chicago.

Zelizer, B. (1998) *Remembering to Forget: Holocaust Memory Through the Camera's Eye*, University of Chicago Press, Chicago.

Zuckerman, P. (2003) *Invitation to the Sociology of Religion*, Routledge, New York.

Index

activist groups, *see* protest movements
Adorno, Theodor, 10, 21, 83–4
advertising, 42
aesthetic public sphere, 195, 197–8
aesthetics, 157, 163, 169
    aestheticization of economy, 171–2
Albrow, Martin, 124
Alexander, Jeffrey, 25, 27–8, 35, 40, 41–2
alternative lifestyles, 7
    see also counter-culture
American
    cultural sociology 25–9
    social thought, 10
American Sociological Association, 26,
    51
animal rights, *see* protest movements
anti-Semitism, 79, 83–4
Apartheid, 77, 78, 85
Ariès, Philippe, 92, 94
art
    schools, 13
    sociology of, 9, 27
Arts Council (UK), 5
asylum seekers, 86, 87
    see also immigration
atheism
    new 140
    see also religion
Augé, Marc, 183

Austen, Jane, 195
authorship
    individual, 15
    see also copyright
autonomy of culture, 27–8
avatars, 66, 98

Back, Les, 158
Bambaataa, Afrika 33
Barrett, David B., 134
Barthes, Roland, 10, 42, 60
Bauman, Zygmunt, 24, 84–5, 191
BBC, 5, 13
Beck, Ulrich, 24, 30, 179
Benjamin, Walter, 10
Benn Michaels, Walter, 89
Bennett, Andy, 152–3, 159, 160, 161
Berger, Peter, 136–7, 147
Beyer, Petr, 131
bio-politics, 92
biopower, 73
Birmingham Centre for Contemporary Cultural
    Studies, *see* Centre for Contemporary
    Cultural Studies
Black Power movement, 8
Blair, Tony, 14
blogosphere, rise of, 15
Blumenbach, Johann Friedrich, 81
Blumer, Herbert, 167, 169

Cultural Sociology: An Introduction, First Edition. Les Back et. al. © 2012 Les Back, Andy Bennett, Laura Desfor Edles,
Margaret Gibson, David Inglis, Ronald Jacobs and Ian Woodward. Published 2012 by Blackwell Publishing Ltd.

body, 91–104
  embodied interaction, 98
  embodied subjectivity, 97–8
  fashion and, 165
  gender–body nexus, 100
  identity and, 91
  medical-technological construction of, 102–3
  political economy of, 92
  self–body nexus, 92
  self-formation and, 92
  sexuality–body nexus, 100
  social order and, 92
  sociology and, 92–6
  symbolic/representational, 92
  see also avatars
Bordo, Susan, 100
Bourdieu, Pierre, 10, 22–3, 30, 55–8, 94, 96, 156, 167, 171
  theory of practice, 58
  see also cultural capital, cultural tastes, habitus
Bové, José, 182–3
brands, 127, 172, 173
Brecht, Bertolt, 10
British
  cultural debates, 26
  cultural studies, 26, 59, 111, 112–14
British Humanist Association, 140
British Sociological Association, 11, 23
Brown, Murphy, 195
Bryant, Kobe, 174

campaign groups, *see* protest movements
Campbell, Colin, 146
Cantor, Muriel, 27
capital
  forms of, 23
capitalism
  differentiation of, 52–3
  people's, 53
Castells, Manuel, 131, 185
Castoriadis, Cornelius, 87
Centre for Contemporary Cultural Studies (CCCS), 8–9, 21
Chaney, David, 23–4, 25, 30, 32, 157, 162
Chayefsky, Paddy, 196
Chicago
  as home of the blues, 153–4
Chicago School, 33
Christianity, 135, 143, 146
  progressive, 135, 148
  media, 135
  merchandising, 143

fundamentalism, 137, 146
  symbols, 139
  advertising, 140
cinema, 4, 8
Clark, Terry, 52
class, 47–61
  analysis, 48, 51–5
  cultures, 13
  declining relevance, 47, 51–3
  definitions, 48–51
  historical inequality, 49
  inequalities, 13
  life chance, 49
  lived culture, 58–60
  Marxist tradition, 48, 49–50
  opposition, 58–60
  political category, 49–50
  reproduction, 55–8
  social position, 49
  social, 48, 51
  subjective location, 48–9
  Weberian tradition, 41, 50–1
Clinton, Hillary, 118
clothing, 163, 164, 165–6
  see also fashion
CNN, 126
Coca-Cola, 127
codes, 38–40
collective consciousness, 94–5
colonialism, 82–5
colour line, 77, 85, 86–7
community
  popular music and, 152, 160–1
  fashion, 169–70
consumer society, 6, 22, 47, 99, 152
copyright
  changing notion of, 15
cosmopolitanism, 125
counter-culture, 7
  middle-class, 7
  see also protest movements
Cox, Oliver, 79–80
Crane, Diana, 27
creolization, 130
cultural
  agency, 28
  autonomy, 29
  capital, 55–8, 156
  change, 4, 12–16
  consumption, 29, 55–8
  divisions, 6–8
  fragmentation, 152

frameworks, 28
heterogenization, 122, 132, 181
homogenization, 122, 132
policy, 195, 198–9
politics, 111, 117–19
project, 8
tastes, 56, 57–8, 96, 157–8, 163–76, 170
cultural economy
aestheticization, 171–2
fashion, 163, 164, 170–5
cultural elites, 5
in mass media, 6
orthodoxies, 12
cultural imperialism
globalization as, 126–7
cultural production, 28, 29
as reflexive process, 31
cultural performance, 41–2
politics and, 108, 109–11
Cultural Sociology, 20
cultural sociology
approach to politics, 109
definitions, 19–30
differences from cultural studies, 20
insider–outsider research, 33–4
local vs global, 32–3
methodology, 31–43
theoretical development, 31
cultural studies, 10
British, 26, 59, 111, 112–14
differences from cultural sociology, 20
heterogeneous discourses, 4
cultural turn 3, 9, 16, 19, 20–1, 22, 24, 31
impact on music 152, 162
culture in practice, 28
culture wars, 140

Daily Show, The, 108, 194
Darwin, Charles, 81–2
Dawkins, Richard, 134, 140, 141
de Gobineau, Comte Arthur de, 81
de Saussure, Ferdinand, 38–9
language studies, 39
deconstruction, 66
de-industrialization, 22
dementia, 100
democracy
culture of, 199
democratic principles, 90
performance of, 110
demographics, 157
demonstrations, *see* protest movements

deterritorialized places, 183
Dickens, Charles, 195
difference, 77–90
DiMaggio, Paul, 27
Disney Corporation, 127
digitalization of cultural goods, 15–16
DIY cultural production, 158, 162
DJ Kool Herc, 33
Douglas, Mary, 92, 94
Dowd, Timothy, 159
Dreyfus, Captain Alfred, 83
Dreyfus Affair, 83
Du Bois, W.E.B., 77, 78, 86, 88
see also colour line
Durkheim, Émile, 35
collective consciousness 94–5
on religion, 134–40, 142, 143, 145, 147
view of body, 92, 93–4

eating, 177–88
obesity, 179
see also food
Elias, Norbert, 10, 92, 94
elite culture, *see* cultural elites
elite–mass dynamic, 167–9
empathy, 31
Engels, Friedrich, 142
English Literature departments, 5
epiphenomenal perspective, 11–12
ethics, 139
see also religion, spirituality
ethnicity, 25, 28
ethnocentrism, 125
ethnographic observation, 169
European
City of Culture, 16
cultural sociology, 22–5
social thought, 10
everyday
cultural sphere, 23, 32–3
production of culture, 20
experts
culture of, 95–6, 198

factory farming, 179, 180
Fair Trade distribution, 186–7
Fanon, Franz, 78, 86, 90
fashion, 13, 163–76
aesthetics, 164
blogs, 175
branding, 172, 173
celebrities and, 165, 173

fashion (*Continued*)
    class differentiation, 169
    collective aspect, 166
    as communicator of cultural ideals, 167
    communities, 169–70
    consumption, 174–6
    cultural economy, 163, 164, 170–5
    cultural mechanisms, 167–71
    cultural power of, 166–7
    as cultural process, 164
    cyclical nature, 167
    defining, 164–66
    denim, 173
    display, 167–8
    as dynamic process, 166
    elite–mass dynamic, 167–9
    ethnographic research, 169
    functions, 167–71
    imitation, 167–8
    individuality, 164, 166
    interactional mechanisms, 169
    logic of, 163, 164
    marketing, 174–6
    mobilities of, 167
    networked objects, 172–3
    novelty, 164
    producing desire, 174–6
    sneaker, 173–4
    social class and, 170–1
    social power of, 166–7
    street style, 173, 175
    temporal nature, 167
    transformative power, 167
    working-class culture, 173
    see also clothing
fast food, 122, 127, 178, 182–4, 185
Federal Communications Commission (US), 193
feminist theory, 63
field
    as other, 31
    relations, 33–4
    research, 31
Fields, Gracie, 7
Flinders, Carol Lee, 144, 145
food, 177–88
    Americanization, 182–4
    animal breeding massification, 179
    crises, 178, 179–82
    cultural conventions for consumption, 178
    cultural meanings, 178
    dialectical symbolization, 185
    factory farming, 179, 180

    genetically modified crops, 181
    globalization of production, 178–9
    heterogenization, 184–8
    homogenization, 182–8
    ontological security, 187–8
    organic, 186–7
    preparation, 178
    production, 178, 179
    prohibitions, 178, 182
    Slow Food movement, 186
    symbolic significance, 177–8
    trans-Atlantic transactions, 187
    see also eating, fast food
Ford, Henry, 93
Fordism, 93
Formby, George, 7
Foucault, Michel, 10, 73
    approach to body and identity 92, 95–6
frame alignment, 115–16
Frankfurt School, 26
Fredrickson, George, 77, 79
French cultural theory, 26
Freud, Sigmund, 97–8, 101–2
    critique of religion, 136, 138, 141, 142–3, 147
Friends of the Earth, 124
Frith, Simon, 151, 154, 160

Garfinkle, Harold, 97
gatekeepers, 33–4
Gay Pride movement, 8
Geertz, Clifford, 38
gender, 63–75
    body and, 100–2
    conformity to norms, 66
    contemporary diversification, 65, 69
    as corporeal process, 64
    disparities, 70–1
    distinctions, 64
    essentialist politics of, 65, 68–9
    heterosexual orientation, 64
    intersexuality, 64, 75
    language and, 69–72
    mediation of, 64–5
    online representation, 66
    as psychic process, 64
    representation in advertising, 65–6
    sex–gender distinction, 67–9
    as social construction, 65
    social expectations about, 63–4
    socialization, 67–8
    style, 64
    symbolism and, 69–72

trans-gender identity, 64, 68, 73, 74
transsexual identity, 74
genocide, 82–5
genre, 40–1
Ghosh, Jayati, 86
Gibson, Mel, 147
Giddens, Anthony, 24–5, 30, 73, 124
Gilroy, Paul, 78–9, 87–8, 89–90
global
    capitalism, 123
    citizen, 180
    culture, 127–9
    events, 125
    financial crisis, 122
globality
    construction of, 125
    see also globalization
globalization, 121–32
    anti-globalization movement, 182–3
    changes to space and time, 124
    complex nature of, 122–3
    cosmopolitanism, 125
    creolization, 130
    cultural complexity, 130–1
    cultural heterogenization, 122, 132, 181
    cultural homogenization, 122, 132, 178, 182–4
    as cultural imperialism, 126–7
    defined, 121–2
    disembedding processes, 124
    ethnocentrism, 125
    food production, 178–9, 182–8
    global capitalism, 123
    glocalization, 130
    hybridization, 130, 131
    reduced geographical constraints, 124
    undermining of national power, 123
glocalization, 130
Goffman, Irving, 92, 98
Gramsci, Antonio, 21, 111, 112–14
    see also hegemony
Grazian, David, 153–4
Great Chain of Being, 81
Great Exhibition of 1851, 4
Greenberg, Clement, 126–7
Gross, Terry, 141
Grosz, Elizabeth, 101
Guggenheim Museum, 16

Habermas, Jürgen, 10, 195–6
habitus, 22–3, 55–8, 96
Hage, Ghassan, 86
Hall, Stuart, 9, 59, 78, 86, 112–14, 160

Hebdige, Dick, 59–60
hegemony, 21, 109, 112–14, 127
    challenges to hegemonic order, 21
Held, David, 124
Hertz, Robert, 92, 94–5
heterosexual
    orientation, 64
    social order, 71, 72–3
high culture, 3, 5–6
    privileged status, 13
    see also cultural elites, low culture
hip hop, 33, 159
    Canterbury Sound, 154
    as global cultural form, 33
    origins, 154
historical materialism, 93
Hitchens, Christopher, 134
Hobsbawm, Eric, 128
Hoggart, Richard, 8–9, 21, 59
Holocaust, 83–5
homology, 156–7, 160
homosexuality
    narratives of, 66–7
Horkheimer, Max, 21, 83–4
humanism, 140
    see also atheism, religion
humanization of commodity, 93
hybridization, 130, 131

identity, 91–104
    bodies and, 98–100
    categories, 99
    construction, 20, 24, 158–9
    fashion and, 165
    local, 25
    mediation of, 99
    popular music and, 152, 155–9
immigration, 85–8
    anti-immigration sentiment, 78
    global stock of migrants, 85
    line, 85, 86–7
    Pacific Solution, 86
    within Europe, 86
imperialism, 82–5
industrialization, 6
inequality, 51–4
information technology
    changing role, 14–15
    see also Internet
intellectual property
    music and, 162
intellectuals, organic, 112

International Sociology, 52
Internet
    impact on music, 154
    impact on sexuality, 67
    online embodiment, 98
    online representation of gender, 66
    see also avatars
intersexuality, 64, 73, 75
iPod, 166, 171
Irigaray, Luce, 69, 101–2

James, Allison, 186
James, William, 136, 138, 143–5, 147
Jameson, Fredric, 171
Jefferson, Tony, 160
Jim Crow laws, 83
Joe the Plumber, 107–8, 109–11, 116, 119
Jordan, Michael 174
Jordan, Winthrop, 80

Kopytoff, Igor, 166

Lady Gaga, 127
Lamont, Michele, 58
    criticism of Bourdieu, 58
Lazarsfeld, Paul, 26
Leavis, Q.D., 4
Lee, John, 80
left-wing political affiliation, 54
legitimate authority, 111
leisure-based society, 22, 47; food and, 186
Levi's, 127
Levis, F.R., 5
Lévi-Strauss, Claude, 35, 39–40
    classification, 39–40
    linguistic systems, 39–40
Lewis, George, 157–8
Liddle, Kathleen, 159
Lien, Marianne Elizabeth, 181
life politics, 54–5
    see also post-materialism, third parties
life-course trajectory, 51, 60
lifestyle
    practices, 20
    theory, 25, 32
linguistic systems, 39–40, 69–72
Linnaeus, Carl, 81
Lipset, Seymour, 52
literature
    sociology of, 9
local culture, 127–9
    interpretation through, 129

Long, Edward, 80
Lorimer, Douglas, 82
low culture, 3
    see also high culture

Maffesoli, Michel, 160
Malbon, Justin, 160
Mann, Michael, 26
market exchange, 51
Markula, Pirkko, 96
Marx, Karl, 50
    analysis of capitalism, 50
    critique of religion, 136, 138, 141–3, 147
    historical materialism, 93
Marxist tradition, 10, 35, 92–3
    cultural Marxism, 21, 26
mass
    audience, 5
    culture, 4, 5
    entertainment, 4, 6
    ideology, 4
    persuasion studies, 26
    style, 59–60
mass media, 112
    Americanization, 199
    citizenship, 198–9
    as cultural imperialists, 126
    elites in, 6
    French model, 199
    impact on politics, 116–17
    in United States, 198–9
    US hegemony of, 199
    US model, 199
    see also media, television
material culture, 42
Mauss, Marcel, 35, 92
McCain, John, 108
McDonalds, 122, 127, 182–4
    McDonaldization, 178, 183
Mead, George Herbert, 92, 97
media, 189–200
    entertainment, 189–90, 193–8, 200
    impact on politics, 116–17
    meanings of, 189
    news, 189–90, 193–5
    sociology of, 27
    see also mass media, publics
mediatization, 152
    of politics, 116–17, 118–19
    of public life, 116–17
Melly, George, 6
Miller, Daniel, 129

Miller, Toby, 174
Minow, Newton, 193–4
modernism, 11
modernity, 4
    breakdown of control of cultural relations, 24
    fashion in, 165
    fragmentation, 98
    reflexive, 24–5
    representation in, 11–12
    social complexity, 98
    see also epiphenomenal perspective
monotheism, 69–70
Moore, Barrington, 26
moral panics, 112
Morgan, David, 100–1
Mosel, Tad, 196
Mosse, George, 82, 84
Muggleton, David, 152, 160
multiculturalism
    death of, 86
music
    blues and roots, 153
    classical, 152
    heavy metal, 156
    jazz, 152
    sociology of, 27, 151
    see also hip hop, popular music

narrative, 40–1
national cultures, 4
National Public Radio (US), 141
nationalism, paranoid, 86
Nazi Germany, 77, 83–5
Nelson, Maheno, 159
networked objects, 172–3
New Left Review, 8
newspapers
    changing role, 14–15
    see also mass media, media
Nike, 127
Nirvana, 153
Nisbet, Robert, 51
non-places, 183
norm
    conformity to, 66
    moral force of, 64

Obama, Barack, 78, 89, 109–11, 135, 148
obesity
    social construction of, 96
objectivity, 31
Olympic Games, 125

Pakulski, Jan, 52
pandemics, 180
para-textual goods, 16
    marketing of, 16
Paris '*les évènements*', 8
Park, Robert, 26
Parsons, Talcott, 26
party
    concept of, 51
passional economy, 174
Payne Fund Studies, 4
Pearl Jam, 153
Pepsi, 127
performance of cultural text, 15
    changing role, 15
    copyright and, 15
Persinger, Michael, 145
    God Helmet experiments, 145
Peterson, Richard A., 27, 161
Pieterse, Jan Nederveen, 130
place
    popular music and, 152–5
    trans-local mobility, 159
political sociology, 109, 111–16
    and organization of state, 114–16
politics, 107–20
    celebrities in, 118
    cultural performance of, 108, 109–11, 119
    impact of state, 114
    mediatization of, 116–17, 118–19
    rituals of, 108, 109–10
    as taste culture, 157
Pop Art, 6
popular culture, 13
popular music, 151–62
    as art, 151
    audiences, 162
    authenticity, 152
    commodification, 152
    community and, 152, 160–1
    consumption, 152, 162
    DIY production, 158, 162
    festivals, 159
    identity and, 152, 155–9
    impact of cultural turn, 152
    as industrial product, 151
    intellectual property, 162
    mashups, 162
    performance, 152
    place and, 152–5, 159
    production, 152
    queer music scene, 158–9

popular music (*Continued*)
  role of Internet, 154
  scenes, 160–1
  technology, 162
  working-class origins, 153
post-class analysis, 54–5
post-industrialization, 3, 47
post-materialism, 54
postmodernism, 10
postmodernity
  shift to, 24–5
post-subcultural theory, 152, 160
protest movements, 7
  animal rights, 180
  anti-globalization, 182–3
  environmental, 180
  see also life politics
Prozac culture, 102–3
psychoanalysis, 97–8
Public Broadcasting Act 1967 (US), 193
public life, 189–200
  culture in, 190–1
  mediatization of, 116–17, 189–200
  rationality in, 190–1
public service broadcasting, 4–5
public sphere, 189, 190–1
  aesthetic, 195, 197–8
  entertainment media and, 195–8
  news media and, 191–3
  official, 191–3, 199, 200
  traditional model, 15
publics
  informal, 191–3, 200
  official, 191–3, 200
punk style, 59
  see also subcultures

Quayle, Dan, 195, 198

race, 28, 77–90
  classification, 81
  concept of, 78–82
  genetic science and, 81
  Great Chain of Being, 81
  pseudo-scientific theories of, 81
  racial difference, 78
  scientific theories of, 81
  stereotypes, 85
  see also Darwin, Charles
racism, 77–90, 125
  against Jews, 79
  in American South, 77

  in Apartheid South Africa, 77
  changing nature of, 88, 89
  cultural, 86
  in Europe, 78
  institutionalized, 77, 85
  in Japan, 78
  Jim Crow laws, 83
  legacy, 86
  in Nazi Germany, 77, 83–5
  proto-racism, 79
  racial prejudice, 79
  in Rwanda, 78
  simplification of, 89
  terminology of, 88
  see also genocide, Holocaust, slavery
radical politics, 7, 8, 9
radio
  stratification, 5
rationality, 190, 191
rationalization of society, 139
Reagan, Ronald, 118
Redhead, Steve, 160
reflexivity, 66
refugees, 86
  see also immigration
religion, 133–48
  broadcasts, 136
  as business, 135–6, 143
  as delusion, 142–3
  Durkheim on, 134–40, 142, 143, 145, 147
  dwellers vs seekers, 145, 146
  enchantment vs disenchantment, 139–40
  Freud on, 136, 138, 141, 142–3, 147
  functionalist approaches to, 136–8, 139
  gender and, 138
  God Helmet experiments, 145
  as internal experience, 143–5
  Kabbalah, 134
  Marxist critique of, 136, 138, 141–3, 147
  New Age, 134
  in post-industrial world, 138–41
  in postmodern world, 143, 144
  progressive, 134–5l
  religious fundamentalism, 133, 137–8, 140,
    143, 146
  religious pluralism, 133
  religious worldview, 139
  sacred vs profane, 139, 147
  search for meaning, 140–1
  secularization of society, 133, 134, 147
  sexual orientation and, 138
  social change and, 145–7

synthetic, 134–5
this-worldly vs other-worldly, 145–6
Weber on, 133, 136, 138–40, 145–6, 147
Wicca, 146–7
William James on, 143–5, 147
see also spirituality
reproductive technologies, 73
research
  ethnographic, 169
  global vs local, 32–3
  insider vs outsider, 33–4
  material research, 42
  methodological inspiration, 37–42
  methodologies, 35–6
  methods, 35–6
  positivist approaches, 36–7
  postmodern paradigm, 36–7
  post-positivist approaches, 36–7
  qualitative, 36
  quantitative, 36
  surface vs depth, 34–5
  visual research, 42
researchers
  insider, 33–4
  outsider, 33–4
right hand
  superiority of, 95
Riot Grrrl movement, 158
rituals
  political, 109–10
Ritzer, George, 182
Robertson, Roland, 125
Robinson, Gene, 138
Rose, Jacqueline, 102
Rose, Reginald, 196
Rowling, J.K., 147
Rubin, Gayle, 71

Sapir, Edward, 165–6
scenes, 160–1
  virtual, 161
Schaeffer, Francis, 141
Schaeffer, Frank, 141
Schilt, Kristen, 158
Schmidt, Leigh Eric, 144–5
Schwarzenegger, Arnold, 118
scientific method, 140
scientists
  power of, 180
Seattle
  musical influence, 153
secularization of society, 133, 134, 139, 147

sense of self, 99
  vs social identity, 99
September 11 terrorist attacks, 41
Serling, Rod, 196
sexuality, 63–75
  impact of Internet, 67
  importance of sexed body, 68
  individual, 73
  religious control of, 65
  sex–gender distinction, 67–9
  social expectations about, 63–4
  state control of, 65
share ownership, 53
signs, 39, 97
Simmel, Georg, 10, 22, 38, 164, 165, 167–8, 169, 171, 173
Simpson, Tim, 183
Skocpol, Theda, 115
slavery, 79–80
  Atlantic slave trade, 80
  plantation, 80–1
  white slaves, 79
Slow Food movement, 186–7
Smith, Philip, 25, 35, 40
Snowden, Frank, 79
social
  actor, 31, 35
  difference, 47–61
  drama, 40–1
  exclusion, 47, 91
  identity vs sense of self, 99
  imagination, 195–6
  inclusion, 91
  institutions, 22
  mobility, 47
  performance, 41
  stratification, 14
social class
  fashion and 170–1
social relations
  production, 20
  reproduction, 20
Social Text, 29
socialist theory
  reworking of, 8
sociological project, 122
Sociology departments, 9–10
Sokal, Alan, 29
Sokal affair, 29
sotierology, 139
  see also religion
sovereignty, 123

Soyer, Alexis, 177
Spillman, Lyn, 28
spirituality, 134–5, 143–5, 146–8
    belief in reincarnation, 146–7
    Easternization of West, 146
    individual, 136, 143–5
    search for meaning, 140–1
    yogaization of West, 146
sport
    cultural role of, 6–7
Springsteen, Bruce, 153
Starbucks, 183
status, 13
    body and, 92
    dimensions, 51
    groups, 51, 72
Stewart, Jon, 108, 194
straight style, 59–60
Straw, Will, 160–1
strong program, 28, 30, 35
structural determinism, 155
style, 163–76
subcultures, 59
    subcultural style, 59–60, 91
    subcultural theory, 160
    see also post-subcultural theory
surplus value, 50
Swidler, Ann, 27
symbolic interactionism, 97
symbolic order, 69–72
symbols, 97
systems, 38–40

taste cultures, *see* cultural tastes
Tate Modern gallery, 16
Taylor, Charles, 93
Taylorism, 93
Taylor, Jodie, 158–9
television
    as mass medium, 13
    as part of aesthetic public sphere, 197–8
    role in social commentary, 196–7
    see also BBC
tertiary education
    growth of, 9
Thatcher, Margaret, 13–14, 113
theology, 139
    see also religion
Theory, Culture & Society, 9
thick description, 27, 38
third parties
    rise of, 54
    see also life politics, post-materialism

Tilly, Charles, 26
Tomlinson, John, 184
tourism, 13
trafficking of women, 71
trans-gender identity, 64, 68, 73, 74
transnational corporations, 123
transsexual identity, 73, 74
Trinity Broadcasting Network, 36
Turner, Bryan, 92
Turner, Ted, 126

UK cultural debates, *see* British cultural debates,
    European cultural sociology
United Nations, monitoring of gender injustice,
    70–1
urban popular culture, 4, 26, 28
urbanization, 6, 179
    ghettos, 113
US cultural sociology, *see* American cultural
    sociology
US social thought, *see* American social thought

Veblen, Thorstein, 167, 168–9, 171, 173
verstehen, 37–8
visual culture, 42

Waters, Malcolm, 52, 124
Weber, Max, 22, 37–8, 93, 114, 118, 133
    concept of class, 49–51
    on religion, 133, 136, 138–40, 145–6, 147
    see also verstehen
Weinstein, Deena, 156
Welles, Orson, 26
Westwood, Vivienne, 173
Wicca, 146–7
Williams, Eric, 79
Williams, Raymond, 20–1, 59
Willis, Paul, 155–7
Wittig, Monique, 70
    use of the term 'lesbian', 70
women
    as objects, 71
    as property, 71
    representations of, 69–72
    trafficking of, 71
    see also gender
Women's Liberation Movement, 8, 73
working class
    contraction of, 7
    culture, 7
    stereotypes, 7
world risk society, 179
Wright, Erik Olin, 48

Wurzelbacher, Joe, *see* Joe the Plumber
Wuthnow, Robert, 145–6, 147

xenophobia, 78, 87

Yale University Centre for Cultural Sociology, 20, 23, 35

youth cultures, 7, 25, 59
    collective identity, 158
    fashion, 173
    see also subcultures

Zolberg, Vera, 27
Zuckerman, Phil, 138